# Powerful Magic

## LEARNING FROM CHILDREN'S RESPONSES TO FANTASY LITERATURE

## Nina Mikkelsen

*foreword by* LAURENCE YEP

Teachers College
Columbia University
New York and London

Published by Teachers College Press, 1234 Amsterdam Avenue, New York, NY 10027

*Library of Congress Cataloging-in-Publication Data*

Mikkelsen, Nina.
    Powerful magic : learning from children's responses to fantasy literature / Nina Mikkelsen.
       p. cm. — (Language and literacy series)
    Includes bibliographical references and index.
    ISBN 0-8077-4596-0 (alk. paper) — ISBN 0-8077-4595-2 (pbk. : alk. paper)
    1. Children—Books and reading—Psychological aspects.   2. Children's literature—Psychological aspects.   3. Fantasy literature—Psychological aspects. 4. Literacy—Philosophy.   I. Title.   II. Series.
    Z1037.A1M55 2005
    028.5'5—dc22

                                                                                    2005045706

ISBN 0-8077-4595-2 (paper)
ISBN 0-8077-4596-0 (cloth)

Printed on acid-free paper

Manufactured in the United States of America

12  11  10  09  08  07  06  05       8  7  6  5  4  3  2  1

# Contents

# Foreword

I GREW UP IN AN African-American neighborhood and went to school in Chinatown, so my childhood was spent either in one ghetto or another. As a result, I could never get involved in the so-called "realistic" children's books of the fifties because in them every child had luxuries such as bicycles, and yet, despite all their riches, the children seemed to leave their front doors unlocked. That contrasted with my own experience in that no one had a bicycle and everyone employed multiple locks on their front doors. As a result, books such as the Homer Price series seemed absurd and impossible to believe.

On the other hand, I could identify with the children in fantasy novels, who through some magical means stumbled from our everyday world to a new world where they had to learn new customs and even new languages. Like the children in the Oz books, I had to adapt every day to different environments and situations and figure out the behavioral codes that people were following.

So, fantasy books were the opposite of escapism, because they taught me basic survival strategies such as the flexibility of mind that children demonstrated in the pages of these fantasy novels: I saw how they adapted to the strange and even uncomfortable and, more importantly, what happened when they guessed wrong.

Children have an emotional reality that is no less valid than their physical reality; as a child, fantasy spoke to my emotional reality. When I read fantasy books, I was able to confront issues that I would not have if they had been thrust at me in contemporary settings—and, anyway, in the fifties Chinatown and African-American neighborhoods were not the subject of credible children's books.

Moreover, even though I had friends in both ghettoes, there were also other times my upbringing made me feel like an outsider, moments which, spanning two cultures as I did, made me feel as if I belonged to neither one.

Therefore, beyond teaching me social skills, fantasy also taught me that it was possible to find a place for myself. Other people, living within one culture, stepped into a niche that was already constructed for them. There were times when I had to build a place for myself.

If, as Freud said, dreams are the royal road to the unconscious, then fantasy is the royal road into childhood—not as it appears physically, but as it exists both emotionally and psychologically.

LAURENCE YEP

# Acknowledgments

MANY CHILDREN HAVE CONTRIBUTED to my learning about children's responses to literature through the years. My own two children, Vinny and Mark, led me into and through the field of children's literature from infancy on. Children in my neighborhood and in Vinny's first- and second-grade classrooms became my next—and some of my best—teachers. Children in other settings through the years continued to add to my knowledge, helping me to see more about children and their books. All of these children and the moments of response that run through the pages of this book stand as indispensable—and irreplaceable—light-givers on the spectrum of response.

I am grateful for the teachers who have invited me into their classrooms to read aloud to children, to elicit responses, and to conduct research that contributed so much to my learning. I am also grateful to the many forums that have allowed me to present papers and publish essays focused on children's responses to literature: the National Council Teachers of English, Canadian Council Teachers of English, National Association of Teachers of English (England), Children's Literature Association, American Educational Research Association, International Reading Association, United Kingdom Reading Association, International Federation for the Teaching of English, Modern Language Association, and Boston University Conference on Language Development; and to the editors and reviewers who have contributed greatly to my knowledge in these ventures.

I am especially grateful for classes in children's literature with Charlotte Huck at Ohio State University, which produced a lifelong quest to know more about this field and to emphasize—and honor—children's responses to literature in my work. Additional seminars, workshops, and institutes with educators like Donald Graves, University of New Hampshire, Lucy Calkins, Teachers College, Columbia University, and Margaret Meek, Don Fry, and Harry Rosen, National Association of Teachers of English, have also contributed to my knowledge of literature, literacies, storymaking, and reader response. I thank Virginia Hamilton for her special insights about multicultural literature and for writing so many mind-expanding children's books, including the one that concludes the studies of this book. At Teachers College Press I thank, Dorothy Strickland and Celia Geneshi, Language and Literacy Series editors, Carol Collins, acquisitions editor, Wendy Schwartz, development editor, Aureliano Vázquez, Production Editor, and Jessica Balun, Publicity Coordinator for all their valuable insights, suggestions, and publishing knowledge. And I thank Laurence Yep for writing the Foreword to this book.

I first came in contact with Yep's work in Charlotte Huck's children's literature classes. Reading *Child of the Owl* (1977), I was fascinated by the way that he had woven a Chinese folk fantasy tale into the plot to show contemporary Chinese American children caught between two worlds but growing stronger from cultural knowledge handed down in family stories. Later I would discover two more books with Yep's signature folk fantasy embeddings: *The Star Fisher* (1992), Yep's story of his mother's growing up years in my own home state of West Virginia, and *Dragonwings* (1977), a masterful blending of realism and fantasy, details of which began emerging in the deep structure of my older son's responses the summer we read it alongside *The Hobbit* (see Chapter 6).

Yep has written in nearly every genre, including autobiography (*The Lost Garden*, 1991), play script, mystery, folk, quest, transformation, multicultural fantasy, such as *Dragon of the Lost Sea* (1982), historical fiction about Chinese immigrants in a variety of precarious situations in America, like his two Newbery Honor books, *Dragonwings* and *Dragon's Gate* (1993), and folk tale retelling (Yep has taught Asian American studies and creative writing at the University of California, Berkeley and Santa Barbara). In fact, very few—if any—other American multicultural writers for children and young adults are producing as many thought-provoking, artistic, authentic, and innovative books. For *Powerful Magic*, he tells me he focused on what fantasy meant to him in his own childhood—and what better way to open the doors of this book.

Finally, I thank my family for living so patiently with children's voices playing endlessly on the tape recorder as I listened into the worlds of children, hoping to make sense of it all—and most of all for being those voices.

# Introduction:
# Children's Ways of Reading

LOUISE ROSENBLATT (1994) SPEAKS of the reading "transaction" as an "active process lived through during the relationship between a reader and a text" (p. 201). What brings a work of literature "alive" for readers is not simply a matter of finding meaning in a text, nor finding meanings for textual "signs." It is a "live circuit set up between the reader and the text" (p. 14).

In the same way, what brings *children's* books alive is not merely adult readers finding their own meanings in texts, nor is it adult guesses about how children might respond. It is instead a cycle of response that emerges when children are shaping meaning from texts and adults are tuning into their worlds and seeing more as a result. It is what happens when adults become "word-catchers," observing, describing, and preserving children's responses to literature—and when adults help children become word-catchers, too. As observers of their own reading, describing their own ways of seeing and knowing, children learn more about themselves and their books.

Children may have less formal education than adults; their life and literary experiences are certainly less extensive than adult experiences and therefore very different, and it is these differences we need to know more about if we are to understand what children are thinking, feeling, and seeing in their literature. As literacy educator David Dillon (1985) states: "We still know very little about the culture of childhood, what [children's] worlds, constructs, and values are—which will determine their experience with literature as well as be shaped by it" (p. 166). Far too often we leave children's ways of knowing locked away in a separate place. Thus we prevent ourselves from knowing about their worlds—their interests, ideas, preoccupations, understandings. What if we called forth these secrets of response?

Children can show us the most about what their literature means in terms of their own cultural lives. For this reason, they should be admitted to the "conversation" as equal partners in learning. Children have a great deal to teach us about their literature, literacies, and child worlds. This is a book about children learning through literature and adults learning more about both children and books from eliciting and studying their responses.

In *Powerful Magic*, I rely on my own work as a literature and literacies researcher as the basis for discussion about how children reshape literature (particularly fantasy) in terms of their own child worlds and how their worlds—personal, social, cultural, and narrative—converge on their literature. Reading with my own two children from early childhood on and hearing their responses led me to begin sharing books with their friends and classmates and to invite their responses, and to observe and describe the literature and literacy process, in terms of their feelings and ideas. At the same time, I was discovering narrative, reception, and cultural theories and incorporating them into my learning.

I have found especially important Louise Rosenblatt's (1994) transactional reading theories, Wolfgang Iser's (1978) analysis of the act of reading, Roland Barthes's (1985) semiotic narrative theories, Margaret Meek's (1988) ideas about the way texts teach, Harold Rosen's (1984) emphasis on the importance of story and storying from the home culture, Shirley Brice Heath's (1983) studies of children's culturally divergent storytelling worlds, Jerome Bruner's (1986) concept of adult–child conversations as "negotiable transactions," Wayne Booth's (1988) ideas about ethical reading and nurturing characters, Sheila Egoff's (1981), Jane Yolen's (2000) and Laurence Yep's (1995) theories about fantasy, Paulo Freire's (1973) studies of cultural and critical consciousness, and Anne Haas Dyson's (1989, 1993, 1995) ideas about the many worlds—social, imaginative, real, symbolic—converging on child writers.

In the chapters of *Powerful Magic*, the strands of these different theories weave together so that ideas overlap, enrich, and inform one another and readers explore many ways of seeing, particularly *children's* ways.

## EMPHASES OF CHILDREN AND FANTASY WORLDS

Three major ideas weave through this work:

1. When children hear or read fantasy literature, they respond easily and often at length, producing full and rich responses from which we can glean more about their ways of reading the world, and the world of literature. Although children need a full diet of all literary genres, their responses to fantasy are crucial for opening up the richest vein of knowledge about their worlds and their ways of

transacting texts. (If we want to learn more about children and books, fantasy opens the door.)

2. "Live circuits" of response arise from an intersection of a "field" of *multiple* literacies (generative, personal/empathetic, sociocultural, literary, intertextual, narrative, and critical) during conversations in which adult and child, as partners in thought, negotiate complexities of text and world to make greater sense of things; explore personal ethical choices; and research their own learning.

3. Children shape and reshape literature (in talk, storymaking, art, and role-play), in terms of the narrative coding they notice and use to make sense of the worlds within and beyond the story.

I begin with animal fantasy and wordless picture book fantasy and proceed to transformation, quest, and multicultural fantasies, having noticed from the beginning of my research that children reading fantasy produced rich and abundant responses. Fantasy gives them new and different images to think with; at its best it gives them exciting, inventive ways of shaping and reshaping their worlds. It takes them to places far from their own worlds, giving them freedom to explore and create, and it releases their imagination in full and expressive ways. Children have a *need* for fantasy, I have observed, and to ignore that need is to lose contact with child worlds and the secrets of those worlds.

From the beginning also, I identify an array of literacies that I have observed arising naturally in children's reading and storymaking processes and that I previously described in *Words and Pictures: Lessons in Children's Literature and Literacies* (1999), chapter 8, "Authorial Signposts and Reader Response." Readers, at different times and with different books, and passages of books, have different "ways" of approaching texts. They engage with stories in individual ways, noticing different shades of meaning and gaining unique pleasure and insights from their encounters. When they share different reactions, they help one another to see more. Settings that allow multiple literacies to emerge and interweave in children's responses produce *responsive* readers. Children's different "ways" of approaching and engaging texts emerge as the literacies listed in Fig. I.1.

We often see theorists and researchers emphasizing one of these ways of reading, based on their interest in or preference for that perspective. Rosenblatt has spoken often of an *aesthetic* experience in reading and has produced a definition of *critical* reading (1994) that I have found helpful for my work. Freire (1973) has also contributed an important perspective on critical thinking. Booth (1988), Meek (1988), Fry (1985), and Paley (1997) describe the conditions for what I am calling *personal/empathetic* reading, but Rosenblatt's theories about *aesthetic* reading intersect readily with it.

## FIGURE I.1.  A Field of Literacies

**Generative Literacy:** Reading, writing, listening to, storying about, or viewing a work to build the big picture of it; sorting out the text (story, poem, picture) in order to make meaning of it; putting the pieces of the literary puzzle together to see what's happening or what has happened. *Preliminary and ongoing meaning-making.*

**Personal/Empathetic Literacy:** Discovering something about a character that connects to the reader's own life; a natural ability readers have to understand what others are feeling or experiencing that draws them into text and pictures quickly and easily. *Understanding implicitly why a character does certain things or feels a certain way.*

**Sociocultural Literacy:** Reading texts in terms of the reader's developing picture of what the world is like (based on the reader's beliefs, ideas, values, ideologies). *What readers' lives cause them to see in the story world.* Also understanding—or "reading"— the world differently after having read or viewed a text, sorting out the world through developing pictures of what a textual world is like. *What the text or pictures cause readers to see in the world.*

**Literary Literacy:** Uncovering patterns of meaning, in structure, style, and subject, in a story, poem, or picture; using the author's signs, signals, or clues to see how the text and pictures work and what they are saying in terms of themes and ideas. *How the text works to produce meaning for readers.* Within this literacy, or closely related to it, is **Intertextual Literacy:** Seeing connections among different texts. *How texts work in related ways to produce meanings for readers.*

**Narrative Literacy:** Telling stories about the author's story as that story unfolds or after; walking about the story as one of the characters and enlarging or expanding on the author's story in order to frame it with a new story "picture." *What a text makes readers think about, imagine, or create.*

**Critical Literacy:** Refusing to accept everything about a piece of literature, no questions asked; reading against the grain of the text to clarify what the reader feels and knows about the world and what the reader would do to create changes in the work—or the world—based on those feelings or that knowledge, as they are set in motion by the work. *Resisting the text or the world of the text; thinking about what matters in the world, as the text activates those thoughts.*

**Aesthetic Literacy:** Becoming actively involved in imaginative participation in the work, which leads to searching for meaning and ideas, and discovering a deeper understanding of what it means to live in the story world. *Living through a work with full absorption and strong engagement in forming mental images about characters, settings, and events.*

**Print Literacy:** Acquiring the skills to decode or encode fictional and nonfictional print (newsprint, dictionaries, encyclopedias, textbooks, letters, advertisements, signs, tickets, menus, recipes, stories, poems, cartoons). *Taking in what is presented in printed materials; making one's way through the text and the world to assign a "fixed" or stable meaning.*

Rosen (1988) speaks often of the way readers tell stories about the story as they read, and Meek (1982b) and Paley (1997) also contributed to the idea of *narrative* literacy, or the way that readers walk around in stories, telling stories about the story. Chambers (1993) and Meek (1988) have traced the ways that readers notice and respond to patterns in authorial coding—what I call *literary* literacy here. Paley (1997) and Dyson (1993, 1995, 1997) often pay particular attention to what I call *sociocultural* literacy in their research. We see what I am calling *generative* literacy in discussions by Wells (1986) of parent and child negotiating texts together. And Brian Cambourne's (1992) ideas about reading to make our way through the world, or function in it, inform my notions here of *print* literacy.

The problem is that we seldom see theorists presenting more than one or two of these ways of reading—the way that we see Freire, Dyson, and Paley blending *personal/empathetic, sociocultural,* and *critical* literacies (Mikkelsen, 1999). Seldom do we see them noticing that, given the right circumstances, such as exploratory conversations and other spontaneous, natural response events, these ways can work together so that children read the world (and the story worlds) in fuller, richer ways. Throughout *Powerful Magic,* I describe and discuss reading events in which multiple literacies weave together through children's responses.

Beginning with chapter 4, I also explore the way that multiple literacies intersect with the different Barthesian codes in children's literary transactions and the way that various kinds of fantasy emphasize particular narrative codes. I have also discussed and described the Barthesian (1985) codes in *Words and Pictures* (1999).

> *Actions* coding allows readers to notice important actions, behaviors, conversations, and inner stories that characters or narrators tell as readers trace the plot of a story or attempt to make meaning of it. *What is happening here? What are the big scenes in this story? How do these scenes move the story along?* (Often intersects with *generative* literacy.)
>
> *Semic* coding causes readers to notice small details about setting and characters that flicker through a story, poem, or pictures in order to transmit ideas. *What threads of meaning are weaving through this story? What do I continue to notice? What is it all adding up to?* (Often intersects with *personal/empathetic* and *literary* literacies.)
>
> *Cultural* coding plays upon readers' unexamined assumptions about the world (the author's or the reader's world) that relate to general knowledge of the world itself, knowledge connected with a particular time or place, or unreliable (limited, skewed, or biased) "knowledge." *What am I noticing about this story world, and how do*

*the ideas and values of it relate to my picture of how the world is, or should be?* (Often intersects with *sociocultural* and *critical* literacies.)

*Enigma* coding places mysteries (gaps and blank spaces) in the work, filling it with suspense and intrigue. *What do I find puzzling? What do I continue to be curious about? What questions remain unanswered as I close the book? What do these puzzles conceal from my ongoing or ultimate understanding of the story?* (Often intersects with *narrative* literacy.)

*Symbolic* coding involves ideas that result not from logic, reasoning, or experience but from implicit pieces of meaning threaded through or embedded within the work that enable us to see larger patterns, make connections, and produce final pleasure that we have brought completion to the work. *What sense am I making of this story? What do I see in it? What do I finally understand after closing the book? What does it cause me to think about?* (Often intersects with *literary*, *intertextual*, and *aesthetic* literacies.)

## FOCUS AND PLAN OF THE BOOK

My response studies with children involve a variety of settings—home, school, neighborhood. Because of the current emphasis on literature-based teaching, there has been a great deal of discussion about ways of teaching with children's books. But we cannot really talk about children's books in the classroom if we have not first conducted in-depth investigations with children—portraits of response rather than mere snapshots. Such studies must take place in both personal and social contexts, and often they must occur outside the classroom in settings where adults have additional "spaces" to evoke, listen to, and extend children's responses to literature, especially their responses to fantasy.

The studies presented here also involve a mix of age levels, genders, and cultural and experiential backgrounds. The book begins and ends with studies of my own two sons, and because I am taking readers along in my own journey as a response researcher, I begin at the beginning when they were ages 5 and 7 and end as they were taking off into their teen years, ages 11 and 13. Between those two points are chapters and parts of chapters that focus directly on female children and children of different experiential and cultural backgrounds.

The book has three parts, each of which focuses on what takes place when "live circuits" of response are set in motion in what I call a cycle of response. Part I, "The Child and the Book" focuses on the way the cycle begins: children encounter books and make full, rich meanings of them, in terms of multiple, intersecting literacies, if the books engage them in terms of their own child worlds, as they react to the author's narrative coding.

Part II, "The Reading Transaction," focuses more specifically on children reading the signs of an author's narrative coding and responding spontaneously and naturally in terms of the child worlds that converge on these texts, especially when adults invite children to engage in exploratory, "transactional literary conversations."

Part III, "Children as Research Partners," focuses more specifically on that aspect of the cycle when children and adults are learning more about children's worlds as partners in research, and the way the next cycle begins with children's revisiting the response setting because they are taking pleasure in new understandings and inventions and growing through response. (see Fig. I.2 for a visual representation of this cycle.)

Chapter 1 presents my first response study, undertaken with three children on the home front, my own two children and my nephew, responding to Leo Lionni's *Alexander and the Wind-Up Mouse* (1969) and the way the study grew into further encounters with the same book later that year, when the two younger children read it again.

Chapter 2 investigates the area of children's preferences and examines what happens when many different children respond to a wordless picture book, Raymond Briggs's *The Snowman* (1978), and it becomes increasingly clear that one size doesn't necessarily fit all.

**FIGURE I.2.** A Cycle of Response

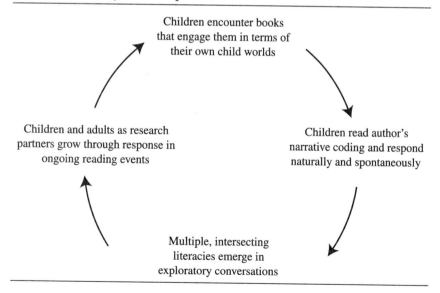

Chapter 3 describes a classroom experience with second-grade children responding to *Alexander and the Wind-Up Mouse*, and it demonstrates how exploratory conversation with children reading the "real" book—not a basalized version—produces multiple, intersecting literacies, and children's growth in responsive—and at times resistant—reading.

Chapter 4 unfolds more about children's preferences, this time focusing on a child dealing with narrative complexities during repeated readings of a book she chooses and continues to revisit—Arthur Yorinks and Richard Egielski's *Louis the Fish* (1980)—the result of deepening *aesthetic* literacy.

Chapter 5 describes what happens when children in a classroom setting examine this same book and a "transactional literary conversation" unfolds, with children discussing what matters in their lives.

Chapter 6 involves children researching their preference for fantasy—or a particular favorite, J. R. R. Tolkien's *The Hobbit* (1965)—and engaging in exploratory conversations that yield more information about how they read the world in terms of personal ethical choices.

Chapter 7 involves the same two children assisting me to answer a question that children have special knowledge about: Is this book a *children's* book? In the process, they negotiate complexities of text and reflect on ethical and sociocultural issues that arise from a challenging multicultural fantasy novel, Virginia Hamilton's *The Magical Adventures of Pretty Pearl* (1983).

In each of these chapters, the focus is on literature at the very moment children are living through it, catching the "tune" of it, and, in response, playing "music" of their own making: becoming engaged with characters; noticing patterns of sound and sense in stories; understanding more about themselves, others, and the world; and learning about literary conventions and complexities of narrative coding. They are responding to stories with talk and stories, in order to step more deeply into literature. And they are, at the best of times, getting lost in books and becoming responsive readers and partners in research.

Each chapter focuses on children's worlds—personal, social, cultural, and narrative—as they produce children's unique ways of seeing and knowing; each is about valuing—honoring—children as insightful readers. We can learn a great deal about children and their worlds from the way children puzzle out the mysteries of their books, and we can learn a great deal about children's books if we are listening for the child's "tune." When we engage in responsive reading with children, they reveal for us more about their literature, their worlds, and their ways of experiencing the world of literature.

*Powerful Magic* is a book for those who want to know more about how children shape literature in terms of their own child worlds: researchers in the areas of literature and literacy, cultural theorists, literary critics, reviewers, teacher educators, teachers and prospective teachers, librarians, authors, parents, or those, like I, who may suddenly find themselves with a special interest and curiosity in children, books, and child culture, as I focus on next.

# PART I

# THE CHILD
# AND THE BOOK

WORKING WITH CHILDREN, we need to know which books to share. Often, if we simply observe children reading or listening to stories, we learn quickly which books are the "right" ones for our purposes. But more often we need to listen to children's responses in order to see that although some books seem a good match for many children, especially at particular times in their lives, not all books are right for all children.

Once we know how children react to books and what they see in their literature, we have better ways of deciding how we will use classroom time to foster children's growth into literacy. Will we continue to privilege our own perceptions and interventions and our overriding concern that children become more like we are—and as quickly as possible? Or will we open up time for spontaneous reactions to books so that we learn more about children, their worlds, their books, and our ways of sharing them?

More knowledge about child worlds will give us more confidence to take less traveled roads in our teaching; it will also help us defend our choices against those who would place lockstep, standardized teaching approaches above children's natural ways of learning.

*Chapter One*

# Stepping into Response:
## *Alexander and the Wind-Up Mouse*

THE WORLD OF CHILDREN'S RESPONSES opened up for me as I shared a little mass-market picture book with my first child, Vinny, just six months old, and discovered that he was totally absorbed (even nibbling at the pages) each time I read it aloud. What did he see in this book? What was he thinking as he heard the words about Susie and the big dog and gazed at the pictures? Questions about *his* world continued to fascinate me when I shared books with him and later with him and his younger brother.

There were even more questions when Vinny went to school and I became a volunteer story reader in his first-grade classroom. Twice a week I took a welcome break from teaching college writing classes to visit his school with a handful of picture books. At this point, I had taken classes in everything from *Beowulf* to Virginia Woolf. But the more I read to children, the more I wanted to learn about child readers and *their* books. The next summer I enrolled in graduate classes in children's literature, where I conducted my first response study.

The assignment was to observe a child or group of children responding to literature, in talk, art, or writing, and I decided to share a book with my own two children, Mark, age five, and Vinny, age seven, and my nephew, Brian, age nine. Browsing through my sister's bookcase, I found Leo Lionni's *Alexander and the Wind-Up Mouse* (1969), an animal fantasy picture book. Filled with danger, magic, risk-taking, and a joyful ending, it seemed just right.

When two mice, a real one and a wind-up, become friends, the real mouse, Alexander, who faces constant danger from angry humans, soon begins wishing he could be just like Willy, a safe, beloved child's toy—at least until the little girl, Annie, throws Willy away. If Willy is to live, Alexander sees, he must make an important wish that the Magic Lizard grants him. And he does: the last page shows the mice—with Willy turned real—dancing happily together in the garden.

I wanted to see if any one of these children, with his different experiences and preoccupations, would respond, with deepest engagement, to the book. Which child, or children, would "become" one of the characters, the way Vinny and Mark often became Batman and Robin as they watched their favorite television cartoon? It was not my plan simply to compare children's responses at different ages or developmental stages to see which child had the "best" ideas. I was not trying to develop—or "improve"— the children's understandings or responses. I was not studying these children to see how they were entering more competently into *my* world—or how I could help them become more experienced, adult-like readers. I wanted to see how their own child worlds (their different perceptions and sensibilities) affected their readings of the book, and I hoped to learn if any child's engagement with the story was stronger because of something about the book, the child, or some mysterious alchemy of book and child.

"An intense response to a work," says Rosenblatt (1976) "will have its roots in capacities and experiences already present in the personality and mind of the reader . . . [and] choices in literary materials must reflect a sense of the possible links between these materials and the student's past experience and present level of emotional maturity" (p. 42). Following this line of reasoning, we would not study children's responses to see how "complete," comprehensive, or adult-like they were but to see how—and particularly *why*—children became involved in a book. Knowledge of children's responses would therefore broaden and deepen our perspectives about both children and books.

### DIFFERENT WAYS OF SEEING

I read to the children separately, pausing to open up the story for meaning-making. Some stories are more openly interpretive than others; they have more of what Iser (1978) describes as gaps and blank spaces and thus more freedom for readers to speculate on the author's clues and signals—and on their own feelings, ideas, and associations. Following Barthes (1974), we call such works "writerly": readers take on an equal share of the creation of stories when they fill in gaps and spaces to make meaning.

"*What happened?*" The story opens with a picture of cups and saucers flying (a human has apparently seen a mouse). "The mouse made a noise and all the cups fell" (Mark). "The spoons and cups fell and the little mouse is running to his mouse hole" (Vinny). "The mouse got up on a counter and knocked something off" (Brian). Each child focused on Alexander as the main character. Both Mark and Brian saw the mouse as proactive (Alexander causes the cups to fall), but Vinny saw the mouse as reactive (the cups fall, scaring the mouse, who scampers off); thus he focused most directly on Alexander's role of protagonist (it is Alexander whose life is at stake, he implies, when he decides, in this "writerly" scene, that the mouse was off and running for safety).

*"How are the two mice different? (Does one have something the other doesn't have?)"* The story continues with the mice noticing and getting to know each other. "One mouse has feet and the other has wheels and a key" (Mark). "One is man-made and has love and one is nature-made. This gives him strength" (Vinny). "Willy has friends and comforts. Alexander has rights to the whole house, and he can move freely" (Brian). Again Vinny focused on Alexander as the one whose fortunes we are following when he focused on the "nature-made" quality of Alexander giving him "strength." (When your fate is at stake and you don't have love, you need strength.)

*"Which mouse would you rather be?"* "Alexander because I like him better" (Mark). "Willy. He has wheels and can go real fast" (Vinny). "Alexander. He can move whenever he wishes and I'd like to scare people" (Brian). Mark's feelings for Alexander might have arisen from sympathy; Alexander is the less fortunate mouse at this point. Brian was attracted to Alexander's "magical" power to scare people. Vinny chose to be Willy, just as Alexander wants to be at this point; thus he revealed his strong empathy with the main character. For the moment he has *become* Alexander (he knew what Alexander wanted to have and be—and he wanted to have that fun time, too).

*"What will Alexander wish for?"* Willy tells Alexander about a Magic Lizard that can grant wishes. When each child predicted Alexander would ask to be a wind-up toy, I asked why: "He wanted to be loved" (Mark). "He wanted somebody" (Vinny). "He wanted friends and comfort" (Brian). Mark emphasized one side of Alexander, his need for safety and love; Vinny and Brian emphasized another side, Alexander's need for a friend. When he heard what Alexander really wished, Vinny said: "I thought it was nice when Willy turned into a real mouse because he [Alexander] wanted him turned into one." His empathy for Alexander was again evident, as was his emphasis on friendship.

At the end of the story, I asked the children what the story was about to them: "Mouses" (Mark), "Alexander and a wind-up mouse" (Vinny), and "A lonely mouse and the friendship of a mouse and a mechanized mouse and how one would change the other instead of himself" (Brian). Then I asked them to show what the story was about to them, with words and pictures.

I recorded each child's answers to the questions, as well as their spontaneous comments and nonverbal activities both during and after the reading and drawing. Each child's picture focused on a different emphasis of the story, thus producing a different insight: Mark focused on the small, vulnerable aspects of the mice. Filling a huge expanse of page filled with sky, outside world, and tall cave (with a large open door), he drew a picture of two tiny but well-defined mice lost in the mountains, trapped for twenty years in a cave by a fox. "Then they got saved [an intriguing gap]. And they laughed "blah blah, blah—all the way home."

Vinny focused on the mouse friendship, drawing Tom and Jerry sneaking watermelon and having a contest, a scene that made him laugh as he drew. Brian focused on the sacrifice that each animal made for the other, or the idea of friendship-as-responsibility. His comic-strip story told of a frog, Herman, and his frog friend who gets sick, causing Herman to go to Neptune "to see if his underwater friend can be spared." Neptune tells him to go home and "take care of your frog friend," and when he returns, his friend is well and he is "eternally grateful."

Each of the children was producing tentative meanings for the story, or engaging in what I have called *generative* reading. And each was bringing to bear his own experiences of the world in what we might call *sociocultural* reading. Mark was small and had become lost one day at the mall, a scary time for him, but he persevered and was at last found; Vinny had watched and enjoyed many Tom and Jerry cartoons; and Brian had a pet frog, Herman.

Brian used a great many of Lionni's signposts in his picture-story, thus revealing strength in what we might call *literary* literacy, the ability to weave threads of story into meaningful and satisfying textual patterns. Mark's story was equally strong in what we might call *narrative* reading, or the ability to invent himself as a storyteller as he listened to the story, puzzling out what the author and he together were making of the world. Lionni's story had given him much food for his own creative thoughts.

But it was Vinny who appeared to take control of the story and the storymaking with the greatest degree of pleasure, thus revealing strength in what, following Rosenblatt's terminology, we might call *aesthetic* literacy, the ability to become deeply and actively involved in the story, living through the experience with the characters. While drawing, he was very content, very absorbed. He sang and laughed. That night he became engaged in imaginative play, entering once more into *becoming* Alexander, in terms of what we might call *personal/empathetic* reading. "I'm Alexander getting into my little hole," he told me as he continued to play for some time under the bed. It was also Vinny who asked to hear the book again several months later.

Based on the obvious pleasure Vinny took in creating his story and playing through the story later, I concluded that his alignment with the book was the strongest of the three children. Mark was attentive and productive, and Brian produced a mature response in terms of cognitive complexity. But Vinny's strong absorption and personal involvement enabled me to see quite visibly live circuits of response.

## EXPLORATORY CONVERSATION AND INTERSECTING LITERACIES

When summer ended and the school year began, Vinny, now seven years, nine months, asked to hear Lionni's book one night at bedtime, and because this was now a more natural, conversational setting, I found myself asking the same questions at times—but differently. This time Vinny was no longer a response *subject* but my response partner; I was no longer interviewing him, I was talking with him about the story. Soon I saw that conversation could open up many different literacies at once, producing expanded meaning-making.

At the beginning of the story, I found myself asking, as before, "What happened?" But conversation allowed Vinny this time to respond by weaving a small story: "He [Alexander] got in a kitchen cupboard. He opened the door and everything fell out." (Before he said merely that the dishes and cups fell down and the mouse was "running to his mouse hole.") Telling more now enabled him to start building, piece by piece, a satisfying meaning base for the story. At the same time, he could build strength in reading the text on his own terms—or what we might call *generative* literacy.

When we reached the scene of the mice talking and becoming friends, I wondered as before how the mice were different, and as before, Vinny said that one was "nature-made" and one was "man-made." But this time he added more: "Willy is mechanical. Alexander is a live animal. Everyone loves Willy. Everyone hates Alexander because he's like a troublemaker." He was sorting out why the humans strike at Alexander with a broom—or looking at things through *their* eyes.

"Why a purple pebble?" I asked Vinny (when Willy tells Alexander about the Magic Lizard). "It means magic," Vinny declared. (When the lizard tells Alexander he must find a purple pebble, Vinny decided that purple was part of the lizard's magic.) "He [the lizard] will turn him [Alexander] into a mechanical mouse." This was a surprising response. Vinny had in several months forgotten details of the plot, but the lapse in time was fortunate for his growth in *literary* literacy, or his ability to notice recurring patterns signaling meanings. As he became reengaged with familiar story patterns, he constructed them in different ways—or with new eyes. What was significant now was how closely he was aligning himself with Alexander, that is, engaging in *personal/empathetic* literacy (the ability to become deeply involved with one of the story characters, usually the main one).

"Which mouse would you rather be?" I asked again this time. Before he had said, "Willy. He has wheels and can go real fast." Now he said, "The real mouse. Then no one would have to wind me up. I'd be free." When I wondered why Alexander doesn't see how great it is to be free (Alexander wants to be Willy, the toy cuddled and loved by Annie), his response was equally interesting for increased strength in *sociocultural* literacy, or the way we read when we use our knowledge of the real world (our values, beliefs, and ideologies) to understand the story world. "He's thinking more about Willy than about himself," Vinny answered. "He wants the key and two wheels, too; that makes him move. And they could run together and be cuddled."

How do stories work to achieve a successful bonding of reader and story character? Booth (1988) says that stories invite readers to care about nurturing characters who nurture them in return. From this perspective, we would say that Vinny cared about Alexander, who cares about Willy, who in turn cares about Alexander. And both story characters were "nurturing" Vinny, an empathetic reader.

Margaret Meek (1988) similarly says that a character's predicament engages us because of our concern for the character. We meet this character, she adds, and we ask not just what will happen next, but what will happen to this character? In this case, Alexander is himself a nurturing character, but he also invites nurturing: he is an endangered creature who causes readers to ask intuitively, *What if this were happening to me?* Literature, in other words, helps readers to know themselves, others, and the world better for having entered the character's time, place, and predicament. Thus it fosters important *personal/empathetic* learning

But even though Vinny empathized strongly with Alexander, he was able to shift to another perspective as he read the story this time. He began to see through the eyes of the human brandishing the broom in the picture. Thinking about how the two mice were different, he explained that humans would see Alexander as a troublemaker. In response to my comment, "People don't want to cuddle Alexander, do they?" he replied, "No, he might bite."

Such shifts are important for children's growth in multiple literacies. Forming a strong relationship with the central character produced Vinny's deep engagement as a story participant and enabled him to respond from an empathetic core. Increased *personal/empathetic* literacy produced pleasure in the literary process, which took him more deeply into the story itself, living through the experience with the characters—or engaging in *aesthetic* literacy. When he responded with empathy toward a very minor character, the human adult who was frightening Alexander or bashing him with the broom, he was building a stronger meaning-making structure from the story patterns (*literary* literacy) and from his knowledge of and beliefs about the world (*sociocultural* and *critical* literacies). And he was becoming deeply engaged as a co-creator of story (*narrative* literacy).

With *literary* literacy, we see Barthes's (1974) "readerly" role in action (the reader is making meaning of what the text appears to be saying); with *narrative* literacy, we see what he calls the "writerly" role (the reader is making meaning of what the text leaves unsaid). This story was drawing Vinny into both roles and both literacies at once, perhaps because Lionni's narrative coding was balanced evenly between readerly and writerly roles or because some combination of Vinny's age, social relationships, and personal constructs was a good match for the book. And because Vinny was filling gaps of meaning in new ways each time he revisited the story and because his empathy for the characters was so strong, the story was fostering his *aesthetic* literacy.

When we reached the scene in the lizard's garden at midnight, when Alexander faced his big moment of choice, I found myself asking as before, "What will Alexander wish for?" And Vinny replied as before: "To be a mechanical mouse like Willy." Again his empathy for the main character was so strong and his emotional immersion in the story was so complete that he did not change his earlier prediction (Lionni's talent for producing a suspenseful—or unpredictable—story at work). "What could happen if Alexander did become a mechanical mouse?" I asked, and Vinny replied with strong meaning-making: "He'd get thrown away. He might break. They'd be together," he added, "but they might be thrown away in two trash cans."

"What will happen now?" I wondered when Alexander raced back to the box of cast-off toys, one of which contains Willy. With more of the details of the story now emerging, Vinny predicted, "He'll be alive."

"But they already threw him away," I said.

"He'll be in the baseboard," he assured me. "He jumped out of the box and ran into the baseboard."

Judging by Vinny's earlier picture creation, in which both mice (he now called them Tom and Jerry) were living as real mice in Annie's house (his story "sequel" to Lionni's story), the ending of the book was especially important to him. He saw friends helping one another to survive; each was happy that the other was alive, but they were also having fun.

That Vinny remembered the ending of the story during this revisiting of the book appears to support the conclusions reached by Fox (1993) in her research with preschoolers. Drawing from Bartlett's theories (1932) that personal interests and individual temperaments are what enable readers to recall certain aspects of stories, she decided that her preschoolers remembered best what they found meaningful in stories. They transferred what they saw as the "powerful parts of strong stories" (p. 128) to their own stories in various re-created ways. Then they were able to relive important story moments.

If we consider Vinny's earlier story-picture in the light of Fox's theories, we see more clearly why he made his baseboard mouse hole beside Tom (or Herman, as he later renamed him for Brian's pet frog) so large in relation to the broom. By the end of the book, the mouse hole had become a safe home for Willy, and Vinny wanted a similar safe place for his own story mice, Tom/Herman and Jerry. To signal this safety, he made Herman's mouse hole exceptionally large. In his role as author, he found ways to control the danger to the mice from the broom; thus he could produce—and sustain—the humorous tone he wanted for his story.

Vinny's responses as he revisited the story revealed a burst of interwoven literacies. He was sorting out plot and characters, building a tentative framework for meaning-making (*generative*). He was developing understanding for the characters and their actions (*personal/empathetic*). He was interpreting characters' actions and behavior in terms of how he saw the world working (*sociocultural*) or how he thought it should work (*critical*). He was thinking about what the story meant and what ideas it emphasized in terms of repeated patterns he noticed in the story (*literary*). He was filling in gaps of story with stories of his own and thinking about how stories are told (*narrative*). He was making emotional connections between the text and his own personal life, and he was becoming absorbed in what the characters were thinking, feeling, seeing, and hearing—or living through the story with the characters (*aesthetic*).

Each of these ways of responding emerged from a generative base. Equally strong as a base for all the other ways was his empathy with Alexander, which set all the other literacies in motion. His personal affinity at this time for a small, threatened, but clever fantasy animal with its ability to conquer danger—and have fun doing so—and his high priority for having and being a friend were important factors for his bonding with story. But the author's part in eliciting reader empathy cannot be overlooked, nor can Vinny's drawing, storymaking, and free play during the earlier events, all of which helped deepened his empathetic response and his aesthetic reading.

## CHILDREN'S RESPONSES AND SOCIAL CONTEXTS

Several months later, on a February day, when Vinny was eight years and two months old and Mark was five years and seven months, I happened to be reading *Alexander and the Wind-Up Mouse* to both children together and inviting their responses in talk and drawing, as I often did.

As they listened together, I found myself asking the usual questions I had at certain places in the story. And the meaning-making continued to expand as we all read together.

When I asked, "Which mouse would you rather be?" Vinny again chose the real mouse, but now he expressed another reason for his choice: A real mouse could get cut and "pretty soon be better" (the cut could heal like a human cut would), but a crack in the mechanical one would "stay there all his life." Mark stated firmly that he would rather be the mechanical one: "He can't die" (his emphasis on vulnerability/danger/smallness was still intact).

This time instead of asking "What will Alexander wish for?" I said, "If you had a friend who had something you didn't have (like wheels), but you had something special, too, something you or your friend's life depended upon (like feet), what would you wish for?" Vinny said, "To be like me because he is my friend." Mark agreed: "Be like me"; then he added: "Sometimes you shouldn't care for yourself. You should care for other people" (an idea that might have been growing out of his concern about dangers facing the mice, or any small creatures like himself).

Finally, when I asked, "What was the story about to you?" Mark said, "Helping people," and Vinny said, "Friendship." Their answers clarified their earliest responses to this question, when Mark said, "mouses," and Vinny said, "Alexander and a wind-up mouse."

Mark's picture-story this time revealed a "doughnut man" (drawn to look like Lionni's Magic Lizard) who was turning two mice, one real, one mechanical, into doughnuts, perhaps his way of showing how helpful the doughnut man/lizard was. The picture shows two happy—and as Mark said, "yummy"—doughnuts dancing together. He solved the problem of Lionni's story (Willy's lack of feet) by transforming both mice friends into dough. The danger and vulnerability of the mice seemed erased now, unless you remember, as Mark implied, that doughnuts exist to be eaten.

Vinny's picture-story emphasized the value of helpfulness as his earlier story had done, but now he revealed more clearly that being helpful was not just a funny and fun time; it could be a lifesaving experience (he was no longer deemphasizing the dangers in life for the small creatures). He made his lizard a real mouse—Mikey—who, like Lionni's lizard, had magical powers. But as a mouse, his lizard was still too small and vulnerable to fight the cat bully (his interest in Tom and Jerry surfacing once more), so Mikey needs the help of his mouse friends (named here Willy and Alexander also). And like Mark, Vinny was emphasizing magic as a way of keeping friendship as full of fun as possible—no sacrifices necessary.

In his first reading, Vinny had wanted to be Willy (to have wheels and go fast). On the second reading, he said he wanted to be like Alexander, who was free to move as he liked. This time he again chose Alexander because he could mend himself if cut or "broken." Then as he drew, he managed a way for the mice to have the best of both worlds. "They figure they are going to be like Willy except they are going to be like him in another way," he said. "Instead of wheels on the toys, they are going to have roller skates and skateboards."

A comment Mark made during the reading when I asked how the two mice were different seemed to be inspiring Vinny. Mark had replied: "One has wires inside; the other has brains." The mice in Vinny's story use brainpower to have both freedom and fun: He gives them feet for mobility and wheels for speed. Yet Vinny's own personal perspective, beginning with the first reading, was still intact: His mouse friends are having fun, just as he was having fun watching them and bringing them to life in his own stories.

Vinny continued: "A third mouse, Mikey, a little guy, is riding in the sky making magic and swooping Willy and Alexander up into his spaceship so the cat can't get them and also so they can help Mikey fire tomatoes and eggs on the cat's head." Giving help, he implied, is the force behind friendship, help that at times needs a little magical push.

As before, their picture-stories revealed more about their own child worlds: the need to have fun, the importance of friends caring about one another, and the need for many helpers at times when a great deal of magic is needed.

## REFLECTIONS

When children are deeply engaged with fantasy literature, we see "live circuits" of response that reveal more about the books children read, their ways of reading and composing, and their own child worlds. But what causes their deep engagement? If the child's empathy with the character is at the base of all the other literacies—and if playing the becoming game is an important step into *aesthetic* literacy—what enables a child to respond from this empathetic core, or to *want* to play the becoming game? What enables rich responses to emerge and grow during a reading event? What causes a child's *aesthetic* literacy to deepen as his or her responses evolve?

It all begins with the child and the book. And my question—what caused Vinny's strong engagement with the book?—left me thinking there was no way to separate the two. Authors shape stories by creating patterns, says Meek (1988), and by eliciting reader empathy. But it takes child readers to make meaning of these patterns, to bring them to life, to step into the shoes of a nurturing character.

Adult mediating strategies are particularly important, too. I was discovering there was no way to separate the book and the child from the circumstances of the particular reading event. Conversing with children about books opens up the way for stronger meaning-making. Inviting their comments at moments that occur to us naturally as gaps in the story is a good place to start. Drawing, storymaking, and free play during or after the reading event all help to deepen children's empathetic response and their aesthetic reading. At the same time, I discovered that children playing the becoming game was an important step into narrative literacy. Feeling what their characters are feeling is what authors must do first: they must *become* their characters, and child readers must do the same. Each of these children found some aspect of Lionni's characters to become; thus they were better able to extend Lionni's story with picture-stories of their own.

Equally important is that we elicit children's responses in social settings so that we evoke the richest array of interwoven literacies and encourage children to become not merely our research *subjects* but our partners in response. When I stopped interviewing children and began conversing with them, the lights went on, responses began to flow, and I saw a cycle of response—or "live circuits"—moving in a circular, often recursive, pattern of events (see Figure 1.1), in which readers did the following:

- selected or encountered books (or, in a more mystical vein, the books "found" them);
- noticed signposts of the author's narrative coding in many different ways, in relation to age, gender, personal constructs, cultural experiences, and social contexts;
- responded spontaneously and naturally with talk, art, storymaking, and role-play;
- engaged in conversations that resulted in multiple, interwoven literacies;
- negotiated narrative complexities and explored personal ethical choices and social and cultural issues that mattered to them in terms of their worlds;
- produced rich responses that enabled them to learn more about literature, literacies, and child worlds;

**FIGURE 1.1.** A "Live Circuit" of Children's Response to Literature

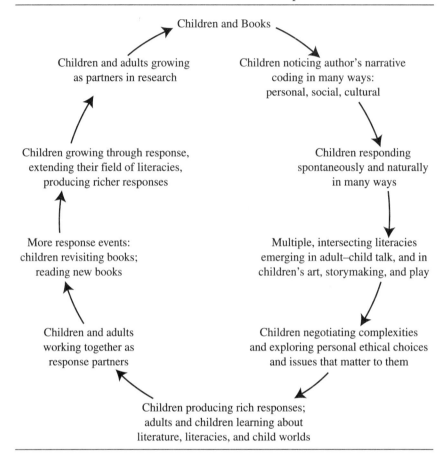

- worked together as response partners, learning from one another; and
- engaged in more response events as they were growing through response.

Just as the cycle of response begins with the child and the book, it ends there, too—the live circuit returning to its starting place, with the next reading event waiting to begin. Vinny's empathetic personality mirrored easily the empathy that both mouse characters felt for one another, and his preoccupation with friends having fun was also mirrored on many pages of the book. Thus he found the story just right for hypothesizing, storymaking, play—and revisiting. He was not intimidated by the vulnerable condition of either mouse; he had experienced enough of the real world and the world of cartoons and comic-strip conflicts that he was able to construct trickster plotting for his fictional mice.

Reading and drawing later with Vinny, Mark seemed less over-whelmed by the emotional content of Lionni's story. Even though he continued to emphasize vulnerability and danger for the mice because of their small size, and even though he made comments about the need for caring about people and about dying, these emphases seem to indicate preoccupations arising from his own personality construct and his prior experiences, which in no way prevented him from negotiating complexities of text or bonding with the book in subsequent readings.

Often as educators, we lament, rather than celebrate, differences of response; thus we expect reading events to produce convergence of responses rather than divergence, variety, or many ways of seeing, all of which emerge when we value natural and spontaneously reading events. But I was discovering that children reading, talking, storying, and playing the "becoming" game together could stretch and nurture one another's imaginative capabilities.

It is important for children to see—and to show us what they see; it is also important that they help one another see more.

*Chapter Two*

# Inside the World
# of *The Snowman*:
# Different Ways of Seeing

WHEN VINNY BECAME a second-grader, I volunteered as a storytime reader again. I was hooked on children's books and children's responses by this time. The previous summer I had learned about wordless picture books in my children's literature class and had purchased Raymond Briggs's *The Snowman* (1978). It certainly presented a challenging read-aloud situation; the children would have to "read" the story to me. What would they notice? I wondered. What would they "tell" as the story? Would they even like a wordless book? Would it "work" in a classroom setting?

## *THE SNOWMAN*: ADULT PERSPECTIVES

In this wordless fantasy, a boy makes a snowman one day; then, at midnight, the boy runs downstairs to let the snowman into his house, where the snowman discovers lights and running water, the fun of toys and a freestanding freezer, before he takes the boy on a magical flight. Returning at sunrise, the boy returns to his warm bed, the snowman to his post outside the boy's house. Waking, the boy runs outside to see coal eyes spilling over a heap of snow.

To tell this story, Briggs displays a sequence of pictures, small to full-page (no two pages have the same format). A number of techniques from film, filmstrip, cartoon, and picture books spin the plot, convey motion and movement, introduce important details, foreground high points of the action, mark the passage of time, and interject enigmatic gaps. The story takes place in a twenty-four-hour span of time. But the major events take place at night, when the boy and the snowman each explore the other's world.

Briggs leaves important signposts along the way in soft-crayon, impressionistic drawings to signal meaning. "Hot" colors—red, yellow, and

26

orange—signify the heat threatening the snowman's life; "cool" colors—blue, purple, and gray—fill the snowman's natural world of snow and sky. Green tones—earth, life, and growth—fill the boy's world and bring his time with the snowman to an end, in the tiny final picture. So picture size is also significant. Several large pictures stand out: the parents sleeping, the snowman trying on the parents' clothes, the snowman staring happily at a cluster of balloons, sitting in the family car, headlights blazing, climbing into the freezer, and sitting down to a candlelight supper. In the largest pictures boy and snowman soar wordlessly over a landscape dotted with nature and culture (two double-page spreads).

Literary critic Sheila Egoff (1981) has expressed reservations about wordless picture books, saying that words are more effective for presenting a plot (and a punch line) than are pictures, although she also admits that this genre rises out of the "tradition of the pictograph, humanity's primal form of literacy" (p. 255). Therefore, this kind of picture book, she says, would enable children to perform as readers all the while they were becoming more adept in the reading role. On the other hand, Egoff warns, pictures do not allow anyplace "for the mind to hide" (p. 255), as words do, if a picture (or an idea embedded in a picture) becomes frightening.

Furthermore, she says, although a book like *The Snowman* may be the shining example of its particular form, if it is so "tightly controlled in its cartoon-strip visual images," it might "negate the interjection of the viewer's imagination" (p. 255). Even Egoff would agree, however, that the last picture of this book—the boy staring at the quickly disappearing snowman—certainly packs a dramatic punch. The way that Briggs has arranged pictures—juxtapositions of large scenes to slow down and stop the action and small scenes to keep it moving quickly along—also provides strong signals for the plotline, compensating effectively for the absence of words.

## *THE SNOWMAN*: CHILDREN'S PERSPECTIVES

I had shared wordless picture books with my own two children, but I had no idea how the many small pictures and the filmstrip format would work for a classroom read-aloud time. Would this book foster the children's interest in stories or merely suppress the imagination? Would a frightening idea (a snowman "dying") be oppressive in a wordless format? Or would children find ways to find hiding places of the mind? Of special importance, would sharing this particular type of book open doors into child worlds? What words would children produce, if pictures were the entire text of a book?

I could only discover answers to my questions if children, not I, were
doing the "reading." So as I sat on the floor, with my son's classmates scat-
tered around me, I encouraged them to tell me the story. As they told, I
jotted down their responses:

> He's coming alive!
> Like Frosty!
> Did he turn real?
> I like this book.
> Now he's inside.
> He's going to melt.
> No, he's going outside.
> They're eating ice so the snowman can stay cold.
> Why doesn't he melt?
> They opened the freezer.
> Why did they turn on the lights?
> Why doesn't it have any words?
> He can fly!
> How can he fly?
> The wind lifts him up.
> He's flying!
> The snow just sticks to him like a magnet.
> He's far away now.
> In the city.
> At the North Pole!
> I think it was a dream.
> He [the boy] thinks it melted.
> It did melt.

What the children emphasized in their responses told me a great deal
about the book in terms of its narrative structure, sequence of events, major
threads of plot, story setting, and genre (*The Snowman* is not just fantasy
but dream fantasy, and it becomes interesting to see how, or when, children respond to this nuance of plot). In fact, their reactions revealed what
Rosenblatt (1994) calls the "lived-through evocation [calling-forth] of the
work" (p. 70), the "evocation" being the first "stream" (p. 48) of responses,
the second being the reader's evolving interpretation of the work. Readers
are "generating the work of art" (p. 48) when feelings and ideas emerge;
at the same time, they are beginning to shape a "tentative organizing framework" (p. 165) of meanings for the work, as these children were collectively
doing. Readers are also responding to the "author's pattern of words"
(p. 53). At least two literacies are therefore at work as readers evoke a work:

what I am calling *generative* literacy (building up or constructing tentative meanings) and *literary* literacy (noticing various patterns of words, images, ideas, and story structure as part of the meaning-making process).

## TEXT AND CHILD CONTEXTS

*The Snowman* has an easily discernable structure, despite the way the scenes "melt" together in a tightly fused sequence. In the beginning a boy wakes up to discover a new snowfall and rushes out to make a snowman. Then just at midnight, as the clock at the boy's bedside shows, the boy steals downstairs to visit his friend. He discovers that the snowman has turned around (he is now facing the boy's front door) and is tipping his hat as if to say hello. These second-graders entered the reading event just at this point with responses about the snowman "coming alive" and a question, "Did he turn real?"

The middle part falls into two sections. In the first, the boy brings the snowman into his warm house and shows him his world; then the snowman takes the boy up into *his* world of sky, cold air, and snowflakes. They fly over the famous English seaside city of Brighton, the Royal Pavilion, and the Brighton pier. (Briggs lives in Brighton, where King George IV had the Royal Pavilion in 1787 constructed with ornate turrets to resemble a palace in India.) These American children, however, used their own cultural knowledge to transport the snowman to the "city" and to the North Pole as they experienced—alongside the boy—the fun of flying.

At the end of this second part, as boy and snowman stand facing a sunrise, viewers do not know what transpires in their words or thoughts (the boy might be telling the snowman about the danger of a snowman melting; the snowman might be explaining why he will soon be gone; or either might be simply thinking about what will happen next). Then boy and snowman turn back around and the snowman hugs the boy good-bye. The children made no comments at this point.

As the book ends, the boy waves good-bye one last time before falling into a restless sleep. The snowman is turned outward now, his back to the boy's house, as at the beginning. Here again the children made no comments. Then, in what might be called an epilogue, the boy rushes out into the morning sunlight to find the snowman turned back into a small heap of snow, his coal eyes sinking into the ground. At this point, one child responded that the story is a dream; the others focused on the melting snowman. And the response about a dream is worth noting.

Had the child noticed the clock hands standing at midnight at the very moment the boy goes downstairs to see the snowman? Had he read other stories, fantasy and fairy tales, in which midnight is often the time when magical impossibility occurs? Or was seeing the story as a dream a way for him to explain the sad fact of the snowman's melting—a way to explain the boy's magical flight, to place the fantasy in a more realistic context, or to "melt" away the suggestion of death?

Egoff defines fantasy as a "literature of paradox" (1981, p. 80). It is "the discovery of the real within the unreal, the credible within the incredible, the believable within the unbelievable. Yet the paradoxes have to be re-solved. It is in the interstices between the two halves of the paradox, on the knife-edge of two worlds, that fantasists build their domain . . . their basic concern is with . . . the integrity of the self" (p. 80). Fantasists, she continues, "wrestle with the great complexities of existence—life, death, time, space, good and evil—and a child's struggle to find its place within these awesome concepts" (p. 80). Yet they are not entirely solemn in their aspirations; as she adds: "Fantasists also indulge in creative play and cele-bration. It is as if they themselves were children albeit godlike ones, rede-signing the universe to make its realities more apparent" (p. 80).

What are we to make of a fantasy when all we have are pictures— details, images, gestures, facial expressions, movements, and size and placement of pictures—as clues? What might children enable us to see? "A wordless book," I wrote after hearing the children's evocation, "encour-ages the opening up of ideas. What are the characters thinking and feeling and saying? With written words there are answers readily available. With no words there are as many answers as readers. But pictures can 'speak' to readers too. We feel something even though we don't have any words. I wonder what these children will write and draw to show what the pic-tures in this book are saying to them."

## DEEPENING THE EVOCATION: WRITING AND DRAWING

To deepen the evocation, I invited the children to think of one picture that was special to them and to write their own special words to tell about it. If they wished, they could draw pictures to accompany their words. The children chose pictures from all parts of the story. Three children wrote and drew about the beginning of the story:

*Tisha:* Snowman and girl

*Cory:* He built a good snowman

*Larry:* Falling Snow Boy Snowman Building a Snowman

Three children focused on the beginning of the middle section (the snowman coming to life, just before he entered the boy's home):

*Katina:* The snowman was alive he came alive when the boy made him I like the part that when he came alive

*Kristin:* The snowman was alive

*Anna:* The snowman was alive he had a boy to play with. Mother call him to eat then he went to the Big City he had on body [nobody] to play with

Five children selected the first part of the middle section (the snowman inside the boy's house):

*Jessie:* The snowman pick up his hat

*Michael:* I like when the snowman took the boy and went in the car and turned on the lights.

*Jerry:* Driving in the snow.

*Brad:* I like the part win [when] he was driving the car he turned on the car light

*Vinny:* I like when the snowman hit the ball. And it went strait back to him and then hes [he's] on the wall and the boy said are you al right? And the snowman said yes and the boy said get up!

Seven children chose the second part of the middle section (the boy and the snowman flying):

*Carl:* Boy Snow Falling snow [the boy and snowman flying]

*Monique:* I like when him and the snowman went right up in the sky

*Cathy:* I like the time when he went up in the sky with the wind

*John:* As they flew over the city of New York in the snow It was a cold night time

*Linda:* I like the windy sky when he went up into the snow sky

*Reggie:* I like when the snowman was flying. They was high in the sky. The snow was falling down from the sky. The snow was little.

*Lea:* Bob said we better go home. But I enjoyed coming to Washington D. C. let's go! Bye Mr. snowman, said Bob.

Two children wrote about the final scenes:

*Chuck:* The boy was seep [asleep] he was so sleepy. I am so sleepy I can fall asleep he light [liked] his pillow and he light his shep [sheet] and his pillowcase

*Patty:* At the end he was sade [sad] becuses [because] his best friend Mr. Snowman melted.

Only one child, Patty, focused on the very last scene of the book (the nearly melted snowman), a picture Briggs has wisely painted as a very small square in a large pool of white space—almost hidden from view. Response researcher Don Fry (1985), in *Children Talk About Books*, tells us that Clayton, age eight, devised his own strategy for keeping the sad outcome of the story distanced: he turned immediately back to the beginning of the book once he came to it. "I don't look at the end page," he says. "I didn't like that piece" (pp. 119–120).

But because at least one child did choose this scene, I saw that young children reading together in a social setting could evoke the entire sequence of a book. As a group they had focused, naturally and spontaneously, on all the different threads of plot—or story parts—with most of their responses focused on the scenes of liftoff and flight. In fact, their focus corresponded to Briggs's own emphasis, if we consider that he created a full-page picture of the flight on one side and two half-page pictures of it on the other, the only such large-scale configuration in the book. The boy's adventure of flying with the snowman certainly seems to be the author's intended high point of the action.

Except for Patty, the responses of the children were divided among the other major parts of the story, and their responses indicated that picture size signaled important scenes of the story to them. In the "middle" section, when the boy and snowman are inside the house, the scenes the children remembered are also those Briggs created in larger format: the snowman tries on the boy's father's clothes, plays with the boy's punching bag, and tries to drive the family car.

The pictures of boy and snowman, boy and mother, and boy and parents produce interpretive "writerly" gaps about who is talking and who is listening. Three of the children introduced dialogue into their story pictures. Vinny and Lea created spoken words between the boy and snowman, and Chuck showed the boy talking to himself.

Rosenblatt (1994) speaks of readers weaving their own responses into a character's words, when they sense a "particular voice of a particular kind of persona" (p. 57). Readers take clues from the text concerning what characters would say, and when children introduce dialogue, they reveal the ability to "hear" different ways to enter in with their own point of view about the story. Dialogue becomes a first step in telling stories of their own within the author's story (*narrative* literacy).

In addition, two children conversed with one another as they wrote and drew. They were extending the story in free and sociable ways, in the same way that Heath (1983) described "Trackton" children (children she encountered in the Piedmont Carolinas who from birth were immersed in a flow of talk, with family members, neighbors, and other children listening and telling stories):

> *Monique:* I like when him and the snowman went right up in the sky. Do you think that when the boy and the snowman went up in the sky was real?
> *Carl:* I don't believe it but it have to be true.
> *Monique:* I know you don't believe it [but] you have to believe things sometimes. You know, I want you to believe it.

Just as Briggs had worked hard to produce believability for his fantasy story, Monique was concerned with drawing a picture that Carl could see as believable. In Rosenblatt's words (1994), literature brings into being "a structure of ideas and attitudes that grow out of and around the concepts of social life" or of "human considerations" (p. 56).

Readers dip into their own "internalized culture" (p. 56) to draw from the story a world similar to or different from their own; they affirm what they want others to believe about life in terms of the story world. Thus we see another literacy—*sociocultural*—emerging in this interchange in which children wrestled with questions like what is real, what is "true" or believable? As Carl and Monique—and all the other children—were struggling to articulate their own meanings and values for the story, they helped produce a more complete knowledge base for the entire group. The more responses—convergent or divergent—that arose from these child readers, the greater this base became. And resistant responses opened up even more doors to child worlds.


## WHEN CHILDREN RESIST THE TEXT

One child did not draw any scene from *The Snowman*. Keith had developed a deep engagement with another book I had read aloud prior to this, *Jane's Blanket*. So he chose to draw about that book, although his accompanying words—"Pink blankets falling from the sky, producing rain"—resonated easily with *The Snowman*.

Written by the famous playwright Arthur Miller and illustrated by Emily McCully, *Jane's Blanket* (1963) is a lyrical story about a little girl giving up her baby blanket so the birds can have a warm nest. There is nothing in this book about rain, but Keith's picture-story (actually a haiku) reflects the gentle tone of the words and the pictures of birds flying through the air carrying pink wool threads. Perhaps he was also blending scenes of falling snow from Briggs's book with Miller's spring setting.

Keith's response was also rooted in genre preference. Miller's book, a realistic picture storybook, was just the kind of book he thought he should be reading as a second-grader. "Why didn't it [*The Snowman*] have words?" he asked me. "It's boring just to have pictures."

"I wonder why we have pictures in books," I said, to extend his response.

> *Keith:* To know what's going on. With *Pippi Longstocking* [1950, by Astrid Lindgren], you might have to read it all over again if you didn't have pictures. If you stop and then come back, you might not understand it as well.
> *NM:* So it bothered you when this book didn't have words.
> *Keith:* When they open their mouths, you don't know what they're saying.
> *NM:* [turning to the page on which the boy and snowman are flying]: I wonder how the boy felt there.
> *Keith:* Excited. He didn't know the snowman could fly.
> *NM:* Is there one picture you remember better than the others?
> *Keith:* The boy was sad when the snowman melted. It didn't have a happy ending. It was dumb.
> *NM:* So the story was about—

    *Keith:*  A snowman that melted at the end and the boy was sad. I
       don't think it was true. I think he dreamed it.

    Keith's focus on the last page as what the story was about tells us a great
deal. His decision not to draw about this book and his idea that the boy
dreamed the adventure both helped to distance his feelings about the
snowman's "death." His picture of pink blankets might also have been a way
of talking about the snowman indirectly (a comforting way), in that snow is
often seen as "blanketing" the earth. And the idea of rain might have been
his way of reflecting the sadness he felt about the snowman melting.

    The importance of eliciting children's responses is that we learn more
about their worlds, their many ways of seeing, their different ways of reading and reacting to books, and their need to control their own exposure to
disturbing images and ideas. Seeing more of their worlds helps us fill in
the picture of their ideas and feelings about literature and life and form
richer interpretations of children's books. Best of all, inviting children to
talk openly about books helps *them* form deeper and richer evocations of
books—or to grow as responsive readers. As we help them bring unconscious ideas and feelings to conscious awareness, we see that evoking response can foster growth in *multiple* literacies. Thus we become better
teachers or better mediators of their books.

    In my own work at this time, I was learning that the more I let
children's ideas unfold in drawing, talk, and storying, the more I learned
about the complex relationship between children and books and about
the importance of letting them control their exposure to troubling images.
At certain times, a book like *The Snowman* evoked deep feelings and cu-
riosities, and when I observed children wrestling with these feelings, it
helped me know them better and it caused me to ask new questions about
books. Were wordless fantasies valuable for their writerly pictorial
"texts"? Did they evoke a richer array of literacies than other books?
(Wasn't Keith's resistant reading linked closely to *personal/empathetic, literary,* and *critical* literacies? Wasn't it also directly related to the deep
*aesthetic* literacy that he had developed as he read *Jane's Blanket?*)

    At the same time, in the classroom setting, during these brief read-
aloud times, I felt I was seeing only snapshots of children's feelings and
ideas. I wondered if there might be some way to see more, if I returned to
the personal context. I wanted to watch *The Snowman* unfolding in just a
few children's minds, to listen as they storied the book for themselves,
"reading" the sequence of pictures at their own pace, with time for ideas
to grow and bloom as extended responses. What might I learn then about
children, books, and responsive reading? The next week I took *The Snowman*
home with me, hoping to see more.

## OUTSIDE THE CLASSROOM:
## CHILDREN AND *THE SNOWMAN*

One way to study children's interpretations of wordless books is to notice how many of the scenes children select for picture reading. How much of the original story do they choose to tell about? We might assume that the more of the story that a child retells, the better the child has internalized or "comprehended" the story. Or we might realize, as Fry says, that children's stories of wordless picture books are not simply "retellings." They involve a bringing of the original story "to life in words" (1981, p. 20), or the child reader putting "into words of his [or her] own story the feelings experienced through the pictures of the original" (p. 20). So the question may be *which* scenes children choose to tell about or re-create, rather than *how many*.

Listening on the homefront to children's responses to *The Snowman*, I noticed that Vinny (8 years, 3 months) produced a slightly longer story than Mark (5 years, 8 months) and that he responded verbally to more of the scenes. But I also noticed that both children showed a strong interest in one particular part of the story—the point at which the adult snowman enters the boy's house and "plays" in the child's world. Mark's story, although shorter, was in fact filled with color, liveliness, and emotional engagement. So an important question becomes, what draws children into a book? What do their "readings" or "tellings" reveal about their worlds— their interests, preoccupations, concerns, ideas, and ideologies, their cultural understandings (and misunderstandings), their narrative strategies? How do they deal with complexities of fantasy?

### Mark

Mark begins with a global statement that reveals his eye sweeping over the entire page: "Chubby got out of bed." His name for the boy is the same one he often calls himself in stories, a name he likes because he was chubby in his baby pictures, and his parents had often praised his chubbiness (he *knew* himself through this description).

He focuses on the second picture, saying: "He opened his eyes." He skips the third picture, in which the boy looks out the bedroom window, saying again: "He got out of bed." Then he focuses on the fourth picture, saying, "Chubby looked outside. It was snowing." He continues, "He put on his shirt. He put on his pants," an exact rendering of the next two pictures. During the first part of the story, when the boy is making the snowman, Mark sorts out the pictures to put together his own "story" of the story (*generative* literacy).

In the middle part of the book, when the snowman has fun turning on the oven, Mark has fun injecting sound effects. At the scene in which the snowman tries out the boy's skateboard, he produces invented words to express a fusion of sound and feeling. When the snowman falls, Mark says he goes "kerplooey." At times his cultural experiences do not match those pictured in the text. But he pushes forward, his interpretations based on his experiences and what his imagination makes of the story world (*socio-cultural* and *narrative* literacies).

When steam comes pouring out of the water faucet in one picture (an unfamiliar occurrence for Mark), he interprets the lines Briggs draws for the steam as bugs: "The snowman made all these scruffy bugs." When the snowman climbs into the freezer, Mark, familiar with a freezer compartment rather than a freestanding appliance, interprets frozen food packages as gold nuggets and begins spinning a little story of his own: "They found gold—a million dollars—and they got into it and they played all night long." Thus misreading stimulates his imagination and increases his delight in the story.

Mark's experiential level is not at this point a close match for a major thread of story—the danger of heat melting the snowman. Therefore the binary pattern of hot/cold is not what he focuses on, although at the fireplace scene, he does notice that the snowman "runned away from it." The steam radiator is another unfamiliar object to Mark, one that he interprets as "stairs." And for the next scene, the snowman facing a flower painting, Mark produces still another divergent reading: "The snowman looked at a pot of flowers and it made him happy." The snowman stands before the flower painting with downturned mouth, a blank space of meaning (what the snowman is thinking we can never really know). And because Mark is not focusing on the continuous thread of heat and melting that Briggs has woven through the story (foreshadowing the snowman's fate), he cannot really "read" the picture in terms of authorial signposts. When he sees the snowman contemplating the flower, he can only "read" what he himself might feel (he must rely on *personal/empathetic* rather than *literary* literacy). Does he see the snowman's downturned mouth? Possibly, but with no heat–cold symmetry upon which to build an interpretation, he must rely on imagined logic.

Mark is not fearful about the snowman melting at this point; picture clues are not guiding him to feel the same concern the boy feels for the snowman. No matter how many times he "reads" the story, he is unprepared for that particular understanding of it. His engagement is rooted in the idea of *play*. Chubby, he says, makes a snowman. Mark names the boy in these pictures for himself; thus he shows he is already playing the "becoming" game. Then Chubby and the snowman play together all night long. They discover gold together. They fly together. "The snowman runned and Chubby runned with him," says Mark. "And then the snowman said, 'Are you ready?' And Chubby said, 'Yes.' And then they flied off to the moon."

Mark's emotional investment in the story, his narrative competencies, and his narrative confidence are all very strong at this point, so strong in fact that when he reaches the ending of the story and says that "he [the boy] came outside and he [the snowman] was melted," he does not stop there. "I'm going to make up another part for myself," he says: "And then the next snow time, he made another snowman. And it never, ever, melted away. That's all. The end."

With narrative strength and resourcefulness, Mark takes control of a story he likes—and an ending he does not like—and shapes it into something he likes better. Then, as he and I talk, he continues to shape—or reshape—his story, as well as his own cultural learning. In Paulo Freire's terms (1973), he is developing *conscientizcao*, "the awakening of critical awareness" (p. 19). He sees that he can change the story to have what he wants as a reader. Then, in a post-story conversation, as he talks more about the story and his response to it, he brings to conscious awareness what he has been doing to shape meaning for himself. Was there any one part that worried him, I ask. "When he melted, I feel sad," Mark says. "I feel if we [he and Vinny] made a snowman, it would melt, too. And I thought the father would wake up and see the snowman getting into his clothes. The snow would drip on his clothes." (That seems to worry him; the snowman would be in trouble!) These are legitimate and interesting concerns from the child's perspective, and in verbalizing them, Mark can begin to reshape the story to resolve them.

Turning to the last page, he begins creating another "draft" of his earlier story revision: "When he runned outside the house, he saw the snowman was melted. Where was the [snowman's] nose? And he was so sad he builded another one." Now Chubby doesn't just wait until the "next time" to make another snowman; he makes it right on the spot, a solution that reveals Mark is gaining strength in *narrative* literacy, or in dealing with a story problem by revisiting—and reshaping—it.

When we turn back to the scene of the snowman in the parents' room trying on the parents' clothes, Mark says he knows his own father would not want to wake up to find all his clothes drenched in snow. But he sees comic aspects of the snowman's bumbling, too. He sings a song to accompany the pictures of this part, which he also finds humorous: "The snowman putted on the glasses. The snowman putted on the tie. The snowman putted on the overalls. And the little tiny tie!"

I ask if he would like to be Chubby. "Yeah, he got to fly," he replied. "[And] he got to show the snowman what he could do: how to eat, how to turn on the light, how to make ice, how to make scruffy bugs, what a sink was, what toothpaste was, what a fireplace was, what a TV was, how to play tap-tap, how to get dressed like his father." (Chubby gets to inhabit—and play in—two different worlds, his own and the snowman's.)

"What would he like to do as Chubby?" I ask. "The part when he made the snowman [the beginning]," he tells me. "And the part when the snowman came in the house, because me and him could have a fun time. I like his face." So I see that Mark's interest in the story is evenly divided between the first and middle part. The author's created child's world corresponds closely with Mark's own world, at the heart of which is "fun." And a "fun time" for Mark means showing the snowman *his* world. (They are friends.)

But a fun time also means making something or remaking it, putting something back into the world that was lost or nearly lost. When I ask, "Was there one part that made you feel happy?" he replies, "When the boy made the snowman. Then you can build the [second] snowman and make it look like him [the one that melted]." Later this day, Mark does just what he imagines. We had been reading Briggs's book on a snowy day, and talking more about the story gives Mark the idea to go out and make his own snowman. Just as he could make—and remake—a story as many times as he wanted, he could make a snowman without any fear of the sad ending. If it melted, he could make a new one.

Mark's storying, coupled with the post-story conversation, produced an important intersection of *generative, narrative, sociocultural, personal/empathetic,* and *critical* literacies. It introduced another literacy, too, one that we might call *lifelong* literacy, in which children revisit or reinvent the reading experience because they find it pleasurable to do so (life and literature connect for them in important ways when they read). What would I see, I wondered, if I invited responses from Vinny, who was a little older, with different life experiences—and prior experience with this particular book?

## Vinny

Unlike Mark, Vinny begins with the storybook phrase "Once upon a time," revealing that he sees Briggs's book—and his own story of it—as part of a larger collection of literature generally (*literary* and *narrative* literacies combined). In his opening sentence, he describes what he sees in Briggs's first scenes: "A little boy named Charles lived in a house." (He names his character for one of his best friends.) His next sentence summarizes and interprets the story quickly and easily: "And he woke up that morning and looked out the window and got dressed." (Because this reading follows his classroom evocation, he needs less time for preliminary meaning-making.)

Vinny sends Charles running outside "not knowing the wind blew his hat right off his head," unlike Mark, who had said, "And when he came outside to play in the snow, his hat fell off his head." Whereas Mark is concentrating on reading pictures, Vinny, in this second reading, has moved from puzzling out the story (*generative* literacy) to active involvement with the story-character (*personal/empathetic* literacy). His story-character, Charles, is so preoccupied by the snow, he doesn't even feel the cold.

Like Mark, Vinny's interest picks up as the middle part of the story emerges, and so does the liveliness of his response—as well as the complexity of his understandings and his narrative competencies. "I'm trying to make the boy say something," Vinny says aloud at this point. "What would he say?" he continues. Then he has Charles ask the snowman an important question for character development: "Would you like to learn something?"

Mark also has seen the teaching/learning aspect of the boy–snowman friendship, saying in his post-story reflection: "He [the boy] got to show the snowman what he could do." But Vinny, at the outset, makes Charles's role a very active one. Charles invites the snowman to become his friend, and friendship in this case involves responsibility.

Vinny continues telling in this strong teacher role, his narrative voice filled with confidence and authority:

> He looked at the fire and everybody knows that fire melts snowmen . . . And then Charles turned on the lamp and then he turned it off. And then the snowman tried it. And then Charles got mad at the snowman. And then the snowman got sad and looked at the flower picture. Then Charles got happy again and forgived the snowman and said, "Come on Snowman. Let's find out something else."

Why does Charles become angry when the snowman turns on the light? A look back at the picture tells us what Vinny may be inferring— that Charles may very well be reminding the snowman that heat melts cold, or would melt him. But the snowman does not listen; like any child, he is exploring and having fun: he wants to turn on the lamp once again. Vinny might interpret the snowman's downturned mouth as sadness that erases Charles's anger. Charles continues to act with care and responsibility, reminding the snowman, whenever necessary, that heat can melt. When the "snowman was getting very hot," Vinny says, a few scenes later, Charles "opened up the icebox to get him cold so he wouldn't melt." When the snowman causes a flurry of paper towels to unroll, Vinny includes dialogue that shows he understands the boy's need to take care of the snowman; thus he deepens the picture of their developing friendship (*narrative* literacy): "And the snowman said, 'Help! Help!' And the boy said, 'I'll help you.'"

One of the most complex interpretive moments of Briggs's book is the scene in which the boy and the snowman have exchanged roles: The snowman has taken the boy up into *his* world, and finally they have landed back down on the earth on the pier. The snowman is pointing to something. Vinny doesn't tell what he thinks the snowman sees at this point. His snowman merely says, "Oh no. Let's go." But we can guess, from the hot-cold pattern in Vinny's story, that the boy or the snowman is worried about the sun melting the snowman.

The rhythm and sweep of Vinny's language carry his story along as the "facts" of the last scene emerge:

> Then the snowman said, "Come on." And then the snowman went out the door, started running and liftoff! Swisssh. And away they went. And they were flying over everything . . . The snowman pointed. He said, "Oh no. Let's go." . . . they landed. The snowman walked the boy to his house. And they hugged and waved good-bye.

Because Vinny's storymaking ends with words that are quick and to the point ("Then all of a sudden he woke, got up, ran downstairs, opened the door. And the snowman was melted"), I wonder how he feels about the last page. "Kind of sad because it melted," he says. But his sadness does not cause him to rewrite the story as Mark did. He leaves the story as Briggs created it (he doesn't resist it), perhaps because he has read the signs and is prepared for the ending. (He accepts the reality of a boy and a snowman living in two worlds that cannot meet—except in a magical, fantasy sense.)

"Would you like to have the same experience?" I wonder. "If I could be alone and be like Superman," he replies. "This way it is the snowman and his assistant, Vinny. The other way it is just me, Bat Boy" (his interest in the comic book/TV cartoon characters Batman and Robin surfacing).

Vinny reveals a compelling relationship with *both* characters—the boy and the snowman—as his "reading" of the story unfolds (*personal/empathetic* literacy). He fears the snowman will melt; therefore he slips easily into the role of protector during the house scenes and also on the flying adventure, when he warns the snowman about the approaching sunrise. He wishes to be in charge in both settings—home and sky world. As the boy, in his role as protector, he teaches the snowman; as a snowman-superman alone, with no need of any assistant, he becomes all-powerful. And there is still another role he takes on, a fusion of man and boy that occurs when the snowman tries on the boy's father's tie and his suspenders. The part that made him feel happy, he says, is "when he [the snowman] put on those clothes" because "it makes me think of me when I dress up like Daddy."

## *THE SNOWMAN* AND CHILD WORLDS

At eight years, Vinny stands at a pivotal place in terms of life experiences, or between the upper end of what Howard Gardner (1983) describes as the *school-age* child (the six-to-eight-year-old) and the beginning of the *middle* childhood one (ages 7 to 12). Because he still reveals characteristics of younger children, he relishes doing what he does well. As Gardner explains, children at this time enjoy "the things [they] can do—and the degree of success with which [they] can execute them" (p. 249). To be alone and to be Superman, rather than the snowman's assistant, is just what many children at this point would wish to be, because taking on skills and competencies at this time is most enjoyable—and natural—for growth in self-knowledge. But because Vinny is also taking on characteristics of older children, he has moved beyond the place at which Mark now stands so firmly: the *school-age* child focusing intently upon his own condition, and seeing things "in a certain way, because of his own perspective" (p. 248).

Taking on more traits of middle childhood, Vinny, as older child, has strong sensitivity to the motivations of others, or the "heightened capacity to place oneself into the skin of specific other individuals, as well as of unfamiliar 'generalized others'" (p. 250). At this time of middle childhood, Gardner also says, "children become more deeply invested in friendships and will go to considerable lengths to maintain a personal relationship" (p. 249). So it is not surprising that when I ask what part of the story he likes best, he says, "Building the snowman. If you have a real good toy, someone could come and break it. But the boy had a friend." (Vinny's prior reading of *Alexander and the Wind-Up Mouse* may be surfacing here.)

His answer reveals still another role for the child reader. He is not only protector of the snowman now, nor is he merely the protected one; he is a co-creator—not a superior nor an inferior position—but an equal one. As friends, the boy and the snowman create one another in the sense of expanding each other's worlds. In Vinny's terms, or in terms of his own child's world, they do "nice" things for one another. Each at one point or another takes responsibility for the other. Each cares about the other; each learns from the other. Ultimately each lets go of the other and lives with the reality that you cannot always keep what you make (a snowman or a friend)—

nor can you really replace either one when it disappears. Vinny's Charles doesn't go out and make a new snowman; he accepts the loss and that's the end of the story. What counts is the moment of sharing that neither friend would have had without encountering the other. This is a complex idea for a child, which might help to explain why children often find the ending of this book particularly sad.

Vinny's response, like Mark's, is important for teaching us more about children's worlds at younger versus older ages and for showing us another rich burst of intersecting literacies: *literary, narrative, sociocultural,* and *personal/empathetic.* But even though their evocations are strikingly dissimilar, neither child's response is "better" than the other. (Neither child is the "wrong" age for the book; each is simply "right" for it in a different way.) Thus it is *difference* we must celebrate here. Briggs has created a book that serves as *wordless picture book* for Mark and as a *picture book for an older child* for Vinny—two very different subcategories of the picture book genre, as these responses reveal.

To open up the book for the widest possible child audience, Briggs structures his narrative as four short, semi-independent tales within a larger framework of binary patterns (young/old; child/adult; boy/man— or snowman; host/guest; teacher/learner; earth/sky; hot/cold; freezing/ melting): The boy wakes to a snowy day and builds a snowman; then he runs downstairs at midnight and discovers the snowman has come to life; he shows the snowman his house and the snowman shows the boy his world in the sky; finally, he wakes up to a sunny day and discovers the snowman is melting.

The binary pattern of old/young, parent/child, host/guest that Mark sees is equally important to the hot/cold, freezing/melting, teacher/ learner one that Vinny incorporates into his storymaking. Mark stops short in linking these two patterns together (or of seeing that the boy is teaching his guest about heat/cold and melting), as Vinny is able to link them. As a younger reader, Mark seems to understand stories in terms of incidents, or episodic "chunks" with characters as "linking devices" (p. 248), as Maureen and Hugh Crago (1983) have theorized, based on their study of their daughter Anna's responses at ages two through five. Mark focuses on the episodes or "chunks" of fun the boy and snowman each have, rather than on the thread of danger for the snowman that runs through Vinny's story.

Children of various ages, according to the experiences, emotional engagement, and understandings they bring to a reading, help us to see more. And the more data that can be gathered about children's responses to books like this one, with its delicate balance between "readerly" and "writerly" aims, the richer our knowledge of children's literature and literacy processes becomes. We need to notice not only experiential levels and developmental stages but also areas of cultural difference, such as gender.

## MORE CHILD WORLDS: FEMALE RESPONSES

There does not appear to be anything particularly sexist about *The Snowman*, except that rarely do we hear about a snow *woman*. A cultural lapse—or is there some inherent reason why there are so many snow*men* in the world? Briggs's book reveals a *male* child making a snow*man*, inviting him into his house, and showing him something of his own *male* child's world: he tries out a punching bag in the boy's bedroom—a toy or piece of sports equipment generally associated with the *male* sport of boxing. What do female children make of this book, I continued to wonder for some time after I collected Vinny and Mark's responses.

I remembered Tisha, in Vinny's classroom, drawing a picture of a snowman and a girl, to bring her own gender into play. But other females, like Monique, Lea, and Patty, became easily engaged in the story in a classroom reading event, to the extent of Lea including dialogue as part of the response. Did a social setting facilitate their engagement with and understanding of the book—from a male perspective? Did it preclude seeing themselves as reading differently—or capable of doing so? What would a more extended female response in a personal setting reveal?

### Lolly

When my next-door neighbor Lolly turned six years, five months, I asked her to "read" me this wordless story:

> One day there was a little boy who was making a snowman.
> He decided to make him Frosty the Snowman. So he found an old
> tie and tied it around his neck. And an orange for his nose. And
> then he found some coal and he looked like a real snowman and he
> said, "I'll call him Frosty the Snowman." One day the little boy
> peeped out his window and the snowman didn't move. The little
> boy's brushing his teeth. It kind of looks strange to the little boy.
> [Beginning]
>
> One morning when he went outside, "Hi!" said the snowman.
> "Hi," said the little boy. "Shake my hand. Would you like to come
> in my house?" "Ok. Oh, no, light will make me melt," said the
> snowman. "Don't put me in that bed." [She is viewing the sofa.]

"Ok," said the little boy. The little boy took him to the kitchen. "Would you like to have something to eat?" "Yes," said the snowman. "And something to drink, too." And then after we play the game, they had some Popsicles. And the snowman was catching toilet paper. And the boy took him to the top with him. "Oh, look at that picture. That's just like you." And they went into the mother and father's room. And they dressed up and they'd better be careful. He could melt. He said, "Follow me downstairs. Do you want drive my father's car?" "Yes," said the snowman. "I know how to drive." And he did. "Do you like to rock?" "Yes," said the snowman. "Would you like to run with me up here?" [said the boy]. "Yes," said the snowman. [Middle, Part I]

"Would you like to fly?" said the snowman. "Yeah!" said Jamie. "Look at all those countries" [said the snowman]. And he took the little boy into the bridge. "Oh no," said the little boy. "Where is my Mama and Daddy?" And they flew back. "Well," said the snowman. "Bye." And he gave him a big hug. And he walked away. [Middle, Part II]

Next morning he woke up. He didn't see no snowman. "Oh, oh, where's my snowman?" said the little boy. And he walked out and saw the snowman [pause] melted. The end. [Ending]

Different aspects of response are noticeable immediately. Unlike Vinny and Mark, Lolly names the snowman, but the name she gives him—Frosty—is one that arises out of songs and mass-market picture books titled *Frosty the Snowman*. Her generic name might therefore reveal only a surface attachment for the character. At the same time, she names the boy Jamie, thus strengthening the personal note, although her stance is not the strong personal one of Mark, who gives the boy his own nickname, or Vinny, who names the boy for his best friend.

Like Lea in Vinny's classroom, Lolly also includes a generous amount of dialogue for the story, revealing her own extensive knowledge of authorial choices, and there is a strong sense of narrative voice in this telling, especially the words "And they'd better be careful. He could melt."

Like Vinny, Lolly does seem to understand the concept of heat/cold/melting that runs through the book and foreshadows the ending. But unlike him, she places the snowman, rather than the boy, in the role of teacher. Lolly's experience of the world at this time—that adults know more than children and *they* do the teaching—seems to be guiding her through the story. Thus she does not include any notion of the boy's warnings to the

snowman in her storymaking. She sees the snowman as cautious, saying,
"Oh, no, [heat from the] light will make me melt," when the boy asks the
snowman into the house. And this interpretation of the snowman as all-
knowing carries over to other aspects of her snowman's words and actions.

When the snowman dresses up, Lolly says they should be careful because he could melt, and she seems to be saying, as Mark does, that the
snowman could melt and soak the clothes. But she might also be saying
that like Frosty, a snowman can come to life like a human. Therefore clothing could trap his body heat and cause him to feel hot or "melt."

When Lolly's snowman says he knows how to drive, she shows that
she sees him as a fatherly person, rather than as a creature from another
world who needs to be taught about human activities. Lolly seems to see
the snowman as the paternalistic male adult of so many stories—strong,
protective, all-knowing. Her character Jamie is, in return, simply a courte-
ous and friendly child. "Where is my Mama and Daddy?" Jamie asks at
the pier scene in her story. "Would you like to have something to eat?"
Jamie asks his houseguest, Frosty. Thus Lolly's story cannot focus on the
comic aspects of the snowman blundering through a human world.

Her story is also shorter than either Mark's or Vinny's (346 words
compared to their stories of 804 and 964 words). Thus she responds to
fewer of Briggs's scenes (34 compared to 67 by Mark and 78 by Vinny).
*The Snowman* did not appear to be one of her favorite books; she did not
choose to examine it again. And her disinterest might have been the result of gender, if we consider my neighbor Charlotte's at age seven and a
half.

## Charlotte

Charlotte's response produces a much longer and more detailed story than
Lolly (1,026 words with responses to 79 of Briggs's scenes), and she certainly appears to be producing a close and engaged reading. Yet here we
see the same interpretation as Lolly's: that the snowman is all-knowing
and the boy is less a teacher than a follower of the snowman's bidding.
Thus her telling, like Lolly's, ignores the comic/ironic contrast of child-
as-teacher and snowman-as-child-learner.

In Charlotte's story, the tone is more formal than any of the other
children's and the story language is more highly developed: she names
neither the boy nor the snowman; the snowman speaks as a much older,
nonplayful person; and there is none of the peer fun that we have seen in
the male children's stories. All of these qualities of telling seem to result
from her patriarchal interpretation of the snowman. When the boy invites
the snowman into his house, the snowman says, "I'd be honored to." When

he falls back from the fireplace heat, Charlotte infers that the boy "helped him up," as he might do for any elderly gentleman or grandfatherly figure.

Charlotte's perception of the snowman as all-knowing causes her to treat the boy as the snowman's helper rather than his teacher: "Then the snowman wanted to watch television. He tried it but it was too light and might have made him melt. The boy turned it off immediately. Then he showed him a light. The snowman looked at it and he said, 'It might melt me, too.' So he [the snowman] turned off the light."

She infers that the snowman knows about his vulnerability from the beginning and that the boy is aware of the snowman's plight and cares about it. But there is no anger, no frustration for the boy, as in Vinny's story, when the snowman begins playing with the lamp or bumbling around fixtures and appliances that project heat. At the radiator scene, Charlotte recognizes this object (her own home is heated by steam heat and radiators), and her snowman says, "No, it will burn me." Her male child character says in return: "Ok. Come on out here. Come into this room. They have a neat flower." But because she has not interpreted the snowman as a learner who is gradually discovering things about his "life" and his fate around heat, she doesn't comment on the snowman's downturned mouth: "And the boy got him into that room and they look at the flower. And he said, 'Come into the kitchen.'" Thus she doesn't infer any sadness.

Similarly, at the pier scene, immediately after the snowman has pointed at the sunrise, Charlotte shows us a strong, all-knowing, elderly father figure who does not shrink back in fear or sadness. Instead he simply knows his limitations and guides the young boy home accordingly: "They looked at the horizon coming up. The snowman said, 'Oh, no, it's the light. I will get burned. Come, come, boy, we must fly away.' So they flew away, back to the boy's home."

Briggs's writerly scene can be read in different ways. The boy might be standing on the pier saying nothing to the snowman, with the snowman doing all the talking. Literacy educator Judith Graham (1990) focuses on this scene in her study *Pictures on the Page*, saying the snowman's "concern that they should return home before dawn is indicated by two arms coming up to the mouth and the little coal eyes fastening on the boy's" (p. 32). The snowman's "concern" might arise from either the boy's warning or his own. But Graham also sees the snowman as childlike learner: "[T]hrough the simple line of the mouth, the movement in the head and again through the use of the arms Briggs allows us to meet this polite, naive, incorrigibly curious, generous and imaginative snowman" (p. 32). Therefore the snowman would be heeding the boy's advice.

Taking this other path, seeing the snowman as adult teacher rather than child learner, Charlotte, like Lolly, has less "fun" with the story than Vinny and Mark, who both revel in the topsy-turvy experience of a child leading an adult-sized, childlike figure through their world, then taking a grand adventure with this same figure who is, at the same time, a magical creature. Even though Charlotte appears to be very much in command of the story line on a first reading, she has only a perfunctory interest in it. When I ask her what she thinks the story is about, she says quickly and confidently, "a boy who makes a snowman and he thinks—he dreams—that the snowman comes alive. Then he wakes up and the snow melted."

Her telling of the story is in fact a very polished "performance": well detailed, highly articulate, filled with strong narrative competence. At the end, when she tells about the snowman melting, her voice changes, becoming soft and sad. "Is the story sad for you?" I wonder aloud. "I just didn't like it that much," she replies.

Her telling, despite its literary sophistication, is neither lively, humorous, nor intriguing for her, as many of her other story responses were. Her interpretation of the snowman as formal father figure may, in fact, be erasing all tension, suspense, and reason-to-be from the story. How a child brings life knowledge to bear on the story (*sociocultural* literacy) can therefore become a significant influence on meaning-making and nuanced interpretation, or in this case on *generative, literary, narrative,* and especially *personal/empathetic* and *aesthetic* literacies. Charlotte's knowledge about gender differences, in life and other stories, seems to be causing her to "read" the snowman as not only male, but as a patriarchal male figure. Thus she produces a gendered reading, one that affects the pleasure of the story for her.

## REFLECTIONS

We might easily see Charlotte's rendering of Briggs's story as an accomplished piece, and if we never questioned her further, we might even think that her polished performance produced evidence of deep engagement with the book. If we never elicit, study, and compare male and female children's responses, we miss discovering the possibility of gendered readings that might be far more authentic than any speculations or hunches we might have about gender and children's books. In addition to patriarchal readings that female children produce of male figures in stories (even snow figures), problems may arise if male authors create male child characters with male preoccupations and interests that do not engage female children.

There is of course no reason to discard *The Snowman*; we could search for books like Suteev's and Arnold's *The Adventures of Snowwoman* (1998) to read with Briggs's book. Or as we share *The Snowman*, we could set up hypothetical situations for children to ponder or turn into stories of their own: What might happen if a snow*woman* came to life in your yard? What would you show the snowwoman if you brought her into her home? Where might a snowwoman take you if the two of you set off for an adventure?

Or we could simply invite children to produce stories of their own after hearing *The Snowman*, and female children might produce their own role-reversal reshapings with female characters in the same way that two female children in a second-grade classroom turned the mouse Willy into a female after I read *Alexander and the Wind-Up Mouse*, as I tell about in the next chapter. Often children find ways of their own to deal with gender imbalance, if we give them opportunities for talk and storymaking responses.

Just as it is important that females see themselves as capable of seeing differently, it is crucial that all children know they will be "reading" details in pictures in individual ways. "Some children read more in the detail of illustration than others," says Fry (1985), "not only in what they closely observe and pick out, but in what they deduce from the drawn expressions of motivation and inner thought. In this way, the [child] tellers reveal their sense of place and their understanding of character" (p. 110). And since variations in observational tendencies are very likely related to gender, individual interests and preoccupations, experiential background, and personality construct, children's ability to empathize with story characters will be different. As Rosenblatt (1994) notes, "given the same text, readers differ in their degree of empathy" (p. 67), a situation that might seriously affect whether children love—or simply tolerate—literature.

It is therefore important that children have opportunities to respond spontaneously and naturally to picture books like *The Snowman* in which the artist has taken pains to make a careful selection of patterned details—and to do so in social settings so that they see a range of responses. If children notice a downturned mouth or two arms rising up to a mouth, they will be more likely to weave this expression or gesture into their storymaking. If they do not notice an artist's nuanced patterning, we can invite them to do so by wondering what the snowman might be feeling, what might he be saying to the boy, what might the boy be replying?

It might take several readings before children are able to sort out characters' feelings clearly. So it is particularly important that children with strong interest in a book have ample time to revisit it, to learn more about how authors reveal feelings through gestures, movements, and facial expressions. Children also need time and opportunity to deal with the feelings that characters are evoking in their own minds. Fry's child respondent Clayton made a response *spiral*—telling, talking, writing—through the book and back again many times, until he was able to work through the emotionally uncomfortable aspects. And Mark reshaped Briggs's ending because he felt comfortable to do so.

It is equally important that children like Charlotte and Lolly, who have little interest in a book, move on to other books and that children like Keith and Clayton, who have strong aversion to a book, have opportunities to visit alternative books and talk more about their feelings. Because pictures allow little space for children's minds to hide, when the idea behind them is frightening, as Egoff says, adults need to provide ample opportunity for classroom conversation with wordless picture books that explore complex issues.

It is also important that adults consider multiple perspectives when they try to puzzle out why a book "works" with some children but not others. Not only is it true that children differ in their observational tendencies, it is also true that children who are deeply engaged with a book tend to be close observers of details in pictures. In this case, their observational tendencies reflect the pleasure they are taking in story events, setting, or characters and lead them, in turn, to even deeper engagement and continually evolving insights. Thus it is important that children have freedom to choose books of greatest appeal to them (as Keith preferred Arthur Miller's book) and opportunities to return to and respond in many different ways to books, in order to deepen their engagement and grow in responsive reading.

Other factors play into theories about engagement, too. That Vinny enjoyed *The Snowman*—and read closely the pictorial details—was probably, at least in part, connected to gender. Vinny particularly liked the punching bag scene, and as a boy, he felt quite comfortable to assist, befriend, guide, and be guided by a male snowman. But his pleasure might have also been connected to age and place in the family structure. As an older sibling he knew perhaps more about the guiding/teaching role than his younger brother, because he had been called upon many times to be the teacher. And not to be ignored is a child's prior experience with a book. When Vinny produced his "telling," he had already viewed *The Snowman* in his classroom at least once; thus for this reading, he could step more easily and confidently into the story.

Gender, personality construct, age, experiential background, and prior contact with the book all might have enabled him to empathize more strongly with the story characters and therefore to take greater pleasure in the story. Or his engagement might have arisen from all of these factors tied to the condition of childhood itself, or of a child learning the subject matter of *himself*. As Hugh Crago (1995–96) reminds us:

> It is not the case . . . that children "gradually learn to make sense of the world" or "learn the rules of story." Rather, they learn themselves and in so doing learn story, in just the same way as they learn significant others through

themselves and themselves through others. As they learn their own boundaries, so they learn to recognize boundaries in stories, and between stories, and between stories and "life." As they comprehend the complexity of self, so they come to appreciate the complexity of characters in books. A sense of the "wholeness" of story (its shape and completeness) emerges simultaneously with a sense of the "wholeness of self." (p. 189)

The sense of "boundaries" in and between stories for Vinny at this time might also have involved what we might call *intertextual* literacy—the ability to see connections among several different texts—considering his many readings of Leo Lionni's *Alexander and the Wind-Up Mouse*. When we place these two picture books side by side, we see similar patterns in *characters* (childlike "people" as friends), *setting* and *plot pattern* (home and away), *mood* (play as risk-taking adventure), *theme* (friendship as helpfulness and responsibility), *genre* (a fantasy world in which something not human comes to life), and *insight arising from the fantasy* (you can wish, build, create, dream, or story a friend into being). As Vinny had said earlier about *Alexander and the Wind-Up Mouse*, having a friend was better than having a toy, because even with a "real good toy," "someone could come and break it." The best part of *The Snowman* for him was "building the snowman . . . [because] the boy had a friend."

All of these children's revelations about child worlds have a great deal to tell us about commercial materials that group stories around one-size-fits-all "main ideas" like "Special Toys," "Friendship," or "Magical Wishes." Given the tendency of reader responses to be so different and unique and of adult and child responses to be equally divergent, adults are better off listening to children's responses and then collecting books related to what children *at that moment* show them they see in a particular book. Responses that children generate during their own reading events produce the most authentic guides for teaching.

Children do see differently, their divergent responses emerging from differences of all kinds. And no one adult, no one committee of adults, no commercial company, no textbook manual, no standardized test can determine or predict what a child should—or will—produce as a response. Only when we set up live circuits of response can we see the wealth of possibilities for learning about children, their books, their worlds, and the best ways of teaching them.

*PART II*

# THE READING
# TRANSACTION

CHILDREN'S RESPONSES TO LITERATURE are crucially important when adults are in the role of reading teacher. Those adults must not only choose a particular approach for helping children make their opening moves into literacy, they must also know which books are the best ones to facilitate this process. Situated between the teacher and the book is the important part. Here we find children and what they bring to the "table": their own associations, experiences, feelings, competencies at the moment that they encounter particular books, and the "transaction" that emerges from this matching of child and book. As Rosenblatt (1994) explains, an inseparable condition emerges at this time when teacher and text "are aspects of a total situation, each conditioned by and conditioning the other" (p. 17).

The reading transaction, in other words, involves an engagement of child and text, in which each is changed in the process. The text changes the child and the child transforms the text; neither is left unaltered. The child constructs a text rather than simply "receiving" it, and the text is expanded, or destabilized, by the child's response. (The readerly interpretation, as it fills in gaps of the writerly text, changes all other readings.) Will we know about either of these changes, in child or text, if we aren't collecting and

studying children's responses? (If a tree falls in the forest . . .)
If we aren't listening to children's responses to literature, our
notions of their books cannot be forever altered by what they
discover, thus adding to our own perceptions. And our
notions of how to release those texts—and our learning—
will be nonexistent.

*Chapter Three*

# *Alexander* in the Classroom:
# Many Voices, Many Literacies

SEVERAL YEARS AFTER my initial steps into the world of children's responses, I noticed *Alexander and the Wind-Up Mouse* anthologized in a reading series in a second-grade classroom. I remembered my son's responses at this age and applauded the reading program for its choice. If any book seemed "right" for children at this age, it was this one. Upon closer examination, however, I was more than a little concerned. The number of pictures had been reduced; the original layout was therefore changed. Even the cover picture was different.

In addition, the collection displayed the usual horrors of basal texts for response enthusiasts: The program was directing teachers to tell children what the story was about before they had a chance to sort it out for themselves. Even worse, the story was being used as a vehicle to teach vocabulary, skills like sequencing, competencies like inferential thinking, and literary elements like the concept of fantasy. Teachers were supposed to determine at the outset if children knew what fantasy was and if they knew that Lionni's story *was* fantasy, rather than trusting the story to produce a fantasy world that children could enter naturally, believing and accepting that world and the characters as real in the context of that world.

Instead of encouraging children to enjoy the story—to slip easily into the "becoming" game, to learn naturally what a fantasy is—teachers interrupted the story constantly to quiz students about causal relationships, word meanings, and definitions of fantasy. In other words, the basal program was using literature to transmit information, what Rosenblatt (1994) has described as "efferent" teaching or learning rather than to allow "associations, feelings, attitudes, and ideas" (p. 25) to arise for readers as they lived through a story for their own narrative pleasure.

I wondered what would happen if a group of second-graders responded naturally to the original picture book, taking what Rosenblatt has described as an "aesthetic" stance, before they encountered this story in their reading class. I asked the classroom teacher if I might elicit children's responses to the "real" book, and she agreed to this plan, plus a post-story time during which the children could deepen their initial responses. I decided to use a conversational, large-group format. I would simply read the book with the class, so that before the children were bombarded by word-attack skills, they could experience the *pleasure* of reading a real book for children just as it was intended for them—in all its narrative richness and complexity.

## EXPLORATORY CONVERSATION AND CHILDREN'S RESPONSES

The reading began with an examination of the cover picture and my invitation to the 17 children to tell me what they saw. And the burst of talk that followed led them to use naturally many skills and competencies of the basal lesson, such as testing assumptions, producing hypotheses, making contrasts, formulating definitions, drawing conclusions, and seeing causal relationships.

First they noticed the mice, the real and the wind-up, the Caldecott Honor Medal embossed on the cover, and what one child described as a "cookie jar." I explained a little about the medal since they were labeling it a "coin." And as I began talking about the *matrioska* doll, I was happily surprised when a child took over my explanation, telling about having such a doll (or toy, as he called it) at home. I asked how big this toy was, since one mouse (Alexander) is playing in the lower half of the broken-apart doll in the picture. This question led to the children noting differences in the real and mechanical mice and to their conjecturing (with no questioning from me) about how the artist might have drawn the wind-up mouse to show he was not real. ("They could have put a patch on him," said one child.)

Looking at the half-title and title pages, one child noticed the right-to-left direction of Alexander, and they were led easily by Lionni into the first page of story. (The text reads, "'Help! Help! A mouse!' There was a scream. Then a crash. Cups, saucers, and spoons were flying . . . Alexander ran for his hole." The picture shows the mouse running off the page in the same right-to-left direction as the previous two illustrations show.) I asked, "What happened?" and a speculative discussion followed, setting the stage for talk later that day, during math, about size, proportion, and ratio:

"The table."

"He probably jumped on the table."

"The table tipped."

"The mouse got up on the table and knocked everything
    down."

"A mouse could not tip over a table."

"And then the cups—"

"It takes about three mice."

"And then the cups and stuff—"

"It takes about three mice."

"A mouse cannot tip over a table, only if the mother got
    scared."

At this point I noticed that the children had taken a side path, filling
blank spaces of text with stories of their own in order to build theories about
the author's story (*narrative* reading). As they constructed a meaning base
for the story (generative reading), I called attention to these seeds of story
with a descriptive comment: "You've got another story going on behind
this one, don't you? That the mother was in the room and she got scared
and knocked the—"

Suddenly Sid broke in, "Hey, there's *two* different stories going on
here—actually *three*!" But before I could ask him what he saw, Elaine entered with a fourth story idea: "A rat could have knocked down the table."
Then Sid entered her story "space" to speculate that "It would take three
rats to tip over one of these tables." Others entered in at this point to continue on this *generative/narrative* reading route:

"Anyway, I've seen glasses hit the floor and they didn't
    break."

"Probably a hundred mouses!"

"The mouse could have gone up and knocked it down."

"No, the mouse can't."

"I doubt, even if it knocked it down, that it broke."

"Probably a hundred mouses knocked it down!"

"It's probably a plastic cup."

As the children proceeded to the next opening (the scene of the broom chasing Alexander), Sid continued growing his own "seed" of story: "I wonder where the mother is right now."

"Whose mother?" I asked. "The human or the mouse mother?" A child answered, "*His* [Alexander's] mother." And the potential for two stories about mothers now emerged. *Narrative, sociocultural,* and *personal/empathetic* reading (see Fig. I.1) would soon intersect when Amy, viewing the story through the lens of her own social experiences, interpreted the picture of the broom as a rake and speculated that "They're [the humans are] gonna rake his butt." Thus stories were building as the children engaged in reading pictures of the world beyond the story words.

The next picture heightened Amy's fears, since she saw the mice as visibly dwarfed by a large stuffed bear and a toy penguin, whose large, dark, staring eye seemed to present a threat for the mice: The children expressed concern that Alexander was so close to the animals. Two children declared that the animals did not look real, an attempt perhaps to reassure themselves that the mice would not be hurt. And their concern—and empathy—for the real mouse (and the choice that Lionni made in placing the mice face-to-face) produced a new idea for Bethany: "He saw his friend."

When I asked what made them think Willy would become Alexander's friend, Elaine answered, "Because he's [Willy's] not real." Bethany added, "And he *wants* to be his friend." Amy, however, traveled farther into the world beyond the textual words from an empathetic core: "And also because if you knew somebody like a mouse and you saw a wind-up mouse, you'd think it was a real mouse, so you would want to be its friend, and you would think it would want to be your friend. And the two of you could knock down the penguin. This time they could both get their butts whipped." (The mice will become friends, Amy hypothesized, because of their mutual need for survival in the face of the penguin, a toy that she seemed to see as a threatening force, just as the human with the broom is threatening Alexander.)

Examining the next page, Bethany predicted that Alexander would climb on Annie's bed with Annie's doll and Willy (the two friends would strive to be together or to become like each other). At the scene following this one, the picture of the mice climbing into the shoes to play, the children's comments led naturally into both a discussion of fantasy and a way of exploring the deeper implications and patterns of text—or a natural way into *literary* reading (see Fig. I.1):

> *Bethany:* They look like they're climbing in boots.
> *Rhoda:* And hiding.
> *Bethany:* Playing hide-and-go-seek.
> *Elaine:* The wind-up mouse is fantasy.
> *Adult:* Do you think he is?
> *George:* It's not real.
> *Adult:* Whose fantasy is it, do you think?
> *George:* The mouse's.
> *Adult:* The real mouse?
> *George:* Yeah.
> *Adult:* The real one [Alexander] is imagining him [Willy]?
> *Clay:* The wind-up mouse can't talk.
> *Sid:* The real mouse can't talk.
> *Adult:* It can or it can't?
> *Sid:* Can't.
> *Adult:* Except maybe in a [pauses to think]—
> *Sid:* A play!
> *Amy:* Or in mouse talk! But not in people talk.
> *Clay:* It's like my uncle. We had rats in our house once and my
> uncle was doing his homework and a rat came and sat down
> beside him.

Clay's comment about his uncle was less a story sprouting *within* Lionni's book than a story of its own that he could cause to grow on its own later. So I read on to the scene of Alexander sitting in his mouse hole thinking of Willy and wondering why he [Alexander] cannot be cuddled and loved, too. I asked which mouse the children would rather be, the real one or the wind-up, and the answers and explanations led more deeply into *sociocultural* reading—one in which the readers' lives inform their interpretations—as the children began sorting out their own preferences in terms of their own experiences:

> *Bethany:* The wind-up, because I wouldn't have to go to school.
> *Bill:* Neither one; I'd want to go to school.
> *George:* The wind-up, 'cause the real one gets chased and caught in
> traps.
> *Clay:* The real one, because when he gets chased, he gets food.
> *Rhoda:* I'd want to be cuddled.

At the same time, expressing their preferences deepened their understanding of the characters and the multilayered thematic patterns in words and pictures (*literary* reading). When the scene of the magic lizard appeared,

Sid looked at the collage of colors and said, "No wonder he's magic." I asked why the pebble must be purple (a secret of text—or an indeterminacy), a question that caused discussion or problem-solving talk as we read the next pages. The question fostered the intersection of *generative* and *literary* reading, as the children began trying to make meaning of the author's narrative choice:

"He must like purple pebbles . . ."

"You know the lizard who was all colors? It didn't look like he had
      any purple . . ."

"It's [the lizard's body] looks like a rainbow."

"He's got a little purple [on his "coat"]."

"Right there!"

"He looks like he climbed on a rainbow and jumped through it and
      got different colors."

"He didn't get the purple."

When they reached the scene of the toy box filled with old, broken, cast-aside toys, one of which is Willy, the wind-up toy, *sociocultural* reading surfaced once more, as the children decided they would rather be real. They also spied a *matrioska* doll in the toy box and the purple pebble at the base of the box. "How do you think it got there?" I asked. The question fostered additional meaning-making, although I asked it simply for my own edification. I was really wondering myself. One child saw the pebble as one of the cast-off toys, an interesting theory about why the pebble is purple (a purple pebble is not a real pebble; therefore it could be a toy).

## A BURST OF INTERSECTING LITERACIES

I called attention to the *matrioska* doll, wondering aloud if we would ever see the cover picture as one of the pictures within the book. But I did not stop for answers; the momentum of the story was pushing the reading along. I read about Alexander's return to the lizard and the lizard's question for Alexander: "Who or what do you wish to be?" I invited the children to predict what Alexander would wish, and as the children talked together, they worked out a collective meaning of the story for themselves. At the same time, in this social context, they were building a theory about social responsibility, with *generative* and *literary* reading intersecting as they perceived a pattern of surprise or an unpredictable turn of plot (each mouse wishing to be the other)—

"To be a wind-up now."

"A wind-up mouse."

"No, he wants the wind-up mouse to be real!"

"Yeah, I think he *does* want the wind-up to be real."

"He wants to run away."

"He wants to be a wind-up mouse."

"The wind-up wants to be real and the real wants to be a wind-up!"

As I read that Alexander ran back to the house "as fast as he could after making his wish," the discussion, with no prompting from me, led them to a further exchange of ideas, in terms of the complicated web of meanings Lionni is spinning here:

"Cause he wanted to see if the fake mouse was—"

"Would be a real mouse!"

"Yeah!"

*Generative, sociocultural,* and *literary* reading continued to intersect as the children heard the last pages of the book: Alexander tells his wish to the lizard; he runs back to the house; he discovers the empty box (the big moment of surprise); he discovers that Willy is alive, real, and squeaking in the mouse hole. *Narrative* reading also emerged as Sid reasoned out the plot in terms of story conventions he remembered and his imagined happy ending: Willy came to life in the toy box, then ran away as the toys were dumped out:

*Adult:* The box was there, but alas, it was empty.
*Children:* Oh!

*Adult:* What do you think has happened?
*Children:* They threw all the toys away!
*Sid:* No! No. It always turns out good. He got out probably. He
     blinked his eye probably and they dumped it out and they
     didn't notice but he was out. It always happens.

"What do the rest of you think?" I asked. Now *sociocultural* and *narrative* reading intersected as George, wrestling with the grand enigma of the story, saw a new complication for the story, and he and Rhoda began to think about motivation in terms of their own values and beliefs about social responsibility as they filled gaps in the story:

*George:* The wind-up mouse would be a real mouse but he would
     still be in the box.
*Adult:* Why do you think Alexander wished what he did?
*George:* His friend [Willy] was good and he wanted to do some-
     thing for *him.*
*Rhoda:* His friend is more important [than he is].

As the end of the story approached, more *literary, generative,* and *sociocultural* readings intersected:

*Adult:* "'Too late,' he thought, and with a heavy heart he went to
     his hole in the baseboard."
*Sid:* He'll be there [Willy].
*Adult:* "Something squeaked!"
*Bethany:* It was the mouse. It was a fantasy mouse and now it
     turned into a real—
*Rhoda:* Real mouse.
*Adult:* "My name is Willy."
*Clay:* I knew it!
*Bill:* I knew it, too!

At the last scene, the children laughed and sang and applauded. They also continued to talk and make meaning of the story for themselves:

"Did you see that one page?"

"The lizard *was* probably magic and he turned Willy into a real
     mouse."

"Are they gonna get married and kiss?"

"And elope?"

"The lizard was probably real and he probably turned Willy into a real mouse."

"Now they're gonna be best friends forever."

At this point I reread Alexander's last words: "'Willy!' cried Alexander. 'The lizard . . . the lizard did it!'" and I asked, "Did the lizard really do it?" (Is Alexander operating as an agent of free will? Did he make—or choose—the wish that saved Willy? Or is Alexander "programmed" by magic, or a lizard/wizard who grants his wish?) Several children said the pebble did it. Several said the pebble and the lizard did it together. Sid, deeply engaged from the outset, began generating a new story in order to answer my question (*generative* and *narrative* reading emerging from his deep engagement or his *aesthetic* reading): "Maybe the person that got it [the box of old toys] took the little wind-up thing out [of Willy] and put all the other stuff on it [fur] and made it look like a real animal," he said. "Or Willy thought so much that he wanted to be a real mouse that it just happened."

Sid attempted at first to place a literal template on the story, as he explained how Willy could look real. Because his reading program used imaginative stories like this one to teach "efferent" or fact-based reading skills, he could quickly identify a mouse as fantasy or real. At the same time, in terms of his cognitive maturity, he still expected stories, even stories that he had learned to label as fantasy, to have a realistic explanation. So his deep engagement with a fantasy story was disrupted by a need to explain the fantasy rationally or to give it a realistic premise. (At one point he thought that Willy's wish was granted through magic; at another point he thought that a human, the one who found the discarded toys, had put fur on the wind-up toy to make it look real.)

That Sid had a chance to puzzle out the story aloud was especially important for *narrative* reading. His response led Bethany to create a story also—a story-chaining effect: "When the purple pebble appeared," she said, "I think the lizard turned into a toy and he could only be winded up and run around like Willy used to." (The lizard, a magical character, helps or saves Willy by taking his place.) Thus *narrative* reading served to foster both *generative* and *literary* reading for her: Telling a small story at this point helped her sort out further why the pebble is purple and how Willy is turned real, in the context of the fantasy.

In this cooperative learning situation, problem-solving took precedence over "right" answers, producing strong involvement in the story and greater unfolding of character motivation (*aesthetic, personal/empathetic,* and *sociocultural* reading) and deeper understanding of genre (*literary* reading). No one was testing or grading the children in terms of their ability to identify the story genre, list character traits of Willy or Alexander, or determine the main idea of the story. There were no worksheet blanks to fill in, only blank spaces of story to ponder in a social context. Thus *narrative* learning continued to emerge, as it did when Sid suddenly remembered his earlier concern with the mouse mother and wondered where she was.

The children became involved quickly in Willy's fear for Alexander's safety. The new story Sid soon began telling to fill Lionni's blank space of story was one with which they could connect and on which they could build for additional meaning-making. But their empathetic concern for Alexander had been greatly in evidence throughout, beginning with the image of the broom at the story's beginning and the children's fears for Alexander's safety. *Personal/empathetic* concern was, in fact, the base of all their responses:

> *Sid:* And where is the mother?
> *Rhoda:* Yes, the mouse mother, the father, the sister, and brother, too.
> *Sid:* See, the mouse mother was probably just sitting at home drinking tea, saying "Well, he'll be home. Honey, bring the newspaper." I mean it's ridiculous. One mouse can't take care of his own self!

At this point, Sid returned to another question, one I had posed earlier about the cover picture. As he and his friends began discussing the idea of the *matrioska* doll in more detail, *generative* and *literary* reading once more intersected:

> *Sid:* You know something? I noticed this was not mentioned in the story [he points to the *matrioska* doll on the cover].
> *Clay:* It was just in the toy box.
> *Sid:* It didn't look like this [like it looked on the cover]; it should have looked like *this* [doll in two parts, rather than doll fused]. And it should have been in the story [nesting doll in two parts].
> *Adult:* Why do you think he put it on the cover like that [in parts]?
> *Sid:* I don't know but there's one thing you can tell they're not. They're both just fantasy.
> *Adult:* Fantasy?
> *Sid:* Yeah. Nice smile [He points to picture on the last page showing mice smiling].

*Bill:* A mouse [real mice] can't smile.
*Sid:* A mouse can't smile. A mouse can't go like that [mice dancing].

In noticing the cover picture and wondering about its place in the overall story pattern, Sid moved into filling what Iser (1978) calls "empty [or blank] spaces" (p. 220) of text that set the reader's ideas in motion. The author provides nothing to fill a blank space of text, and readers must make their own meaningful connections close up the space, unlike a gap of text that the author eventually fills in for readers at some point. Often an "empty space" produces ideas for readers that develop in light of the whole story. In this case an icon of friendship or mutual needs might emerge for readers, the result of the cover picture, which shows a nesting doll broken apart and two mice, a real one and a toy.

Sid stopped short of unfolding such a metaphor at this point, choosing instead to emphasize the story as make-believe. His focus on the characters as *story* characters served to produce a protective shield or distancing device between himself and these virtually motherless mice, who are creating a family structure for themselves in place of a traditional family, as Rhoda had implied. Then he did not have to worry further about Alexander's safety—or his own.

This day was the last for Sid at this school. He was moving to another part of town and he was facing not only a new home but new classmates—and no friends—the following morning. His fears for Alexander, his teacher explained to me, were perhaps very real; his deep engagement with the story was quite understandable, and his empathetic learning much in evidence. Meeting the "right" emotional content in a story at the "right" time can lead to strengthening of the child's *aesthetic* reading, as Sid's response revealed.

## POST-STORY EXPLORATIONS

A picture, Meek says, "holds the story until there is a telling" (1988, p. 12), and as this read-aloud session ended, I wondered what the children might produce as their own icons of story. I asked what they would like to do after hearing the story: tell more stories, draw, write, create a drama? Sid led a group of children to create a mouse drama, one that quickly turned into a boisterous Ninja Turtle mystery. Several children drew. Others, like Clay, whom I now encouraged to unfold the story of his uncle's rat, told and wrote stories of all kinds.

Amy and Rhoda chose to produce a collaborative reshaping of the Lionni story in which Amy turned Willy the wind-up mouse into a female named Amy, and Alexander remained a male named Birk, Rhoda's own last name (in this case a pseudonym). Thus they played out the romance-elopement idea that emerged right after the story reading (a spontaneous story-scripting adaptation):

> *Rhoda:* Once upon a time there was a little boy named Birk, and he was a mouse.
>
> *Amy:* And there was a little wind-up mouse named Amy.
>
> *Rhoda:* And she was very pretty. One day Birk saw her and he kissed her. I mean he saw her and he thought she was very pretty.
>
> *Amy:* And he wanted her and them to be together. So she said that there is a beautiful lizard that is a boy named Birkalotis. Go to there and you can wish whatever you may wish.
>
> *Rhoda:* Ok. So they went there at dawn. The lizard said, "What do you want?" And Birk said, "I wish to turn Amy into a real mouse." So he did. And in the night, he went there, I mean the lizard told him.
>
> *Amy:* To find a purple pebble and he looked and he looked and he could not find one. And finally he went and there was all these toys gathered up in a toy box and then so Amy told the sad story about she had the birthday party and now all her old toys were going to get thrown away and suddenly—bing—a purple pebble fell right out into his arms.
>
> *Rhoda:* And he saw it and he picked it up and at dawn he went to the lizard and the lizard said, "What do you wish for?" And he said, "I wish for Amy to turn into a real mouse." And the pebble was gone. He went back and he saw the little mouse in his cave and he said, "Who are you?" and the girl said—
>
> *Amy:* "My name is Amy." And he said, "My wish come true!" And finally they kissed and they got married.
>
> *Amy and Rhoda:* And they lived happily ever after!

Amy and Rhoda's story is interesting for the way it reveals children extricating secrets of text. One of the subtle secrets of this story arises from the question or enigma (definitely a blank space): Who—or what—really turned Willy into real? The lizard/wizard as magic agent? The pebble as magical object? Alexander as agent of his own wish? Willy taking action to save his own life when he told Alexander about the lizard in the first place?

Amy and Rhoda appeared to see Alexander as the agent of his own wish. They named the lizard Birkalotus, an extension of the Rhoda's last name Birk and their character Birk, since Amy said the lizard was a boy. Amy never labeled the lizard-boy as magical; instead her character Amy emphasizes the power of imagination to bring about real solutions when she tells Birk he can wish whatever he wants to wish when he goes to the lizard. The magic is inside Birk rather than in the lizard, her words imply. In addition, Amy seemed to see the pebble as a discarded toy that gains some autonomy of its own, jumping as it does out of the toy box and into Birk's arms. So strong is the magic here, in fact, that the pebble becomes in their story an icon for the wish itself, or an extension of their story-character, Amy.

Amy's empathetic responses during the read-aloud time may even tell us how she could later produce the metaphors in her story (a pebble is a toy, is a wish, is a girl mouse). As she said then, "If you [a real mouse] saw a wind-up mouse, you'd think it was a real mouse" [you would see it as a mirror image of yourself]. "You would think it would want to be your friend" and "the two of you could knock down the penguin" [mutual support or friendship bringing strength].

Rhoda and Amy's storymaking also reveals how much richer children's *aesthetic* and *sociocultural* learning become when children are invited to perform as authors, making their own creative choices. The particular details of the original story that these two children included were more important for what they revealed about *sociocultural* meaning-making and *personal/ empathetic* preferences than for what such details would reveal about their ability to retain facts of the story-plot for testing purposes.

Rhoda, for example, did not show Birk wishing or hoping to become like Amy the wind-up toy, as when Alexander wished to become like Willy. But that didn't mean she was overlooking or misunderstanding something in Lionni's story. She had earlier constructed the premise that Amy was pretty, Birk had kissed her, and he now wanted them to be together as real. And her response during the read-aloud time—that Alexander wished Willy to be real because Willy is "more important"—shows that she understood well what Alexander also comes to see during the story—that *real* is better. She knew that her classmates understood all this; she had been a partner in learning with them as they all sorted out the story together. So she did not belabor the point, especially since she and her friend Amy had other priorities: highlighting the romance of their story characters, Birk and Amy.

Rhoda and Amy's reshaping of Lionni's book also reveals how important it can be for *sociocultural* and *narrative* literacy when children have the opportunity for post-story responses of their own choosing. Here storying was neither a directed nor a suggested activity. The adaptation these children chose to create also reveals the importance of the reader's *initial* empathy for a book character. In this case, strong empathetic response to a nurturing male character, Lionni's mouse Alexander, instigated Amy's ability to nurture a mirror image of herself as a nurturing female character.

Producing spontaneously what Stibbs (1993) has called a "role-reversing rewrite" (p. 55), she and Rhoda responded to the absence of females in the story by creating a female character of their own to place at the center of the story (*narrative* and *critical* literacies). And Amy's character Amy plays a strong role in deciding the fate of herself and Birk: She tells Birk about the lizard, just as Willy tells Alexander in Lionni's story.

It is, in fact, interesting that Amy and Rhoda chose to change Willy, rather than Alexander, into the female character. In Lionni's story, like many females in fairy tales, Willy lacks autonomy and therefore [human] dignity, but he, like Amy's character, Amy, assumes the role of empathetic connector or "connected knower" (Belinky, 1986, p. 113), when he tells Alexander about the lizard, having noticed that Alexander is lonely and troubled and filled with the need to reinvent himself. And perhaps it was something about Willy as connector rather than merely his lack of autonomy, that drew Amy and Rhoda to "borrow"—and transform—him into a female character.

"Integration" is a word Paulo Freire (1973) uses to explain what is distinctively human—the ability not merely to adapt to the world, but to make choices and transform the world, the result of humanity's "critical capacity": the ability to reflect on oneself, one's responsibilities, and one's role in the world, as well as on the power to reflect, which produces "an increased capacity for choice" (p. 16). For children, this capacity emerges in talk and storymaking such as we see in Any and Rhoda's story. And the more we invite storying from children, the better able they will be to bring to conscious awareness this critical capacity.

## REFLECTIONS

Reading with children in the classroom this day illuminated for me the intricate interrelationship of children and books. Lionni's narrative strategies were especially important for eliciting the children's empathy for the characters and thus stimulating a burst of intersecting—and interwoven—literacies. We have ample evidence in Rhoda and Amy's storymaking, in Sid's deep engagement with the story, and the overall reception of the entire group to Alexander's plight. And Lionni's authorial expertise was especially important to the children's meaning-making process. The book is subtly complex; it contains deep reading "secrets," in Meek's terms (1988, p. 19). And children are quite adept at uncovering such secrets; therefore it is especially important that they read the book as it was originally intended to be read, with every picture intact and every picture placed in the position that the author had planned. Cut and rearranged as this book had been in their basal reader story (Lionni, 1989), the word and picture pattern, so beneficial in books for emergent readers like this one, was broken. Consequently, where pictures might have assisted in the reading process, they could not do so. In the basal story, the picture of the mice playing in the shoes (or boots) had been taken out of its natural sequence to become the cover picture.

It seems ironic that a commercial reading program, which places so much importance on the sequencing skill, would have placed so little value on the author's own sequence of pictures. The responsibility may lie with the way educators generally have devalued pictures for fostering *print* literacy. Susan Lehr (1991) notes: "Reading researchers have had a tendency to separate text from pictures in research situations in order to focus on the child's ability to read text without picture clues" (p. 93).

Here the editors might actually have been thinking of picture clues when they discarded Lionni's original cover of the mice playing in the *matrioska* doll and replaced it with his picture of the mice playing in a pair of shoes (shoes being the more familiar object). But sacrificing the nesting doll figure also sacrifices thematic meaning-making: the doll suggests the unity that exists in a true friendship more effectively than the pair of shoes. Children can see from the picture that the nesting doll parts fit closely together to make one solid object, foreshadowing the peer solidarity of the mouse friends.

In addition, although this reading program retained both pictures of Alexander and the lizard and three of the seven scenes in which Willy and Alexander are shown together, it deleted all of the pictures in which Alexander is alone and at risk. The impact of Alexander's lonely state is weakened, the binary tension of together and alone is deemphasized, and the subsequent empathetic feelings Alexander's condition evokes in child readers is likely to be weaker. Therefore to retain the two pictures of the magic lizard (as icon of connector) seems futile as far as meaning-making goes, since *what* the lizard is connecting has been left out.

When textbook editors cut pictures from their original book-length state, they sacrifice *generative, literary, narrative, critical, personal/empathetic,* and *sociocultural* literacies for what they think is the "best" route to *print* literacy. In the process, even print literacy is sacrificed, because children understand stories holistically, as we have seen. And piecemeal learning surely occurs when advance "organizers" announce what the story is about, when decontextualized vocabulary lists precede the story reading, when the story is interrupted for "comprehension" questions, and when pictures are not allowed to illuminate texts.

Closely connected to the importance of children responding to the book in its original state is the context for the reading event. Of crucial importance here, children encountered the book in a social setting in which they were free to produce divergent responses—or multiple perspectives about the story. With the adult functioning as supportive listener and co-participant, the children were able to converse in natural, spontaneous, and dialogic ways, to open up mysteries of text, to generate theories, and to create story texts of their own. Thus Lionni's story was a springboard for personal and social learning rather than simply a vehicle for assessing comprehension, sequencing skills, story recall, or knowledge of story grammar.

In addition, *sociocultural* and *critical* literacies—or awareness of what the world is like and what part we can play in shaping it—were not taking a backseat to *print* and *literary* literacies. Literature was not being used to teach comprehension skills or literary "elements" such as how to label a story fantasy or realism, as so often happens with the teaching of anthologized textbook stories. Instead multiple literacies were emerging—and intersecting—naturally when the children were free to respond naturally—in sociocultural ways.

We can see *sociocultural* literacy at work if we examine and celebrate story retellings in light of what has been changed by the teller as well as what has been retained. Then, as Rosen (1988) explains, we see what children are investigating in terms of their own values, interests, and cultural differences. The high point of emotional intensity is what children notice, remember, emphasize, change, and resist in their stories, as Amy and Rhoda were doing. Thus it is vitally important that we invite children to respond to stories (the author's or peer stories) with resistant or critical readings.

A critical reading, says Rosenblatt (1994), is one in which the reader refuses "to accept everything unquestioningly" (p. 39). Too often these days, critical reading has come to mean whatever the adult refuses to accept about an author's perspective and therefore what the adult decides children should notice, reexamine. In other words, literature is used to teach curriculum topics of the adult's choosing. Of equal or even greater importance could be a critical way of reading that arises naturally and spontaneously from children's own responses. Before we, the adults, muddy the waters with our own concerns, preoccupations, and agendas, we need to know what children are refusing to accept.

Children who are crossing the borders of gender, class, and ethnicity in classrooms need to "learn to participate in and help build a fair world that can contain them all" (p. 324), says literacy researcher Anne Haas Dyson (1995). Thus they need to help one another see how "fair" texts are—both their own and those of adult authors—as Amy and Rhoda's "take" on Lionni's story reveals. Many voices, many readings, many resistant readings, many literacies, and many intersections with what Dyson (1997) calls "socioideological" perspectives are what we need to learn to determine what makes a particular book "right" for a particular child—or a particular group of children. As children produce new learning for themselves, we learn more about their worlds and how these worlds can transform our own.

Genre was also important. Genre has a natural purpose, and the children experienced it naturally. In this animal fantasy picture book, Lionni's pictures—especially his original intended layout and choices of color, texture, and design—enabled the children to enter easily Alexander's world. And because Alexander is a talking, thinking *mouse*, the children could distance themselves more easily from the disturbing or problematic aspects of his world in order to face their own vulnerabilities, explore their own social responsibilities, and discover significant issues in their own lives.

In this situation, the picture book genre gave children a way to behave as real readers before and during the developing *print* literacy stage. They could "read" pictures as a way to make meaning of texts, and they could talk their way into stories that examined their worlds through a lens of fantasy. The reading of pictures is a crucial but often overlooked process for the making of good readers, and that is why it emerges often here, particularly in the next two chapters. Children reading pictures perform as readers—often, before they can actually read in the *print* literacy sense—as we will see in the next two chapters. In doing so, they grow as readers, with multiple, interwoven literacies emerging naturally in their responses.

*Chapter Four*

# A Deeper Look at Aesthetic Literacy: Brooke and *Louis the Fish*

SEVERAL YEARS AFTER I read with children in my son's classroom, I began teaching children's literature and reading methods classes for preservice teachers. One of these teachers was also a foreign exchange student from London who had brought her six-year-old daughter with her for this year in America. Brooke stayed with us sometimes when her mother went sightseeing. One weekend, Brooke discovered a book that would capture her attention for multiple readings, allowing me to take a deep and extensive look at *aesthetic* literacy, which in Brooke's case was based on her particular way of reading.

Although Brooke was at this time a first-grader struggling with the mysteries of the basal approach, reading in her kindergarten classroom in England had been very different. There she had often "read" books or "read" pictures with a peer partner before her teacher read stories aloud. Her mother had followed this format at home; therefore Brooke was often in control of her own mediating process, choosing her own books, turning her own pages, pausing to turn back and forth when necessary, as any adult reader does, and "reading" the story for herself.

## READING PICTURES

"I want to read *this* one!" cried Brooke, picking up a new picture book I had purchased that day to use in my children's literature classes. It was bedtime, and as she climbed the stairs, she studied the cover picture as I read the words of the title aloud. Then she began chanting the title over and over to herself: "*Louis the Fish! Louis the Fish! Louis the Fish.*"

As she reached the top step, she had already opened the book and was well into her first reading before I had time to jot down her words. What I retrieved, as she climbed into bed, were her responses to the last five "openings" (facing pages) of the book,

Bubble gum! He's got bubble gum! (Opening 11)
Then he changed back to normal. (Openings 12–13)
And then he had two fins. (Opening 14)
Then he went to the store like a fish. (Opening 15)
And then at school he was in here like he was a fish. (Also opening 15)
And then he stayed in there forever, not changing to a little boy again.
   (Opening 16)

*Louis the Fish* (1980), by Arthur Yorinks and Richard Egielski, has on the title and dedication pages wordless scenes of a man, Louis, getting ready for bed. The clock hands show five minutes before midnight, often a sign of magical time. And at this moment, we see fish-shaped clouds swimming past the moon. As the actual story begins, a fish wearing Louis's pajamas is sleeping in Louis's bed, a suggestion, perhaps, of Louis's dream state.

The story continues as a flashback, with backstories of Louis's life. First there are scenes of Louis as a child on his seventh birthday, then of Louis cleaning a fish tank after school. Later Louis is trying to tell his parents he hates meats and loves fish. But they are determined that he take over the family business, which he eventually does. Louis the adult becomes a butcher like his father and grandfather, but unlike them, he hates what he does. He still hates meat and he loves fish, and soon he is imagining that his customers are fish. He sees fish everywhere; he remembers, and remains haunted by, childhood nightmares of the butcher shop meats attacking him. Finally, one night in May (we are back now to the story in present time that frames the backstories), as Louis lies tossing, turning, and dreaming, he turns into a fish. And we see him at the end swimming happily in a pet shop fish tank, the children gazing happily at him.

The picture of Louis swimming in the fish tank fascinated Brooke. In fact, so engrossed was she in the entire book that I asked her if she would like to retell it to me. With both of these readings, she was using pictures to generate her sense of the story, although she might have sorted out a few of the words like "butcher" and "happy."

*Pre-story: Louis, the adult, going to bed the night of his transformation*

Cover picture: Louis pulling down the window shade; fish "swimming" through the sky.
Opening 1 (Title Page): Louis in pajamas and bathrobe brushing his teeth.
Opening 2 (Dedication Page): Louis yawning.
Opening 3 (Words that begin the story; two lines of print).

*Story begins: Louis transformed into a fish*

Opening 4: (Wordless picture page): A fish sleeps in Louis's bed, in
Louis's pajamas.
*Brooke: Louis the fish! One morning Louis the fish was waking up tired. That's
the beginning of the story. This is no words.*

*Story continues: Louis at work just before his transformation*

Opening 5: Picture on left side shows Louis, the butcher, opening up
his shop; words tell about Louis's father and grandfather as
butchers.
*Brooke: Louis was working on a butcher.*
Picture on right side shows two nuns with grocery bags walking past;
Louis tips his hat.
*Brooke: Louis saw some ladies* [she paused] *walking past.*

*Sequence of backstories: Louis at different ages*

Opening 6: Louis on his seventh birthday, holding his grandfather's
present—a gift-wrapped hot dog. He stands beside a blackboard/
easel on which is written, "Louis, 7 years old."
*Brooke: Louis teached the whole class. Louis had a present for Mrs. Class.*

Opening 7: Louis a little older crouches behind a fish tank, playing
happily with the fish.
*Brooke: Louis looked out of his fish* [tank]. *Some popped out of the fish* [tank].

Opening 8: Louis and his parents in the kitchen, his father reading a
newspaper, his mother serving a chicken.
*Brooke: Louis was eating some chicken.*

Opening 9: Louis as an adult sweeping the shop.
*Brooke: Louis had to clean all the whole place up.*

Opening 10: Louis seated in the freezer room of the butcher shop,
drawing fish.
*Brooke: Louis drawed loads of pictures of fishes—like Louis! The fish.*

Opening 11: Louis standing behind the counter of the butcher shop
staring at his customers: a fish family—mother, father, and boy
fish in baseball cap with bubble gum.
*Brooke: Louis was doing* [something in the shop] *and some customers and
the dad, the mom, the little boy* [were there].

*Story continues: Louis the night of his transformation*

Opening 12: Louis in bed tossing and turning.
*Brooke: Louis was like dreaming. He keeps turning around.*

*Wordless flashback scene*

Opening 13: Louis as an older child, in pajamas, standing in front of the
    butcher shop as meat creatures—steaks, salamis, hamburgers—
    cluster angrily around him.
*Brooke: Louis was having a dream.*

*Story continues: Louis after his transformation*

Opening 14: On the bus, a fish with fin-arms wearing Louis's hat and
    butcher's apron stands talking to Al, the pet shop owner.
*Brooke: Louis was the same one. He was the butcher.*

*Story ends: Louis as a fish*

Opening 15: Louis is swimming in a fish tank in Al's pet shop as chil-
    dren stand nearby fascinated by the big fish in the big tank. Al
    stands nearby with arms outstretched, as if introducing Louis.
*Brooke: Louis was at school. Louis was the famous little, the famous big, big fish.*

Opening 16: Close-up of Louis swimming happily in the tank. Text
    reads: "After a hard life, Louis was a happy fish."
*Brooke: Louis was the happiest fish, ever all.*

## PUTTING WORDS WITH PICTURES

At this time I offered to read Brooke the story. But even as we began, she
continued to maintain ownership of her own storymaking. She began by
"reading" the wordless title page (her responses are in italics): *Louis was
brushing his teeth*, the dedication page: *Louis was tired*, and the first wordless page: *Louis is sleepy*. Then, immediately after hearing the entire story,
she told her own version spontaneously. Listening to the words released
her to devote more attention to nuances of picture.

This time she noticed the smile on one of the nuns' faces and her response to the page became: *Louis saw some nice, friendly girls, friends*. She
had heard the word "friendly" used in the text in relation to Louis: "He

was always friendly, always helpful, a wonderful guy." But the nuns are smiling, so she applied the term "friendly" to them and then added a small "story" of her own to fill out the "picture" of Louis: *He said "hello." He was always very kind to people.*

Hearing the words also caused her to reinterpret the blackboard/easel scene as Louis's birthday and to say that Louis got a hot dog, as the text says. Facial expressions in the illustrations also continued to affect her telling, along with the words of the text. At the kitchen scene and at the fish-family-customers page, she introduced the emotion of anger into her own story-picture. First she said: *Louis had some dinner and his mommy was like angry with him.* Actually the mother's anger is directed at the father; she nags him to give Louis a job in the butcher shop so he won't have "to slave over the lousy fish." But Brooke empathized strongly with Louis at this point, and a negative remark about the fish might be, from her perspective, a remark against Louis.

At the butcher shop/fish family scene, she noticed the facial expressions in the illustrations of the fish "people": *Louis saw Daddy grumpy, Mommy arguing, and Boy bubbling.* In this picture the father chomps on a cigar glumly; the mother is turned away from him, her hand raised testily at Louis; and the boy is staring off into the distance. The text leaves the source of the mother's anger openly interpretive. The family unit appears to be a dream displacement for Louis's own family, or his unconscious memory of them, and Brooke might have sensed this.

In the scene preceding this one—Louis sweeping the butcher shop—Brooke generated many more details. The text reads: "Someday this will all be yours" [Louis's father talking to Louis]. Then the narrator explains that Louis's "parents died suddenly" and "for years" Louis worked in the butcher shop. Her response was: *"When the day's gone over, when his dad was sad* [his dad said]: *'This is going to be all yours, when the day is over.' He died.* [Louis's father]. *He* [Louis] *never knew what to say."*

She had not yet assimilated the meat creatures/nightmare scene. She said, *"He* [Louis] *keeped dreaming about his cat. He had to dream."* Then she told me she had also had a dream about cats (therefore, perhaps, she decided that Louis was dreaming of a cat, too).

With these three readings, Brooke was sorting out the story before, during, and after she heard it read aloud. She was also skipping around to find her balance and attain a foothold in the visual and textual shaping patterns of this intricate, innovative book. As the back cover of the paperback edition revealed, *Louis the Fish* (1986) was a *Reading Rainbow* book and a *School Library Journal* Best Books of the Year selection. Here also was a glowing review from *The New York Times*: "Children will find it fantastic and funny." And Brooke in her first three readings had certainly done so.

## NARRATIVE CODING AND CHILDREN'S READING

What choices did the author/illustrator make to produce a confirming (readerly) yet extending (writerly) experience for the child reader? The five semiotic "codes" that Roland Barthes (1974, p. x) uses to describe ways readers process texts—or as Rosenblatt (1994) describes them, the "voices" that produce a "network" through which "the entire text passes" (p. 170)—provide valuable direction here.

With Barthes's *actions* code, a sequence of important acts produces interwoven threads of plot for the story. Conversations, smaller stories or smaller sequences of events within the larger story, and character traits that produce motivation for the action all feed into this code. (In *Alexander and the Wind-Up Mouse*, two mice talk and work together to remain living friends; in *The Snowman*, a boy and a snowman visit each other's worlds before the snowman melts; in *Louis the Fish*, a butcher shop owner who has hated meat since childhood dreams—or becomes—a fish, to escape his disturbing life.)

With the *semic* code, readers notice details or "flickers of meaning" (p. 19) about setting and characters. (In *Alexander and the Wind-Up Mouse*, the artist drew two mice playing in a pair of shoes; in *The Snowman*, the artist drew a downturned mouth. Here the artist has drawn clouds shaped like fish and a fish wearing pajamas.)

With the *cultural* code, readers sifting through the details of the character's world call upon their own habits, values, unexamined assumptions, and unconscious knowledge of the world to test the reality of the story. If the character is living in a different time/place/ethnic group, the reader must "read" the semic coding in order to become inscribed into a new world. (In *Alexander and the Wind-Up Mouse*, a mouse is chased by a large broom; in *The Snowman*, a boy and snowman are flying over a palace; in *Louis the Fish*, a boy is trying to break out of his father's butcher-shop world.)

With the *enigmatic* code, readers notice and speculate about mysteries (gaps and blank spaces) of the text that drive the story and keep it alive. What will happen to a discarded toy mouse? Why does a snowman not melt in a warm house? How can a boy fly? Why does a man become a fish?

With the *symbolic* code, readers find themselves in the realm of ideas that arise out of the entire story, based on patterns they see and connections they make as they go along. And often the patterns are based on opposing ideas that generate meanings: together and alone (*Alexander and the Wind-Up Mouse*), human world and sky world (*The Snowman*), meat and fish (*Louis the Fish*).

We might ask is the story especially rich in any of these codes. Is there strong interplay among them? How does the author balance expectation and surprise (the actions code) or produce patterns of meaning in details of character or setting (the semic code), tap into child worlds with emotional content (the cultural code), create mysteries or gaps in text (the enigmatic code), or thread ideas about the larger world through the events, details, emotional content, and mysteries of the text (the symbolic code)?

From an adult perspective, *Louis the Fish* is an intriguing book, sad yet humorous. Louis resembles Kafka's Gregor Samsa, who was also transformed into a permanent, nonhuman state in *The Metamorphosis* (1972). Louis doesn't "fit." He is an artist, a nice guy, sensitive, pleasing everyone but himself. Louis's choice to become a salmon seems highly appropriate: He is not a shark; he hates violence and brutality, is a pacifist rather than a warrior. He hates the butcher shop, where his grandfather, then his father, and now he spend their days butchering meat. As a child, he dreamed of the meats retaliating: They try to butcher *him*. Ultimately he escapes this childhood nightmare by conscientiously objecting to his life as a butcher: He transforms himself into a new and totally different "self"—a salmon. A fish out of water in his human life, he becomes a fish *in* water (or in a fish tank) as the story ends. Is freedom inevitably impossible, except through imagination—art, fantasy, play, magic, metamorphosis?

We might expect Louis to return to human form, the usual pattern of fairy tales like "Beauty and the Beast" and "The Frog Prince," and the pattern this same author-illustrator team used in their Caldecott Award winner of 1987, *Hey, Al*. But here the transformation is permanent. At the end of the story, Louis is a fish—no turning back. And he is happy in his new state, words and pictures tell us. Was the permanence of Louis's fish condition (losing himself to the human world forever) threatening to Brooke?

Actually, she appeared pleased with the ending. As she made her way through three readings, she seemed to understand—to make sense of—the inverted time scheme, the transformation, and the complex maze of metaphorical implications. The book is particularly rich in the semic, enigmatic, and symbolic codes that Barthes has described. It was also rich in the cultural coding of child worlds; otherwise Brooke, at age six, could never have slipped so quickly and easily into such a multilayered, richly interpretive, readerly and writerly book, with its unique—irreversible and ironic— ending. She could never have found it both funny and fascinating. And she never could have entered this story so easily and remained there so long. What did she see in such a deeply complex story and what did she make of what she saw? How did she reshape the story from her own child's perspective—and what was the author's role in this shaping process?

Several of Brooke's responses during her second reading, before she heard the words of the story, are especially important: "Louis drawed loads of pictures of fishes—like Louis! the Fish." (Opening 10); "Louis was at school. Louis was the famous little, the famous big, big fish" (Opening 15); and "Louis was the happiest fish, ever all" (Opening 16, the last page). At these times, she seemed to find Louis's reinventing himself (as an artist drawing fish and then later as a fish swimming in the tank) a positive action. He was at last happy.

Margaret Meek's ideas about authorial choices and the role they play in children's meaning-making, coinciding as they do with Barthes's theories about semiotic codes, help us see even more.

## HOW TEXTS AND PICTURES TEACH

According to Meek (1988), authors of well-crafted children's books "link what children know, partly know, and are learning about the world, to ways of presenting the world in books." These presentations are lifelike "and the reader senses their relation to psychological reality" (p. 19). In other words, the reader, in Meek's view, "controls the input and gradually makes sense of the way the author has linked things together . . . The interweaving of the reader's meanings and the author's meanings are what we call understanding" (1982a, p. 22). Just how much of the author's meaning is communicated through pictures, we might wonder, since so much of Brooke's meaning-making was emerging through her reading of pictures?

1. Meek says we come to know the character whose "fortunes we are to follow" (1988, p. 8) by encountering that character on each page as "someone to be continuously regarded" (1987a, p. 3). In other words, children turn the page out of concern for the character whose fate is at stake—and in children's books, this character is usually a child. They want to know what happens next to this character. Empathy for the child character therefore teaches child readers to understand the relationship of words and pictures, phrases and scenes, events and episodes, story time and real time (Barthes's actions and cultural codes merging). The break from one picture or one line of text "to what follows on the next page," says Meek, "is a carefully calculated device on the part of the author or artist" (1987a, p. 3) to orchestrate suspense or to create an intended time scheme.

In *Louis the Fish*, the main character Louis appears on each page as a boy, a man, or a fish. Sequentially he appears first as a man, then as a fish-man (a fish wearing pajamas), next as a man, a boy, an older boy, a man, and a fish-man (a fish wearing a butcher's apron), and at the end, he has become a fish. Louis often appears with a fish partner: a real fish he is watching, a fish he is drawing, a fish family he is imagining, a fish wearing his pajamas or his butcher's apron, or fish-clouds floating over his head.

As a result, the child reader can make ideational connections between man (or boy) and fish. The way the illustrator places Louis in each picture—either alongside a fish or as a fish—serves well to emphasize his desire to reinvent himself.

The man–fish connection emerges through a sequence of time shifts. As the story begins, three pictures show Louis as a man in red-and-white-striped pajamas preparing for bed. Then in the next opening (words on white space—no picture), readers hear that one day last spring, Louis, a butcher, turned into a fish. Turning the page, they see the reverse: a word-less picture of a large salmon sleeping in Louis's bed, in Louis's red-and-white striped pajamas.

A second time shift occurs in the next opening: the picture shows Louis the man tipping his hat to two nuns who pass his butcher shop; the words introduce Louis as a butcher whose father and grandfather were butchers. Then a third time shift occurs in the next scene, a picture of Louis as a child. The words tell about Louis in both present time (he is a man who hates meat) and in past time (he always hated meat). On birthdays he received presents of meat instead of toys. The problem (Louis's discontent) sets the story in motion. In the pictures that follow, time proceeds sequentially from past to present. In one, a nightmare "vision," the meat "toys" are attacking Louis the boy, but even here, fish-shaped clouds float over Louis's head, as they do in the cover picture where he is now a man.

2. Meek (1988) says that beyond just recognizing words on the page, children, as they proceed through the pages, pick up the author's view and voice in the author's semiotic coding. Words and pictures on the first few pages of this book signal something important for the entire scheme of the story. Readers see and hear about a friendly, helpful, nice guy who was, as they discover, supremely unhappy as a child. He hated the meat his father butchered and sold. As the son of a butcher, meat was foisted upon him; soon he began to see fish everywhere. A subtle irony arises: Louis is a softhearted, nice guy; the meats that pursue him in nightmare fantasies are salami-thugs and steak-bullies. So to escape them, he becomes what he is at heart—a peaceful salmon.

3. Meek speaks of a page in a picture book as an icon—the author's nonverbal representation of ideas—to be contemplated, narrated, and ex-plicated by the viewer: a picture "holds the story until there is a telling" (1988, p. 12). The scene of Louis's nightmare vision brings to life Louis's deeply buried feelings of frustration, isolation, and loneliness and is espe-cially important as an icon of the meat–fish conflict that begins early in Louis's life and continues into adulthood. Only a small toy cow stands

behind the large glass window of "Lou's Meats." All the other meats have broken out of the shop for their street fight.

The book is filled with glass encasings—windowpanes, meat cases, fish tanks—emphasizing the tension of freedom and constriction: Louis sees in or looks out, but he never is able to escape his conflicted state (semic word and picture patterns intersecting with the symbolic/meanings code). On the cover, Louis stands before a tightly closed glass window. Soon after this, the salmon appears, sleeping peacefully beside an *open* glass window. Meat is tightly enclosed in glass cases and behind shop windows made of glass—until the nightmare scene, when the meats break out. Aggression, hostility, and anger all break loose, along with Louis's distaste for meat. Louis sits in the freezer room in overcoat and earmuffs, and the window opening is particularly small here: he is totally immersed in an inner world. At the end of the story, Louis swims in an open tank in Al's pet store. He is encased in glass now, but he still breathes and moves. Alone in the tank, he is nevertheless still alive. He has escaped the bad guys. He has freedom, within limits, and happily, he has chosen at last for himself. And his choice provides happiness for others, in particular the children who enjoy him as a pet-friend.

4. According to Meek, the artist or storyteller presents children with the familiar in a new guise or makes a logical extension of the real by creating reading adventures with "deep reading secrets" (1988, p. 15), Barthes's enigmatic code. The text means more than it says; it is richly or openly interpretive—unpredictable or, in Barthes's terms, "writerly" (1974, p. 4). Thus it allows readers to produce the meaning, or it is constructed intentionally to invite multiple meanings. Will Louis be able to break out of his limited life and assert himself against the future his parents have chosen for him? Or will he escape it? And if so, how?

We know from the beginning that a fish is named Louis. (Brooke knew this from the title.) But the first words of the book—"One day last spring, Louis, a butcher, turned into a fish"—on a page filled with white space and two lines of text, tell us something else. The mystery of the text is *why* did Louis turn into a fish—and *how*? We discover from reading further into the book that Louis was from the beginning like a calm, friendly fish—rather than like an aggressive meat.

Louis became "himself" at last when he recognized who he was, from his dreams, his drawings, and his visions. So one of the deep secrets of this story may be that when problems in the world arise, following our intuitive urges is the transforming magic that brings feelings, desires, and wishes to the surface—and therefore brings about change. Fantasy, for adults or children, is most often grounded in a physical representation of the mind—a dream state, a mental imagination or vision, even a hallucination. In postmodern picture books, human fantasy often takes the form of surrealistic scenes that reveal the liberated unconscious at work, transforming a problematic world.

The entire sequence of pictures in *Louis the Fish* develops this secret of Louis's complicated inner world. First his parents dominate him, telling him what he must do—and be. But later, after he plays in a fish tank, then draws, imagines, and finally dreams fish, he *knows*, on a deep unconscious level, what he wants to be—a peace-loving fish. And in the surrealistic nightmare scene, when the toy-meats sicken him and the fish-clouds appear, he awakens to this possibility.

5. Meek says authors shape stories by creating patterns, and they "vary these patterns" (1988, p. 14) so that the familiar and the new are juxtaposed. "Skilled writers for children," she explains, "have ways of keeping the reader focused on the moves to be made to keep the story going. At the same time the author tries to intrigue the reader by changing the rules and generating surprise" (1987a, p. 2). Texts set readers up to make predictions: Louis is a fish, as the title states; then they jolt us by reversing our expectations: Louis is a man who becomes a fish, as the first words of the book reveal.

In the picture sequence of *Louis the Fish*, time shifts produce a pattern of *continuous* surprise, or jolts that occur and reoccur. First a fish is sleeping in Louis's pajamas, where we least expect it to be. Then three fish "customers" appear in Louis's butcher shop. After this, meats break out of the shop and attack Louis. Finally we see a fish riding the bus, dressed in Louis's butcher's apron (Louis in transition from man to fish). All of this precedes the final jolt: Louis—all fish—swims around a tank in Al's pet store fish tank.

The shaping pattern of the entire book works to emphasize these nodes of surprise. The front cover shows Louis's real and imaginary worlds fused: Louis getting ready for bed as fish-clouds "swim" overhead. The back cover shows Louis's hat and butcher's apron neatly folded—and consigned to the past—an icon representing the life that frustrated and constrained him. Between these two pictures, man and fish are connected, separated, juxtaposed, and finally fused when Louis breaks out of his conflicted life and triumphs by reinventing himself as artist, entertainer, something—or someone—we watch, respond to, and tell about. Louis has made—or remade—himself, into his own *story*.

A fascinating book, *Louis the Fish* is multidimensional, innovative, and richly interpretive. And even though Brooke produced three readings of it the night she came to visit, I never expected her to think any more about it that weekend. Little did I know.

## BROOKE'S WAY INTO LITERACY

The next morning, after breakfast and Saturday-morning cartoons, Brooke asked where *Louis the Fish* was. She soon found it and began reading it once again, holding the book herself as before and turning her own pages. Thus she continued to control her own reading. Responses that reflect changes and additions from her past two readings appear in italic type below in this, her fourth, reading. The numbers of the openings are indicated in brackets.

Louis the Fish! Louis was brushing his teeth [1]. Louis was tired [2]. This is how the story begins [3]. This is Louis. *He's like a little fish* [4]. He's met some ladies. *He's always nice to people and friendly to people* [5]. *Once upon a time* it was his birthday [6]. He got a little hot dog and a big hot dog *from his mom* [6]. His fish jumped out [7]. The mother was really argued with the son. *"Why are you arguing with the son? He knows what to do"* [8]. The dad said, "You can have this all by yourself" [9]. But the time really went over and his dad died [9]. Each day he drawed some pictures of himself. It was different colors, *any colors he wanted it to be* [10]. Daddy was grumpy; Mommy was grumpy. *But Boy wasn't grumpy.* He had bubble gum. See his bubble gum? [11]. So he dreamed every word [12]. Then he heard some noise. He had *meat, meat, meat, meat,* sausage, meatballs—that these little sausages can't hurt their heads cause they can't hurt so *bad, bad, bad* [13].

A chance remark by me at the wordless nightmare scene took Brooke's reading off in a new direction. "What are these?" I asked about the fish-shaped clouds overhead. Brooke's response, "Fishes!" caused me to say, "Yes, but they're what, too?"

"Fishes-clouds!" she replied quickly. And in producing that response, she saw the way to produce still another metaphor, as she continued to re-create the story and reshape the meaning for herself: *Brooke: On the way he was a fish-monkey* [14]. *But he forgot the time was over. He was a butcher* [15]. *He forgot he ever knew about the butcher* [16].

A great deal of assimilated meaning had taken place by the time of this fourth reading—and not simply because Brooke had heard the words of the book. Of special importance, she had continued to retell the story for herself. Each time she revisited the book, she expanded certain aspects of the story to sort things out more clearly, a process that in turn produced a more complex vision.

If from the beginning she had seen the author's main narrative metaphor (man as fish), here she also began to express this metaphor quite clearly, as she reasoned out the "why" of things for her own evaluative insight: Louis was a little fish, always "nice" and "friendly." The word "little" was significant also. The irreversible transformation was not frightening to her. She felt very much in control of the story ideas from the start.

She was also seeing more of the complex time shifts of the story. She knew that the story began with the first page of print. The author's words "One day last spring" might have had a conventional story-opening "sound" to her. But her own phrase "Once upon a time" at the birthday scene showed that she also saw the story-within-the-story flashback to Louis as a child. And this authorial strategy, what narrative theorist Gerard Genette (1972) has described as "analepsis," is a sophisticated distinction for a child to make.

She said that Louis's mother was the one who gives the hot dog present to Louis, rather than his grandfather, as the text states, possibly because the mother figure was an important and disturbing character to her. In this reading, Brooke again emphasized a family argument during the kitchen scene. She addressed Louis's mother directly, so strong was her empathy with Louis at this point. "Why are you arguing with the son?"she asked. "He knows what to do." As she reasoned out why Louise liked to draw, she emphasized Louis's need for independence and a separate identity. He chose his own colors, (then he was in control). "It was different colors, any colors he wanted it to be," Brooke said. In his drawing, his play, he was happy—not "grumpy" like the fish-boy's daddy.

In this fourth reading, she was for the first time less hesitant to confront the dream scene directly. She rhymed the words, producing for herself something of a nursery rhyme (a rocking-chair moment of comfort and reassurance). Expanding and emphasizing the scene with the pattern she was making of the repeated words "meat" and "bad" produced a meaningful connection for the pattern also: From Louis's point of view, meat was the bully—the bad guy.

Her chant—the patterned repetition of meat/hurt/bad—also emphasized her own concern for Louis's safety and her understanding of his plight. She reassured herself that the sausages are "little"; therefore they can't hurt Louis as badly as, in the dream, he imagines they will. Creating a new scene for Louis's dream, she reassured herself about Louis's safety. In producing a playful Louis who becomes a fish-monkey, she further diminished the threat of the "bad" meats.

Her last phrase, "He forgot he never knew about the butcher," might have indicated that becoming or dreaming yourself into something else— a man-fish, a fish-butcher, a fish-monkey—could help you escape the hurt of death or forget "the time was over" (when Louis's father died). She had told me, during her third reading, more about the meat monsters. "They can't hurt," she said. "They just punch cause they aren't rocks." As we see from the pictures, the spindle limbs of the meat creatures *do* have the soft, pliable look of fabric puppets, which takes the "sting" out of their wrathful looks and gestures.

Walking around the story, telling her own story of the story, as these readings continued, Brooke was able to build on the narrative competencies and critical awareness that she brought to the reading and to produce an evolving interpretation of the authorial coding. In the role of *storyteller*, she extended her range of narrative voices. She talked to the mother as defendant of Louis's actions. And she spoke to an imaginary audience in the fish family bubble gum scene, as stage director or omniscient narrator ("See his bubble gum?").

In the role of *reader*, she continued to reconstruct a sequence of story events. She related these readings to one another as intertexts (each reading response became, for her, a different text); she connected the ending with the beginning of the story; and she continued to engage constantly in inferential thinking. She brought personal associations to the story and applied ideas from her own experiences as she sorted out the shifts in places (home, doctor's office, butcher shop, pet shop) and in time (Louis as man, Louis as boy). And she revealed strong sensitivity to the characters, their feelings, their relationships, and particularly to Louis's predicament. Like all children, who must often contend with being told what to do, she could empathize easily with Louis.

In other words, she was, in terms of Meek's theories, developing concern for a character, when she encountered that character on each page and followed his fortunes. Thus she revealed *personal/empathetic* literacy. She was picking up the author's view and voice and adding an important narrative voice of her own, revealing (*narrative*, *literary*, and *generative* literacies). She was telling what the pictures showed her, in terms of her own *sociocultural* world, and she was uncovering the patterns that the details of pictures made, exploring the deep secrets of the story as she discovered them for herself, in a series of response-texts, and experiencing surprise as the words and picture sequence evolved in her "tellings" (*literary* and *narrative* literacies). Consequently, multiple literacies were all working in tandem with the *aesthetic* literacy that was building from the moment Brooke picked up the book, examined the cover, and heard the title.

In the role of *storymaker* (composer of stories), she revealed knowledge of what words could do to solve story-puzzles. Words not only told stories, she was learning; they could also counter and subvert stories. Her *critical* literacy could expand each time she returned to the book for another reading. In the role of *resistant reader*, she filled in gaps of text when she confronted Louis's mother, when she reassured herself about the meat monsters by composing a chant, and when she re-created Louis as a fish-monkey.

Thus, like Louis, Brooke was escaping constriction. In her case this meant escaping the limits that any book, story, word, or picture imposes with its denotative or connotative "messages." She was not simply and passively receiving text and pictures; she was orchestrating them for her own purposes, as any skilled writer, storyteller, or responsive reader would do. And this orchestration continued.

## GAMES, WORDPLAY, AND NEW STORIES

After noticing the "fishes-clouds" and reinventing Louis as a "fish-monkey," Brooke continued forging her own metaphors for Louis in her fifth and next reading. Metaphor-making, in fact, may have seemed so powerful an exercise in creation that it spurred her to expand the process. Suddenly she began playing a game by renaming Louis and by asking me to repeat certain words:

> *Louis is a fish-doggie* [Opening 4, the wordless picture page of the salmon sleeping in Louis's pajamas]. *Louis saw some fish* [Opening 5, the scene in which Louis opens up his butcher shop and greets the two nuns]. *Louis had hot dogs for his birthday* [Opening 6, the flashback to Louis's seventh birthday]. *His fish jumped out. Say "fish"* [Opening 7, the scene of Louis in his after-school job, cleaning fish tanks in a doctor's office]. *His Mom argued. Say argued* [Opening 8, the scene of Louis's family having a chicken dinner].

Her requests for repeated words like "fish" and "colors" revealed that these were important—or threatening—scenes for her. She wanted the words "argued" and "bubble gum" said loudly, perhaps to drown out the anger of the fish and human families. By juxtaposing something negative (the arguing) with something positive (the bubble gum), she could balance or soften the negative. Brooke's marshaling of the story for her own satisfaction in meaning-making did not end at this point, either. Several weeks later, her most extensive retellings occurred and her *aesthetic* literacy continued to deepen.

In her own home, when my husband and I visited her, she again showed strong preference for *Louis the Fish* above all the other books that I had brought along or that were on her own bookshelves. As she read to me, she continued the game she had created, in her sixth response. But now she interjected the game as a background chorus into the storymaking, perhaps also as a tension release for the more serious issues she was continuing to confront in the story: the arguing of the family members, the death of Louis's parents, and the brutality of the meat monsters. And here, for the first time, she included the nightmare scene as part of the game play.

She had moved from repressing mention of the scene to retelling it, and then finally to toying with it in her wordplay. And in all this time, she had heard the words of the story only once.

Later that same day, still in her home setting, she returned once more to the book, but now her storying took a different turn. In her seventh response, with my husband as the adult partner this time, the game-playing continued. And the result was a branching-away from text entirely. She developed the kitchen scene now as a power struggle, with a very different Louis asserting himself against parental influence, shouting and being "horrible," as she said, and turning the tables to become the oppressor himself: "Louis shouted out to his mom like an old lady and he was horrible. Then he [Louis's father] said, 'Louis, don't shout at your mother or you get a spank!' 'I won't! I'm big enough to spank *you* on the head.'"

Then, at the nightmare scene, she grafted a new story about Louis onto the book-story she had been reading: "Louis was thirsty and saw monsters, bubble gum monsters, hairy, hairy monsters. Louis was a magician . . ." Thus she moved from game-playing and patterned chanting about the meat bullies to literary plotting of her own. Rewriting the story, she could—once again as resistant reader—destroy the book monsters that had been troubling Louis, and perhaps herself. Louis, as magician, conjured hairy bubblegum monsters to fight the meat monsters, after which he turned himself into a fish that could take on the shark.

She broke off her hairy monster story at this point to tell an entirely new story about an old lady who carried a gold stick or paddle or pole on her raft, which she sailed into the shark's teeth, killing the shark: "Open your mouth. Then you're dead! [Spoken very loudly] And that's the end of the story!" [She laughed.] Just as she had previously placed Louis in a more powerful position by enabling him to shout and become a magician, she now created a powerful adult (the old lady) who, unlike Louis, was not transformed into another form. Still, through her own resourcefulness, the old lady—similar to Louis—overcame what threatened her. At school, Brooke had heard Arlene Mosel's story *The Funny Little Woman* (1972), illustrated by Blair Lent, and her old lady character might have been influenced by it.

The game-playing went on, as in the previous readings, with Brooke, the powerful story master now, directing her adult reading partner (my husband) to repeat phrases like "Hurry up the shark!" Her joy in creating and performing was clear. Playing the old lady, she paused for long periods of time to dance around the imaginary pole and to gesture with it. Movement became language at this point. Motion became the story, just as metaphor, rather than plot, formed her narrative structure. She was conquering something as surely as the lady in the story was. The stick, the paddle, and the raft each signified both a way into and through the adventure and a weapon to combat the dangerous forces that were crossing her path.

Literacy researcher Carol Fox (1988) speaks of children's created stories as "metaphorical mirrors" that reflect "several aspects of their inner experiences simultaneously" (p. 62). Such a theory of metaphor as a primary mental process, fused with time-honored notions of narrative as a primary act of knowing (Hardy, 1977), may also cause us to see metaphorical play and storying as a powerful way for children to learn about themselves and the world.

Constructing and reconstructing a telling of *Louis the Fish* and finally grafting her own story onto the book-story base enabled Brooke to mirror her own feelings to herself, but at a safe distance—or through the lens of metaphor—to discharge threatening feelings. Taking control of her own learning from the beginning—reading pictures of the story—she uncovered the metaphorical pattern of the book embedded in the title. Then she was able to build an entire story edifice during her first three examinations of pictures. Each of her readings produced a design, a web of connections—or interconnections—because each of her story designs was superimposed on the preceding one. Placed together one on top the other, the design became a many-layered thing, not unlike the book itself.

That Brooke felt free to play with language, to assume a leadership role by commanding others to repeat lines of her wordplay, to break away from the author's story to extend—and reinterpret—scenes, and finally to create her own story, reveals literary competency. "When we notice that a child has started to play with some newly acquired component of understanding," says Russian children's author Kornei Chukovsky (1971), "we may definitely conclude that he has become full master of this item of understanding; only those ideas can become toys for him whose proper relation to reality is firmly known to him" (p. 103).

## REFLECTIONS

With pictures providing the scaffolding, Brooke's reading proceeded through four stages. First there was *preliminary meaning-making*: her three earliest readings. Next came *deeper exploration of story*: her fourth reading, when a rapid burst of narrative learning—and interwoven literacies—occurred. After this came *toying with text*: her fifth and sixth readings, when a leap of creativity took her into deeper engagement with story—as co-creator of it. Finally there was *expansion of text*: her seventh reading, when she grafted two new stories onto the original story base and engaged further in imaginative play.

## Levels of Response

With time and opportunity to return to a book she found particularly pleasurable, Brooke was also moving through the four levels that literary theorist D. W. Harding (1977) described for children's responses to literature.
First comes "sound," when children respond to the rhythm and rhyme of
nursery songs. Brooke began her long visitation with this book by repeat-
ing the words of the title over and over again. Sound and sense came together for her at the very beginning in the words "Louis the Fish" and the
idea that Louis was, from the outset, a fish. Later Brooke created her own
patterned chant in response to the nightmare scene: Louis had "meat, meat,
meat, meat, sausage, meatballs—that these little sausages can't hurt their
heads cause they can't hurt so bad, bad, bad."

Next comes "event," the stage when children confirm the pattern of a
story or when they find it very satisfying to discover an expected pattern,
and when they improvise upon patterns when they feel secure enough with
a familiar set of events. The intertwined pictures of Louis as both man and
fish and sometimes as both (a fish wearing pajamas or a butcher's apron)
produced the dominant pattern of the story, which set in motion the events
and kept them going in Brooke's responses. Later, she developed so much
strength in her own response pattern that she was able to overturn it, toying with the author's metaphors to produce new ones of her own and to
invent a game in which she set different story patterns in motion.

Then comes "role," similar to what I have called the *becoming* game.
"In free play or classroom drama," Harding says, "children take up the roles
of characters in their stories, or perhaps continue the role playing that the
story involved them in: 'I'm Jack and this is the beanstalk and you be the
Giant'" (p. 381). Sometimes children will replay the story; sometimes reshape and improvise on it, perhaps relating the roles and events more
nearly to their own wishes" (p. 381). Brooke empathized easily with Louis,
as when she stepped into the story to address Louis's mother directly. Later,
in a role as a much more aggressive Louis, she commanded her adult story-
partners to repeat lines of her response and participate in her game-playing.
Still later, she storied a brave magician-Louis who could do battle with a
shark.

Ultimately, says Harding, comes "world," when children begin to talk
about a character's background or that character's relationships with other
characters. At this level, talk, art, drama, writing, and storymaking emerge
and develop, with children organizing elements of the story world and
relating elements of the author's story world to their own worlds. Brooke's
obvious pleasure when she played the old lady with the gold stick, over-
coming obstacles in her path, was the same pleasure she revealed when

she voiced her own strong feelings about Louis's need for independence and creativity. "*He* knows what to do," she had said in her fourth reading. "Each day he drawed some pictures of himself . . . Any colors he wanted it to be." Later she took action in her storying to show what she valued in her own life—freedom to express herself, read her own way, dance her own dance, story her own story.

In these four levels of response, Harding set forth what he thought children were capable of achieving as they grew in their familiarity with literature—or what educators might expect to see in children's responses. Thus his levels imply developmental stages. But Brooke's series of responses indicates that children can move through all four levels during one stage of their lives (for Brooke, this was a matter of weeks) and with one work of literature, if they:

- find the piece of literature particularly engaging;
- have time and opportunity to revisit it and become increasingly familiar with it;
- read at their own pace, in their own chosen way (a liberation stance);
- discover that the story is particularly meaningful to them at that particular moment.

Both the story Brooke heard at this point in her life—of Louis caught in the grip of oppressive conditions—and the story she created of the old lady coming to grips with a threatening situation had metaphorical similarities to the "story" she was living through in her own life. Her mother spoke of the emotional adjustment it had been for her to change to a more structured classroom than her kindergarten in England had been. "At school here she's learning words from her formal reading scheme, not from stories in real books. She's more intense now. She knows when she goes into the classroom she's got to work. But the enjoyment is gone. The teacher might point to her for an answer. There's a different stress level. I know in the beginning she found it difficult sitting still, even having her own desk. She used to say, 'I'm not allowed to walk around the classroom.'"

Dancing that day through her story might have been Brooke's way to react against a more constricted life at school—to mirror her own feelings to herself—as well as to create a way to break through the stress of it. The book and her consequent reading and rereading of pictures—like the old lady's stick, paddles, and raft—provided a way to forge ahead on her learning journey, just as becoming a fish enabled Louis to break through the constriction of his limited and "arranged" life as a butcher.

At this peak moment of literary engagement, Brooke moved easily into the story world in a transformed role. She faced the same constrictions in her new life at school that Louis did when his mother said he should go to work in the butcher shop and when he later took over the shop. Therefore the story was fostering her *personal/empathetic* literacy, just as her personal learning was fostering *literary* and *intertextual* literacies. *Sociocultural* literacy was a big part of the picture, too: The story was giving her own situation more meaning and her own situation was placing more meaning into the book—or enlarging the capacity of the book as meaning-maker. But other literacies were also at work.

Brooke's bonding with the book—her *aesthetic* literacy—had been building from the moment she picked up the book on the stairway, but it became more obvious at this point when her physical movements were at their most visible. Her entire body was engaged, so that voice, gesture, and motion produced a virtual explosion of creative power in her dance-story. In this case, storymaking fostered *generative*, *narrative*, and *critical* literacies, because child and story met and grew together under optimum conditions.

And if fostering optimum conditions for the child's meaning-making is what teaching is all about, we will see Brooke's *way* into literacy—or into literature and literacies—as important teaching of its own. Brooke was never dependent on me, the adult, for her learning. Reading pictures in her kindergarten had taught her to "fish." She already knew how to *read* when she came to visit me that weekend, even though she had not taken on *print* literacy skills yet. What implications does her liberation—and aesthetic—reading have for the print literacy process? And what implications does reading pictures have for teachers who are mandated to teach reading skills?

## What About Print Literacy?

Brooke's reading—even her rich, responsive *reading*—is all very well, some may say. But for all that, she is still making stories of her own about *Louis the Fish*, rather than reading the author's printed words. In other words, it's fine that she's *reading* before she can actually read, but what if this kind of reading proves so pleasurable—so self-absorbing—that she starts preferring it to the hard work of "getting" the words "right"? What, if anything, could adults do to help *print* literacy along, too, in cases like this one?

First of all, they could offer reading lessons from one of the child's own favorite books. But Brooke's behavior with *Louis the Fish* shows us something just a little different, if we consider Northrop Frye's words about readers: "Some want to devour the text; some want to surrender to it; some want to read it; some want to misread it; some want to extract its essence; some want to exclaim its existence . . ." (1984, pp. 990–991). Brooke wanted to devour *Louis the Fish*, but she did not, at this time, want to surrender to it. She extracted its essence, and what she found each time taught her more. She wanted to proclaim its existence; she wanted to build bridges connecting the images. Most of all, she wanted to build new structures in the empty spaces.

Would using this book to teach reading skills damage the pleasure she was finding as a responsive reader? Yes, it very well could; therefore, we should probably find other books to foster print literacy at this time, including the stories Brooke has created for herself. Brooke's stories told in response to *Louis the Fish* could be recorded and transcribed, typed, and bound to produce more permanent copies. Her story about the old lady and the gold stick might make another transcribed story for reading practice. Certainly not every children's book is a book for teaching reading skills. When we elicit and study children's responses, when we give children time and opportunity to revisit favorite books, we see that no one book fits every child at all times, and no one book will necessarily foster every possible literacy.

Richly coded books like *Louis the Fish* are good for eliciting many different literacies. Which brings us to the question: Is *print* literacy the only literacy we should be consider for the classroom reading program? Brooke's responses reveal that reading *well* means developing competency in multiple literacies—each one weaving into the others—and that richly interpretive books are crucial in the classroom, if rich interpretive *reading* is to emerge there. They also show us that responsive and resourceful reading might be the best prelude to print literacy. In other words, must print literacy always precede all other literacies? Could it instead, at times, follow or work in conjunction with them?

Eventually, as the next chapter tells, I took Louis into the classroom to share with emerging, developing, and independent readers who were all in the same workshop, responding together in a conversational format. With this group, I learned still another way into literacy and another criterion for what makes a children's book good. In this case, it was not merely the author's expertise that gave a book its distinction, nor was it simply the growth in *aesthetic* literacy of the liberated child reader. It was a group of children reading together in a social context.

*Chapter Five*

# *Louis* in the Classroom:
# The Transactional Literary Conversation

BROOKE'S RESPONSE to *Louis the Fish* helped me to see, in a developed *portrait*, every stage of her engagement with the book—and to see many ways that the book was *good* from a child-centered perspective. Just as she was extending the book—stretching it—to fit her own meaning-making strategies and her own child's world, the book was extending her field of literacies. And the home setting (mine and hers) was important for giving me this deeper look. Had I been observing Brooke in a classroom, I would not have seen nearly as much in terms of her *aesthetic* literacy.

On the other hand, the classroom has something the home setting does not always have—reader response in a rich social context, with many voices producing many ideas, feelings, and perspectives. What might other children have added to Brooke's vision of the book, I soon began asking myself. What might her interpretation have added to theirs? What might they have all created together, had they been helping one another to see?

Several months after I watched Brooke respond to *Louis the Fish*, I conducted a workshop with a group of seven children, ages five to seven. I wanted to study more closely the connection of literature and literacies in emergent readers. How could we facilitate a more liberated way of reading in the classroom, I wanted to know. And I was particularly interested to see how children reading together in a social context would respond to a complex and innovative picture book like *Louis the Fish*.

College students in my children's literature classes had been worried about the story. If children saw Louis, a boy, turned permanently into a fish, wouldn't they imagine the same thing happening to them? Wouldn't this book cause nightmares? Their fears were not entirely groundless. Any transformation fantasy presents a complicated, perhaps even threatening vision of life for children if the transformation remains permanent. At the same time, as Brooke's reading reveals, this particular fantasy presents a thought-provoking and exciting experience if children have time and opportunity to read it in liberated ways.

Playing a tape of Brooke's picture reading for my college students showed them a new way of reading—a child's way. Listening to her responses, they began to see how resourceful children are in negotiating their fears and in reshaping stories they may find threatening. As Brooke says of Louis, "*He* knows what to do." Of course some children might be overwhelmed by the emotional content of the book. But if many artistic, innovative books are available to children, if they are familiar with books that stretch their imaginations, if they have opportunities to choose their own reading materials, and if they always have freedom to stop reading at any point, we can share these mind-expanding works with fewer worries. Producing independent readers means inviting self-selection rather than censoring liberating books like *Louis the Fish*.

I suggested to the workshop students that we all bring to class favorite books to share; then we would explore what was most mysterious to us. Each day after story time, the children extended group talk about a book with drawing, storytelling, writing, planning a drama, or puzzling out a mystery in the book. *Louis the Fish*, I had learned from Brooke's reading, was heavily coded in authorial strategies and particularly rich in the enigmatic code.

For the shared reading time, I read the book aloud, pausing whenever the children had spontaneous comments or questions, and I participated as a partner, exploring the books with them. The word "with" is important here. If teaching in Vygotskian terms means helping learners enter and progress through a space of emerging development, I wanted to create for this experience what Bruner (1986) calls a "negotiable transaction" (p. 76) and what Rosenblatt (1994) calls a reader's "transaction" (the active process of meaning-making readers engage in as they "live through" a story). I would respond to the children's ideas and they would respond to my own puzzles and spontaneous remarks as well. Exploratory conversation was what I attempted as a liberating and natural way for readers to engage with the story. From a fragment of this workshop, Day Three, I began to see ways that what might be called a "transactional literary conversation" could foster *aesthetic* and *sociocultural* reading. At the same time, I discovered that such a conversation could help the teacher understand children's views of the world and strengthen the expression of their views.

## PRELIMINARY MEANING-MAKING

This day began with the early arrival of Sam, age five, who became interested in a copy of *Louis the Fish* he found lying on the table. (All children of the class were six years old, except Sam and Eric, both five, and Vikki, who was seven.) "A fish in pajamas in bed!" he quickly exclaimed as he opened the book. Then he began shaping his experience of the world to the words he heard and the picture he saw of a fish in pajamas: "Louis isn't really a fish; he's a robot. No man can turn into a fish unless he's a robot. Then he could push buttons and turn into a fish."

Louis's transformation seemed simple and natural to Sam at this point because of his own storying. The readerly aspect of the book fostered his *sociocultural* and *critical* literacies: He could see the book was a fantasy, an "impossible" situation, but he resisted it, finding a way that the story could be real, according to his own understanding of the world. And the writerly aspects of the book—the gaps and puzzles—fostered his *narrative* literacy. When I read the description of Louis as a "wonderful guy," Sam changed the phrase first to "a wonderful fish," then to "a wonderful robot, Louis the Fish!"

The other children began arriving at this point, and I invited them into the conversation, handing out several additional copies of the book. We spent some time discussing the cover.

"Anything look like a mystery here?" I asked.

Ellen, who had seen the book presented on the PBS children's television program *Reading Rainbow*, predicted that the sky would turn into fish. Bess talked about the opening pictures as not really being the story yet.

At the first page of text and the following wordless picture, Ellen told them a little about the time sequence: "He's telling the end. Then he'll tell the story of how he does turn into a fish. I can remember the part [when] he has this dream about other kinds of meat." Then the children began focusing on the kind of fish Louis turned into (a salmon) and on the kinds of fish *they* liked.

As the story began to unfold, we read about Louis as an unhappy child who always hated meat, how he loved his after-school job cleaning fish tanks, and how he would stare for hours at the fish. "What do you think this means?" I asked after reading the narrator's next words: "But a good thing doesn't last long."

Filling in a gap of text imaginatively, as Sam had done with his robot analogy, enabled them to walk around the book—with narrative purposes and competencies, just as Bess's deft use of dialogue produced a small story of her own within the author's story.

*Ellen:* He lost the job.
*Eric:* Maybe he found out the fish were meat.
*Bess:* Yeah, maybe he found out the fish were meat. He said, "I give
    up. I'm not doing this job anymore."
*Eric:* He found out that fish have meat on the inside.

*Bess:* And he didn't like to eat meat and he didn't like to get near meat.

*Ellen:* If he loves fish, why do you think he turned into a fish? I've heard this story, but I can't give the secret away. You have to think, why did he turn into a fish?

*Sam:* Now I get it! He has a dream that there's a lot of food going after him.

*Eric:* He sees a lot of fish going after him, so he sees a lot of fish, so he finds out. At the fish tank he was going fishing for fish to eat it. And then it was actually real.

*Bess:* And he ate so much of it, he turned into a fish!

*Ellen:* You're wrong. You're all wrong.

I read on at this point so that they could see that Louis's mother's feelings about the "lousy fish" were causing Louis to go to work in the butcher shop. At the scene of the fish-family customers in the butcher shop, they began creating stories and theories to explain mysteries in the pictures. A long debate occurred when Eric saw the fish as "crooks" (Eric "read" the picture of the mother-fish's fin as a gun). Suddenly Sam exclaimed, "I think I know now! That's a butcher shop, and fish are meat. So they're getting angry at him [Louis who is grown now and has taken over the butcher shop] and they're telling him, stop selling meat!" Immersion in the group reading event caused Sam to plunge deeply into the transformation fantasy genre that he had earlier resisted—or perhaps feared.

Sam's emergent learning revealed strength in deductive reasoning (meat is sold; fish are in the meat family because they have "meat" on the inside; thus the fish are saying, stop selling *us*) and strength in causal reasoning, both strengths being helpful for the ongoing conversation. His reasoning also caused Ellen to make a distinction between a butcher shop and a fish market, which led to a larger discussion in which I asked questions I was really wondering about and the children responded with their own meaning-making about the story:

*Ellen:* They do not sell fish in that kind of store. Fishermen cut off their heads, degut the guts and put it in [fish] stores to be sold.

*Adult:* Do you mean fish don't like being sold like meat?

*Eric:* They're selling meat and they're made out of meat inside.

*Ellen:* Louis is probably a vegetarian and the only kind of meat he eats is fish.

*Adult:* Do vegetarians consider fish meat?

*Ellen:* I can ask my aunt 'cause she's a vegetarian.

*Adult:* Sam's saying the fish are angry.

*Joey:* The mother looks angry but the father doesn't.

*Bess:* This one's angry, this one's angry [pointing], but this one isn't. 'Cause you could tell by their faces. 'Cause this one's fighting and this one's grinning and this one's walking away.

*Adult:* If these fish are angry at Louis, why are they angry?

*Eric:* 'Cause they're made out of meat and they don't want them to see the meat [in them].

*Bess:* Fish that you eat is not meat anyway.

*Eric:* Muscles are in fish and we have muscles.

*Bess:* But they're not meat.

*Eric:* We eat the muscles in the fish; the muscles are in the fish.

At the scene of the meat monsters attacking Louis, the meat/fish distinction continued to elicit talk:

*Ellen:* Meat is not alive when it's chopped up. Meat is alive when it's in the animal's body. Meat inside of us is alive but when we're dead, it's—

*Bess:* It's dead. It dies the same time we die. They do not take the meat out of the person when they die.

*Adult:* Is there anything mysterious in the picture? Anything we can't figure out?

*Joey:* Why are the meats mad at him?

*Eric:* They're selling them.

*Joey:* And for chopping them up.

*Ellen:* No! They're angry at him because he doesn't like them.

*Adult:* That's three reasons.

*Eric:* Yeah, that's the point, the meat's angry at them because they're selling meat. And they don't want him to sell meat anymore.

*Joey:* Because they're selling them. They're mad.

Then Ellen added a new twist to the theory. "The picture on the refrigerator. I saw something that might have made them really upset [the meats]. He drew on the meats! He drew a little fish on this piece of meat."

The children were focusing on the meat now—how the meat felt (different or rejected)—the same focus they had on the fish and the feelings of rejection the fish might have had. It was a powerful issue for them, at least on this first reading, and one for which they appeared to have greater empathy than they had for Louis's need to assert himself against his parents' demands. The scenes of angry meats and of the angry fish-mother, which mirrored the earlier picture of the angry human mother, produced a strong reaction from them. But as we went on, another focus was emerging in the scene of Louis as a fish riding a bus to work, and in this transition state of fish-turning-human, it was wearing Louis's straw hat and butcher's apron.

## DEEPER EXPLORATION OF STORY

"Anything interesting or surprising here?" I asked as I read about Louis waking up one morning as a fish. "This is all going to be make-believe," said Ellen. "No," countered Eric. Suddenly we were into another mystery now—the dream/reality issue of the book or *how* Louis became a fish. Was Louis dreaming the meat monster scene, the bus scene, and the scene of himself sleeping in bed as a fish?

> *Ellen:* All of it is a dream.
> *Adult:* It says that morning Louis woke up feeling cold. He was a fish now, and Al found him on the bus. Is it still a dream?
> *Eric:* Maybe it's a dream that he woke up.
> *Bess:* He was awake when they were hurting him. That would be stupid if he was supposed to wake up when he was awake. It couldn't be a dream anymore.
> *Adult:* You think he woke up.
> *Bess:* So it can't be a dream anymore. He can't have a dream that he woke up and got on the bus and was a fish.
> *Ellen:* He could have.
> *Bess:* It might have been in his dream. He might have been sleeping and had a dream like that.
> *Vikki:* How in a dream? How could you wake up?

At this point, Bess said that she had a dream like that once: "So he could have a dream like that too." And the ensuing dialogue took them into a new notion that Louis might not have been awake or asleep, but daydreaming.

> *Vikki:* If you're awake in your dream, how can you wake up twice? You're already awake and you're supposed to be waking up in a dream?
> *Eric:* A daydream! He could have had a daydream.
> *Joey:* A daydream.
> *Adult:* Where would he be if he had this daydream? In which picture do you see this?
> *Ellen:* When he starts seeing fish.

When I read the next page (the scene of Louis in the pet store), the children decided that the pet store-fish tank scene was reality rather than Louis's daydream. But was the bus scene also reality, they began wondering:

*Adult:* Of course it's funny to think of a fish being on a bus. I don't know. What do you think?
*Eric:* It's a daydream.
*Bess:* No, it's not.
*Vikki:* Maybe it could have happened if he took a long shower before or if it was raining outside.
*Bess:* For twenty hours? How could you breathe that long under water? How could he breathe if he took a shower all day long?
*Vikki:* He was a fish and then he got under the shower and then he went to the bus?
*Joey:* This isn't true. It isn't a dream either.
*Adult:* The people on the bus don't think it's strange, do they?
*Sam:* I think he was taking a shower and then he turned into a fish and then he got on the bus.
*Vikki:* If he woke up as a fish, how could he turn into a fish in the shower if he was already a fish?
*Joey:* Yeah.
*Bess:* This is what it says at the end [turning forward in the copy she is holding]: "After a hard life, Louis became a happy fish."
*Adult:* Yes.
*Vikki:* If he woke up a fish, how—
*Bess:* How could he get in the shower?
*Vikki:* Could he turn into a fish if he was already a fish?

It seemed clear that the time-shift or flashback aspect of the story was a difficult concept for the children. They were especially puzzled about *when* Louis became a fish. Ellen had a strong sense of narrative time scheme: "The end," she said "is when he starts out being a regular person. But they tell the story of what happened to him and how it happened, and it ends in the beginning and you saw him a fish but he was really a person. He was really a fish sleeping in bed then, but he was there trying to tell a story."

Louis *is* there in the pictures telling his story. The narrator's voice, however, is distanced from Louis, as Ellen indicated by her use of the word "they." It was clear to her from the beginning that Louis was now a fish. Vikki also appeared to have a grasp of the "when": "He turned into a fish while he was asleep, and this is the picture of him." She turned to the first wordless picture opening of the salmon sleeping in Louis's pajamas.

In my own copy, I turned back to the meat monster scene. "But is he a boy or a man here?" I asked. (Louis as a man was doing the dreaming, but in the dream he saw himself as a boy. And the man dreaming and the boy-in-the-dream were wearing the same striped pajamas.) "Why don't we go into separate corners like yesterday and sort this book out, too?" Vikki suggested.

It was time for snack break, and when the class resumed the children had options as usual: to draw, create stories, or work more with book-puzzles. Joey and Ellen returned to the stories they were writing the day before. Sam and Eric drew. Bess read a book Eric had brought. Vikki and Alice decided to work more with *Louis the Fish*. They used the chalkboard for drawing and writing as they proceeded. And as they read, wrote, thought, and talked, the tape recorder picked up their storymaking conversation.

## POST-STORY EXPLORATIONS

Vikki began talking to Alice through a retelling of the book. She was glancing at words and pictures as she made her own story-of-the-story: "Now here he is a very nice man in the butcher shop. Louis is seven years old and he works in a doctor's office with the fish . . . [she continued to summarize the plot, opening by opening]. It all works out . . . all it really is, he liked fish so much that he turns into one and he forgets he was a human being and then it's the end of the story."

By the time I visited their corner, Vikki had discovered a puzzle: "I think this is really weird. I don't know why they put this picture at the front [the fish sleeping in Louis's striped pajamas]. It doesn't make any sense if you include that picture in the story. It should be in the back."

"If it went in a time sequence, it would make sense, wouldn't it?" I said. "Yeah," she answered, "but it doesn't make sense placed at the very, very front." As I left to visit another group, Vikki and Alice began trying to make sense of the time shift, because as Vikki said, "If someone doesn't know how to read and they just want to look at the pictures, it doesn't make one bit of sense."

The book had made sense to Brooke, perhaps because she sorted it out, based on the pictures, before she heard the words—or with only the title as her clue to the fantasy-transformation. Thus she relied on the man/fish metaphor to guide her through the book, and she relied on (or accepted) the idea of *fantasy* to make sense of the story.

"He should be a baby, a child, a man, then a fish," said Alice. "For some reason," Vikki continued, "the fish is first, then the man second, then the child. But that is so stupid." Vikki's phrase "for some reason" was important; it indicated she had entered the realm of the author's crafting choices. Her implied questions were, When do authors rearrange the sequence of a story—or why? What effect are they trying to have on readers when they reorder things? What are they trying to get readers to think about or discover? But I didn't have to ask any of these questions; Vikki was well on her way the next time I dropped by.

"I'm going to write to the publisher about where it should start," declared Vikki. "You hold the pictures up for me," she told Alice, taking the lead in this demystifying process again. "And I'll talk. Louis is a seven-year-old boy and then he gets a job at a doctor's office which he really likes and he helps with the fish and then the mother and father said, 'No, you're not allowed to work in the doctor's office. You must work at the butcher shop.' And I don't think that's fair."

In this second "telling," Vikki condensed a great deal; she began the story with the first scene of the flashback and she subordinated ideas. She focused on why Louis hated meat and liked fish, rather than on the issues the children had focused on during the group discussion. And she produced an evaluative comment at the point of Louis's parents' interference. Alice picked up on this focus, adding two comments of her own for this scene: "The mother's not very nice," and "That is not nice" (the father telling the boy he must leave his job cleaning fish tanks).

"And then he has to take over by drawing," Vikki continued, again focusing on an idea not discussed by the larger group. At this point Vikki and Alice started to draw on the board to clarify their thinking, and the tape picked up their frustration. Three times each child affirmed that this story, or the time shift, was "impossible." "I'm going to write to this person!" they each continued to threaten. Suddenly they were filling up the board with numbers and diagrams (another way of toying with text) that helped them ultimately solve the time problem. And I gained several insights into children's conversational ways of transacting literature.

First, in the large-group discussion, when the children were deciding whether they would return to the book for a second look, the two children who chose to do so were the two who spoke least in the larger group. Vikki became verbally involved late in the session; Alice never entered in at all. Yet both were deeply involved in this small-group partnership as active, critical readers, puzzling out the text and shaping and reshaping their evolving ideas.

Second, the comments about Louis's oppression from parental interference and expectations—the frightening aspects of the mother's anger—were mere suggestions in the large-group discussion, whereas Alice and Vicki emphasized them in their post-story discussion. At the same time, the life-and-death factor of the meat remained a point of interest in both large and small group. In other words, children may be registering ideas on a much deeper level than we suspect when they are listening to and conversing about stories in a social context. Thus time and opportunity for further exploration are crucial to their evolving responses.

Third, the retelling that these two children chose to do was important for showing how resourceful children can be in sorting out problems when they have opportunity to work independently. Consider that these two children used five important problem-solving techniques: cooperative thinking, collaboration, rereading of words and pictures to support propositions, critical thinking (questioning of the book in terms of their own experiential realities), and reflective thinking about their own sociocultural world in relation to the text.

These strategies included, from the beginning, each child retelling the story and then talking about the mysteries or puzzles that either instigated the retelling or emerged as it proceeded. In this case, a purpose emerged out of the enigma coding of the book, in terms of *critical* literacy, and this purpose kept the interpretive process evolving.

Vikki felt that she needed to write to the publisher to recommend a better place to start the story. She had a strong sense that books are *authored* and that authors use strategies to draw in readers—and to keep them reading. She searched out the names of the author and illustrator on the cover and title pages: "We're going to contact Arthur [Yorinks] and Richard [Egielski]," she said (to show these authors a better way to organize the book). In terms of how Vikki and Alice saw the meeting of life and literary realities–or their assumptions of how the world, or the world of literature, works—the authors had not fulfilled their obligations to readers.

Following this first phase of their post-story exploration, Vikki and Alice continued to deliberate about Louis's age at various points in the story, to help determine the time sequence and to sort out the time shifts. What finally emerged was a cooperative venture, a joint "authorship" of their own, a *symphony* of conversation that resulted in Vikki beginning to sort out the problem of the time shifts for herself and an important new idea from Alice:

> *Vikki:* It goes something like this: He [Louis] was a child, a man turned into a fish. Who was 19, 20, and then that would be his man age, and then his fish age would be 23, 24, 25.
> *Alice:* But when he was actually getting chased by the meat, he would be 24.
> *Vikki:* No, because he wasn't a fish yet. He's be 23.
> *Alice:* And actually the boy, it looks like he's a—
> *Vikki:* Child, man—

> *Alice:* Maybe on this page, when he's a man, he could first be a fish
> and then he could just show that and tell you what it's about
> and then the story begins.
>
> *Vikki:* Wait, and then he's a man, no, and he'd turn into a child after
> he's a man. That doesn't make sense. So he must just be kind of
> telling about the story when he's a fish at first *and* a man at first
> and then the story actually starts as a child.
>
> *Alice:* Maybe he was dreaming that he was a man, or that he
> thought he was a child who hated the meat. He always hated
> meat.
>
> *Vikki:* Wait—he always *has* hated meat. [She wrote the word "fish"
> on the board.]

Working out the story as co-authors in this "expansion of text" enabled
Vikki and Alice, as it did Brooke, to see how the author might have been
thinking. Walking around the story, having stepped into the author's shoes,
made them better readers—and "writers"—of this writerly book. Notice
Alice's suggestion for the author: "He could just show that and tell you
what it's about and then the story begins," and the way her words evoked
Vikki's next comment: "So he must just be kind of telling about the story
. . . and then the story actually starts as a child."

Alice's idea that maybe Louis was dreaming that he was a man produced a new possibility for puzzling out the book. "Maybe he was dreaming that he as a man or that he thought he was a child who hated the
meat." Alice's idea confirmed something in Vikki's own thinking, and as
she wrote the word "fish" on the board, she revealed how the pendulum
of meat and fish was swinging easily back and forth in this story, producing endless possibilities for interpretive discovery. And they might
have gone on conquering the impossible that day, but the clock ran out
on their talk. Suddenly it was time to share with the others their chalkboard diagrams—or their "research"—which revealed them responding
to this multidimensional, richly coded picture book with a rich reposi-
tory of literacies.

## REFLECTIONS

In 1989, Marie Clay spoke of the need for rejuvenating instruction for the
first two years of schooling with "the newest discoveries about emergent
literacy." Programs, she stated, needed "to provide rich, whole, complex
experiences with stories and the activities they generate—drama and art,
retelling and rereading, and beginners' inventions of writing . . . [and] to

recognize that there are many different routes to being a reader and writer, and to celebrate each new discovery that children make."

The notion of many different routes to literacy instruction is an inviting one, because we must also ask at the outset, which literacy?

If what counts for us is how we can use an author's story to develop decoding skills (*print* literacy), we will place *Louis the Fish* outside the grasp of emergent readers. We will see a reader's text as a foreign language message to be translated, word for word. And we will bring forth a book like this only when children have passed through preliminary texts having fewer words, fewer unfamiliar words, and fewer distractions like time shifts, flashbacks, and heavily coded pictures. For if we try instead to remove any of these "distractions" from *Louis the Fish*, it is clear from children's responses that the entire structure for meaning-making collapses.

But there are other ways of fostering reading. What counts for us might instead be how literature contributes to or produces learning generally. If so, we will expect to see ideas about story meanings forming in readers' minds from the outset, as they test their assumptions about characters, make predictions about plot, form hypotheses about story puzzles, see causal relationships about conflicts, make contrasts about cast members, and draw conclusions about their actions. We will see the book as an edifice that readers construct from the author's words and pictures, as when these seven children built theories about mysteries they were discovering in *Louis the Fish*.

With young children conversing in large or small groups like this one, or in independent readings such as Brooke undertook, such *generative* literacy would work to prepare a strong foundation for *print* literacy. Brooke was behaving as a real reader before she could actually read; she was an engaged member of the literacy community, already an avid reader. And as these children made meaning of text and pictures together, they created a basis of interest in—or a need for—deciphering words.

Bess argued her way, theorized her way through the story before she read aloud the previous page to establish that Louis did not turn into a fish in the shower. And Vikki and Alice constantly referred back to the book—reading, rereading, debating—using their decoding competencies to support an already highly charged *critical* stance.

On the other hand, what counts for us may be the way that literature produces learning about itself or about *texts*, as when readers see patterns in words and pictures and ideas emerging from these patterns. Literature then seems to be a tapestry readers construct—and deconstruct—thread by thread. *Literary* literacy deepens as readers rework, unfold, or reconstruct stories for consensus-building and multiple perspectives, not just, as with edifice reading, to make sense of story, but to make *greater* sense of it.

What is important for anyone focusing on this way of reading is how—or why—things sound, look, read, or "mean" in stories. Alice and Vikki struggled to remake the structural design of *Louis the Fish* to learn how they thought it should work. And each time Brooke read this story, she constructed what might be described as a "patterned representation of the patterned events that are the story which the narrative realizes," in the words of literacy educator Henrietta Dombey (1982, p. 41).

What counts for us may—conversely—be the way literature helps us to see better who *we* are. It gives us characters that elicit our empathy and stretch us beyond who we are to assume other imaginative roles. At the same time, story characters reflect our deepest wishes, hopes, fears, and ideas. If this way of seeing is our preferred way, we will see literature as showing us more than what we already know, on any conscious level, about what we feel and think and aspire to be. We will read literature to gaze deeply into a mirror in order to see what it has to reveal about ourselves.

With this literacy, the moment when we encounter the work of literature is often as important as the actual work of literature we encounter. At particular times in our lives, we may need stories in ways to which at other times we find ourselves less personally open or receptive. Or at particular times in our lives, we may find we have insights into stories that we would never have otherwise. Our experiences at those moments help us to clarify actions, notice details, detect unexamined assumptions, uncover mysteries, and discover meanings.

Brooke had seen a great deal in *Louis the Fish*—she bonded to it easily and deeply—perhaps because of constrictions in her own life at the moment when she read the book. Time and opportunity for her seven readings produced a clear portrait of her personal learning, one we are not as likely to see—or to see as often—in the classroom, where so many voices are competing for our attention. Nevertheless, in school settings we can still do everything possible to help *personal/empathetic* literacy emerge and evolve. We can invite children to respond to their favorite books as many times as they wish. We can facilitate response conversations in which children feel comfortable making their own personal feelings clear and making discriminations among their feelings, as these children were doing. We can also converse individually with children often about their responses.

Because group settings are so useful for producing social pictures of response, we may find that what counts for us is *sociocultural* literacy, or the way literature relates to us as human beings engaged in a variety of social and cultural situations. Then we will view texts as openings through which readers can pass freely into the *world* beneath or beyond the *words* of text (Freire, 1973), and we will want to see readers uncovering issues and unexamined assumptions and exploring areas of personal and social concern.

Personal experiences have such a strong role to play in social learning, it is probably impossible—or counterproductive—to separate personal and social learning. The children of this group were expressing personal notions of how it feels to be different or to be rejected or oppressed, to have an angry parent—or to be an angry meat or fish. And when they uncovered humanistic concerns for conscious examination, when they explored personal, ethical choices, we saw literature fostering *sociocultural* and *critical* literacies, or the ability to appreciate and value individual expression, multiple viewpoints, divergent or resistant thinking, and to understand concepts about what is "real" or rational at different times, in different places. They were producing a meaningful text filled with gaps, or questions with no easy answers: What is a dream? What is a daydream? What is real? What is fair or right? What does it mean to be "sold" or "chopped up"? How do you change things if they seem wrong?

If what counts for us is that we tell stories about the story as we read—or after—in order to try on new roles and take on new identities, we will expect to see literature fostering, in addition, *narrative* literacy, or greater knowledge about how and why we tell stories. Such reading places a frame around the story-picture as a way of completing it.

*Narrative* literacy engenders a personal sense of selfhood: we put ourselves "together" as we put together the story. We become more ourselves as we "write" ourselves into, and around, a story-character. We become those we envision; our texts become objects to be transformed. Sam saw Louis as a robot; Eric envisioned a crook from the image of a fish fin; Bess remembered a dream she once had and decided that Louis had a similar one; Brooke turned Louis into a magician and herself into a lady with a gold stick. *Louis the Fish,* in the process, became something entirely new.

Finally, if what counts for us—*really* counts—is that we lose ourselves in stories, becoming wholly and completely absorbed in them, as Brooke and Vikki and Alice did, then we are seeing from another perspective, the same one we take with certain paintings as visitors to exhibits and museums. Before them we may stand for long periods of time, gazing each time more deeply into the scene or face and discovering more each time we stop to look. We might step back from the painting to see more, move sideways to gain a different view, or step closer to the picture to focus in on some small detail. No matter where we stand, we are drawn not only to the artist's skill, or genius, in creating a world that illuminates our own but to the emotional content of the work. The picture is one that fixes us, causing us to feel deeply and ponder what we see.

From this perspective, literature is fostering *aesthetic* literacy, or the ability to become deeply absorbed in the author's images and ideas. We might in addition reflect on ourselves in this absorbed state; we might step back and notice our engagement to the extent that we act on it, revisiting the work or discovering the vantage point that gives us most pleasure.

It is not difficult to see that—depending on our own personal, social, and cultural constructs, our own experiences with life and literature, and our own interests and talents—we might emphasize one of these literacies above the others. We might even find ourselves so committed to, or involved with, one of them that we choose to foster that literacy more often with children. We may find ourselves wanting to use literature to help children make meaning generally (*generative* literacy); make discriminations about their own feelings (*personal/empathetic* literacy); make connections between life and literature (*sociocultural* literacy); become lost in a book (*aesthetic* literacy); walk around the story as insiders, telling their own stories about the story (*narrative* literacy); resist the text for any number of reasons (*critical* literacy); or uncover narrative patterns and details for greater meaning-making (*literary* literacy). Or we might be mandated to foster one literacy to the exclusion of all others; thus we would be teaching reading skills and *print* literacy–and nothing else.

Our absorption in, our talent for, or our enthusiasm for fostering one particular literacy is fine, as far as it goes. But it limits the picture of what readers actually do when they read avidly, alone or with others. If we elicit and study children's responses, we discover that *each of these literacies is often deeply interwoven with the others*, and that to isolate one is to lose something important from all the others. If we participate as partners, exploring literature with children, we also discover that what I have called a "transactional literary conversation" enables each of these literacies, in varying degrees, to emerge, intersect, and coexist—and evolve—for a variety of reasons.

Such a conversation is *constantly evolving*, as opposed to structured. Dialogic talk helps to produce cognitive and affective growth in all participants when children make and share new meanings or many possible readings of a story.

It is *open-ended* and *invitational*, as opposed to task-controlled or -directed. The destination of the story-journey depends on the individual route children take during the particular event. Each conversation, like any conversation anywhere, has a life of its own; it is individually crafted rather than assembly-line-produced, packaged, and marketed. Everything remains open as a possibility. The participants are not aware of how things will emerge and do not close down possibilities with a preformed agenda.

One focus may displace another; one book might even displace another as interests change or fade.

A transactional literacy conversation is *descriptive* rather than prescriptive. All participants pay close attention to words and pictures of books, telling about what they see, noting patterns, clarifying words, assumptions, viewpoints, and perspectives. They turn to other texts and prior experiences for help in meaning-making, testing new ideas, and making interpretive choices.

It is *co-authored*—an adult and child partnership—rather than adult-directed. Everything begins and builds from children's responses to words and pictures, with the cover of the book often serving as initiatory stimulus. No adult decides the focus; children and adult do so together as the conversation proceeds. All participants strive to understand what they think and feel; all participants work to clarifiy one another's meaning-making, based on their own ways of seeing. Children have ownership of their own meaning-making process.

It is *democratic* and *egalitarian*. Because children's literature encompasses a child audience, children's authors assume from the outset that children are competent readers, or the ones most knowledgeable about their own child worlds. Adults are neither the only competent individuals nor the most competent readers of these works. Therefore, adults work with children as valued partners in thought.

It is *celebratory*. Responses are seen as opportunities for extending everyone's ideas. Surprise is what the readers value; understanding—or solving the mystery—is what they are after. They are not competing for individual achievement, honors, or "marks."

It is *investigative* rather than evaluative in nature. The adult wishes to expand children's contributions, to draw out their statements for clarification and elaboration, in order to extend their learning and broaden the scope of the discussion, rather than test whether children made some supposedly "correct" meaning. "What if?" "Why?" "What then?" are questions that arise often—and they arise often from the children themselves.

It is *liberating*. Children process a text in their own way, at their own pace, as a primary part of the reading act itself. With text and pictures as the scaffolding for ideas they generate freely, children create their own metaphorical "lens" for the story, especially if the book is multidimensional in nature. They are both recipients and co-creators of the author's story. Voice, gesture, narrative fluency, and meaning-making work together to foster multiple literacies.

Finally, it is *transformative*. Children begin by searching for ideas, bringing to the surface unconscious feelings that reveal values, attitudes, and beliefs, and they end by defining themselves. Response to literature in a social setting becomes ultimately personal and social *action*.

A transactional literary conversation helps adults learn more about child worlds and helps children extend their field of literacies. Therefore it keeps good company with innovative, multidimensional children's books, especially richly-textured fantasies like this one, and it deserves more of our attention when we are searching for new routes into literacy.

This way of sharing books with children was one I stumbled into, in my earliest response work, when I stopped interviewing my own two children about *Alexander and the Wind-Up Mouse* and began conversing with them. It seeped more completely into my thinking as I continued to share books with children in home, neighborhood, and classroom settings. It became my favorite way to share literature with children and elicit responsive reading, and it remains the best way I know to help children grow into literacy and to help ourselves learn more about children and books.

*PART III*

# CHILDREN AS
# RESEARCH PARTNERS

AS WE SHARE BOOKS with children and see bursts of interwoven literacies emerging, as we see children negotiating complexities of narrative coding and puzzling through personal ethical choices, we may wonder, how will we keep this process going? After a successful event, the question arises, what made it successful? Was it something about that particular book (a tough act to follow), something about that child or group of children (and there's no way to clone that special chemistry), something about a particular setting (and no way to re-create that moment)? What can we do to keep children returning to books so that they grow in responsive reading?

One of the best ways is to invite children into the research process as full partners, aware that they are instrumental to our knowing, that they have a great deal to teach us about *their* books and their ways of reading them and of viewing the world. They are the experts, we can let them know, and we need to know what they think. We can invite them into the book selection process; we can pursue the research questions *they* want to know about. It just takes listening carefully to their words—and their worlds—and asking them to tell us more.

When children and adults are working together to explore what matters to them both, the cycle of response spirals up into new events, new readings, new ways of seeing. We are encouraging children to read; they are seeing how valuable it is to do so.

*Chapter Six*

# Fighting the Dragon—and Winning:
## *The Hobbit*

AT THE SAME TIME that I was working in classrooms, eliciting children's responses, I continued to share books with my own children. When Vinny's third-grade teacher read aloud books by Beverly Cleary, we soon began enjoying more of Cleary's books at home. Especially popular with both children were Cleary's mouse fantasies: *The Mouse and the Motorcycle* (1965), *Runaway Ralph* (1970), and *Ralph S. Mouse* (1982). That year we also read Roald Dahl's *James and the Giant Peach* (1961), and I noticed on a more conscious level, for the first time, the strong pleasure these children took in fantasy—and how the book generated talk, laughter, and play.

Mark's third-grade year was also important for literary influences; when his teacher read aloud E. B. White's *Charlotte's Web* (1952), Roald Dahl's *Charlie and the Chocolate Factory* (1964), and Beatrix Potter's stories, he soon began choosing other books by these authors. White's *Stuart Little* (1945) and Potter's *The Tale of Benjamin Bunny* (1904), filled, like *James and the Giant Peach*, with enticing small, resourceful creatures, soon became his favorites.

The summer before Mark's third-grade year, when he was seven and Vinny was nine, I started a neighborhood workshop with children responding to Sendak's *Outside Over There* (1981) and other folk fantasies, a format I extended the next year into a summer program with the public schools called the Gnome Workshop: I read stories aloud and the children responded with talk, storytelling, story-writing, plays, and treasure hunts. To enlist the children as co-researchers, I always asked questions like, What would you like to do (write, draw, role-play) after hearing this story, and What story would you like to tell or write after hearing this one? The second summer of the Gnome Workshop, Mark, Vinny, and some of their workshop friends continued the sessions during the school year, with books from C. S. Lewis's Narnia series (1950–52), which stimulated a great deal of fantasy storymaking and play.

When Vinny was twelve and Mark was just turning ten, we spent part of the summer in Michigan, where their father was attending an institute. With friends and sports events on hold, both children were content to continue the Gnome Workshop routine—reading and storymaking around the kitchen table of the little apartment we had rented in the morning and exploring bookstores, libraries, museums, swimming pool, or arboretum in the afternoon.

I took along books like Natalie Babbitt's *The Eyes of the Amaryllis* (1977), a supernatural fantasy their good friend Jason had recommended, and Mollie Hunter's *A Stranger Came Ashore* (1975), a folk fantasy I thought they might like because of the mysterious selkie character. Each book had instant appeal, and soon we were reading Hunter's *The Kelpie's Pearls* (1964), and Mark was creating a kelpie story of his own.

Alongside Babbitt's and Hunter's books, we continued to read Tolkien's *The Hobbit* (1965). In fact, it seems that we had been reading this book ever since they discovered a cartoon storybook based on this novel (or an animated film version of it) a few years earlier. It had become a staple of the Gnome Workshop, with Vinny often incorporating aspects of it in his stories. *The Hobbit* was in fact his all-time favorite book, with Mark's enthusiasm never far behind; and their responses caused me to wonder what made this book so compelling. Was it something about the idea of hobbits, the adventure itself, the way the emotional content of the story tapped into child worlds, the fact that it was fantasy, or the kind of fantasy it was?

I was also interested in seeing more about the narrative strategies authors used for particular kinds of fantasies. Would one particular way of narrative "coding" (Barthes, 1985) be more important than another in a particular kind of fantasy? And would a particular code—actions, semic, enigmatic, cultural, symbolic—foster a particular literacy, or stronger interplay of literacies, and therefore richer responses? Perhaps children reading—or rereading—a favorite book could tell me more.

## QUEST FANTASY AND NARRATIVE CODING

*The Hobbit* is a quest fantasy, a story in which a hero, on an adventure to find some prize or attain some worthy goal, must find a way to rule—or navigate through—a "high" or mythic kingdom or place that the author has invented as a secondary world. In this case, Tolkien's kingdom of Middle Earth is filled with mysterious legendary creatures—dragons, dwarfs, elves, and goblins—engaged in skirmishes, epic battles, and small intrigues; thus the book, like Hunter's stories, is also a folk fantasy. Actu-

ally it is a literary folk fantasy: Tolkien's leading character, a hobbit (a creature resembling both dwarfs and humans), is entirely his own invention.
Thus the author must find ways of inviting readers into this newly minted
cultural world.

For Tolkien (1965 [in References]), a secondary world is a place that
the reader must see as lifelike and familiar but changed: a transformation
has taken place. The reader must believe in that world while inside it or
believe in the logic of the invented world, and the reader's ability to move
easily through this world is based on the author's ability to create strong,
vivid, powerful images. To produce believability, the author must know
(imagine, *see*) everything about this world—its history and culture, its natural setting, its people, animals, and creatures and their unique behaviors,
appearance, language, values, and preoccupations.

Quest fantasies might depend for their success on readers becoming
deeply engaged with what Roland Barthes (1985) has described as the
"semic" code—the small details that flicker through a story and help readers build a sense of place and characters for the author's created secondary world. Such details are crucial for building a tissue of meanings for
the story, or what Barthes calls a "symbolic" code. In *The Hobbit*, meaning
arises out of the opposing ideas of home and away (being tucked safely
inside one's hobbit hole versus setting off on a risky adventure). The semic
details and images evoke children's imaginings, which we learn about
when we invite their responses, thus setting in motion the intersection of
narrative coding and multiple literacies.

All this I would see as I watched these children entering Tolkien's
secondary world, where a hobbit and his dwarf friends would set off on
a long, perilous adventure to quell a dragon that had long ago stolen the
dwarfs' treasure, after driving them far from their home deep in the
mountains. Filled with determined and courageous dwarfs, a helpful
wizard, Gandolf, and the talents of Bilbo Baggins, a hobbit who takes on
this adventure reluctantly because it seems the "right" thing—or the *only*
thing—to do, the adventure begins.

## SEMIC CODING AND MULTIPLE LITERACIES

Before we left for Ann Arbor, Vinny had embarked on a project of his
own after I said, "I wonder what goes through your mind when you read
a favorite book." He was reading J. R. R. Tolkien's *The Hobbit*, the version illustrated by Michael Hague (Tolkien, 1937/1984) that he had received for Christmas, penciling in responses on the margins, and telling
me his thoughts at other times.

Vinny's *personal/empathetic* literacy quickly took hold each time he began rereading this book. "I'm like a hobbit," he declared this time, in relation to Tolkien's description of hobbits. "I'm short and fat and I laugh after I eat, and I have two things for supper." Fascinated by a creature in some ways like himself (he was short and stocky and certainly loved food), Vinny was soon thinking about other ways he was like and not like a hobbit.

He lingered over the cakes that Bilbo consumes after breakfast, the tiniest of details and one that adults might pass over with little if any attention. "He finishes his cake so fast," Vinny chuckled: "Wonder what kind of cake it is—maybe just a hotcake of something, or maybe a cupcake—or a hobbit-cake." Clearly the semic code was giving him new images to think about, thus fostering not only personal/empathetic but also *narrative* literacy. He wanted to know about buttered scones and seed cakes, and when Gandolf arrives for tea, in Chapter 1, he began recreating the scene for me with a little story of his own: "And he goes, I'll have a poppy-seed cake and I'll have a beer. I'll have red wine, white wine." He laughed, clearly enjoying himself.

When Gandalf announces he is looking for someone to undertake an adventure, *literary* and *sociocultural* literacies soon began emerging, too. The word "adventure" caused me to remember a question I asked the children in the Gnome Workshop several years before this, when we were reading Maurice Sendak's fantasy picture book *Outside Over There*, and the children described the story as an adventure.

"What made it an adventure?" I asked at that time. "It was exciting," Vinny replied. "Very scary, a matter of life and death. I think there's a first-stage adventure with violence, and there's another kind without any violence. Then it's something new. It's mysterious. You don't know how it's going to turn out. Like I took a secret path to Green Springs Park. I had never done that before. It was exciting. You don't know; a snake could be in your path." Vinny and his friends revisited this question often during that workshop and for some time afterward. They seemed to like working out good definitions for the concept of "adventure," year by year.

Now he had new and different ideas:

*Vinny:* You're going to a corner store or you could go outside and you see birds and you think of an adventure like a spaceship flying. Well, it might be a fantasy adventure, but it would be an adventure. Everything's a fantasy; everything's an adventure.
*NM:* If I just look at birds—
*Vinny:* No, birds would be a real-life adventure, like hiking and skiing. Looking for a bird, you're *doing* something. An adventure is just doing something. But maybe to someone else, it's

doing *something*, something big, like climbing a big tree or a
mountain. Sailing a sea.
*NM:* So there are different kinds of adventures.
*Vinny:* Yeah. There's sport adventures, real-life adventures, com-
edy adventures, sad adventures.
*NM:* I wonder what kind of adventure Bilbo's going to have in this
book.
*Vinny:* He'll probably try to get out of most things. He'll probably
have a pretty good one. It will be real to him though. Real to
him but fantasy to us. It'll be pretty big. Most of the things he'll
be trying to get out of—like [he will say], "You go fight the
dragon; I'll go get the treasure. Why don't I just sit here?" He'll
just be trying to get out of it [the adventure].

Vinny was able to step back and think about fantasy now in terms of
how characters and readers felt as they each lived through the story. The
quest was real to Bilbo, he said, "but fantasy to us." Vinny's empathy for
Bilbo was so strong, he saw him as both a character and a person. In fact,
his *aesthetic* literacy was so strong by this time (he had become so engaged
by Tolkien's secondary world) that he decided hobbits were "real." I explained that as far as I knew, Tolkien was the first person to write about
hobbits: "That probably means he had read a lot about dwarfs and elves
and decided to create a creature of his own, the same way you make up
creatures for your stories."

A semic detail related to the dragon Smaug in Chapter 1 produced
another idea for him: authors injecting real or historical figures into a fantasy. That Smaug had settled on their mountain, in a "spout of flame"
(p. 35), routing the dwarfs and stealing all their gold and jewels, caused
Vinny to remember the German word *blitzkrieg* from his interest in World
War II books and movies: "Like lightning," he told me, "and then the Ger-
mans let out a whole bunch of barbs." And he wondered (considering the
book's original publication date—1937) if Tolkien had been thinking of the
dragon as Hitler (the semic and cultural codes were fostering *sociocultural*
literacy). Mark said it might depend on how long he had been planning
the book. I remembered that Tolkien had served in World War I, and
conjectured that he might have been writing about that war, or about
wars generally, and that fantasy writers seemed at times to have strange
foresight—or to be prescient.

The way that real and fantasy worlds were blurring for them here
resonates strongly with the way that Laurence Yep (1995) has defined fantasy. In the Chinese world, he explains, the real and the supernatural are
not opposing forces; they are simply different ways to find or explore truth.

Early historical writers in China used imaginary embellishments to explain events, with fantasy stories later reflecting this blending of the two genres. "[T]he best fantasy is nurtured by the past" (p. 111), Yep asserts, adding that because fantasy takes this longer, historical path, because of its multiple ways of reaching the truth (its versatility), "its rewards are far more satisfying" (p. 111).

## MULTIPLE LITERACIES, NARRATIVE CODING, AND KEY SCENES

Three months later, as I was reading aloud from our small, well-worn, paperback copy of *The Hobbit* (1965b), I noticed—from the range and intensity of their responses—that a key scene had arisen for both children. On the way to slay the dragon, Gandalf leaves the Hobbit and the dwarfs on the edge of the Mirkwood forest with a stern warning, "DON'T LEAVE THE PATH!" (p. 139), and Tolkien describes Bilbo as sitting "on the ground feeling very unhappy and wishing he was beside the wizard on his tall horse" (Chapter 7, p. 137).

Details of the semic code enabled Mark to enter more deeply into Bilbo's feelings and to feel concern: "They have to make it to the woods and some people might die and some people might get lost. And they'll lose more people and when they get to the dragon. You know people are going to die then . . . And that's not right . . . They should send more hobbits." Clearly the emotional content of the story—Bilbo's forsaken feelings and fears—was tapping into the cultural coding of Mark's own child's world. His concern was squarely with Bilbo and the dwarfs—their safety, their vulnerability, the great injustice if the evil creatures swooped down.

Vinny's empathy for Bilbo also continued to be strong, which strengthened his *aesthetic* literacy. Whether he was painting a Dungeons and Dragons figure that he had named Bilbo or drinking his soup with a glass straw saying, "I'm Bilbo with his pipe," he was in role as the hobbit.

With *personal/empathetic* literacy strongly in play, they were both ready to make stronger meaning of the symbolic code. Another key scene that drew rich responses occurred in Chapter 12 when Bilbo Baggins remembers the dwarfs inviting him (in Chapter 1) to become the burglar of the quest-adventure. Now they urge him to take up the burglar role in earnest— to go into the secret passage of the Mountain and decide how they can recover the gold. The stay-at-home, hesitant Tookish part of Bilbo (his mother's side; his mother was a Took) is once again at odds with the adventuresome Baggins side; Bilbo chides himself for putting his foot into this mess at the beginning, then stirs himself with strong words, the narrator adding: "Going on from there was the bravest thing he ever did. The tremendous things that happened afterward were as nothing compared to it. He fought the real battle in the tunnel alone, before he ever saw the vast danger that lay in wait" (p. 205). Through the actions and semic codes, these children could see Bilbo inching forward in the tunnel, which signaled an important question for the symbolic code—What is a hero—and the narrator's implied answer: a person who goes forward even though afraid.

Vinny internalized this narrative coding through *personal/empathetic* recollections that soon drew in Mark. But the question for both children in terms of their own child worlds was, How do you decide whether to go forward when the going is tough—and their implied answer: You have to know what you really want and then keep up your courage—or you might even discover you don't really want the original goal after all (personal/ ethical choices about what you value).

> *Vinny:* If you really wanted to stick it out in a scary movie, you have to ask yourself if you really wanted to watch it. And you're telling yourself that you're brave.
>
> *NM:* Has something like this ever happened to you—that you had to fight a battle alone?
>
> *Vinny:* Yeah, when I was little, not that little, but when I watched a scary movie at Johnny and Mikey's [his cousins] house.
>
> *Mark:* It was scary. I only saw a little of it and I was scared. I didn't win! I was walking up the stairs 'cause I had just finished watching the movie, but I didn't see the whole thing. When I looked around and Vinny was coming up and Vinny came up with me. I lost the battle, and I'm glad I did.

When children speculate about gaps in text, as I noticed from our reading of Babbitt's and Hunter's books that summer, we see the enigmatic code in operation and the way it fosters *generative* and *literary* literacies, which are both important for inferential thinking, drawing conclusions, returning to the text to search for clues (or to notice more details of the semic code), and speculating on—and confirming—theories. (Babbitt's book, a supernatural fantasy, and Hunter's books, both folk fantasies, were all strong in the enigmatic code.)

Whether children solve puzzles of the enigma code, however, is less important than whether we notice the questions they are asking and encourage them to work toward answers—answers, again, that are less important for their supposed correctness than for the meaning-making *process* that evolves on the way to finding them and the fact that what children see as gaps nearly always reveals—to them and to us—what is important for them, in terms of their own worlds.

## KEY SCENES, GAPS OF TEXT, AND *CRITICAL* LITERACY

In Chapter 14 "Fire and Water," we reached the high point of the action—Bard's shooting of the dragon—a key scene rich in semic and action coding. At this point, we also uncovered an important gap of text: Who really defeated Smaug? Or in terms of child worlds and *critical* literacy, who *should* have defeated him? On the surface, the answer is simple; Bard slays the dragon. But Vinny's disappointment—in terms of what he knew and felt about the world and this work—was strong and clear:

> *Vinny:* That's going to ruin it; they [the hobbit and the dwarfs] can't fight him.
> *NM:* Could they have fought him really [considering their small size]?
> *Vinny:* Yeah. Same thing like he [Bard] did; you just go over there and draw a dagger.
> *NM:* Did the hobbit tell them [the dwarfs] that he [Smaug] had a hole in his vest?
> *Vinny:* Yeah.
> *NM:* So the hobbits really did defeat him, didn't they? They talked about it, and the thrush heard it and carried the news to the Lake town people. So it was because of the hobbit that Smaug was defeated.
> *Mark:* Yeah, but—
> *NM:* You wanted to see them do it themselves.
> *Mark:* Yes!
> *Vinny:* Bilbo should have had a fight to the death with the dragon.
> *NM:* Who would have won?
> *Vinny:* Hopefully Bilbo.
> *NM:* Would he really have won or would there have been a problem?
> *Vinny:* Yes, he would have gotten wounded.

Their empathy, therefore their vision of a hero, was invested in the hobbit fighting the dragon. And no matter how clever, courageous, or merely lucky Bilbo was in bringing about Smaug's defeat, if *he* did not slay Smaug, the story lost steam for them.

They were also disappointed because others besides the dwarfs were going to share in the spoils. "That's no fair; the dwarfs don't get any gold,"

Vinny protested. "Well, we don't know for sure yet," I said. "They [the Lake people] are just thinking about how to get it. They used the Elf King's barrels to get down the river. It took a lot of people to defeat Smaug, didn't it? Everybody had a hand in it, and maybe everybody is going to need some of the war loot." (One of Tolkien's subtle "messages," it seemed to me, but these children weren't having any of it.)

With this chapter and the next, "The Gathering of the Clouds," a more complicated part of the actions code emerges. A power struggle between the Lake men and the oldest dwarf, Thorin, arises when the men begin dividing the treasure that through these children's eyes belonged to the dwarfs. Does it? (The dwarf mission and Smaug's retribution ends with many of the Lake townspeople homeless or dead; thus the Lake men's anger with the dwarfs.)

Mark also wondered why the Elf King did not share in the profits. Vinny remembered that the hobbit and Gandolf were friends of the Elf King and theorized, in *sociocultural* terms: "It's like if we had beat Russia and ruled out communism, we would rule it with England 'cause England would help us too." I mentioned that during World War II, it took many countries banding together to save people from Hitler's oppression. Then we began discussing the way different countries took control of Germany after the war, with different world powers on different "teams," as Vinny put it. Quest fantasy, which involves epic battles between good and evil, was providing important opportunities for discussing historical events and debating personal/ethical choices, as they arose naturally and spontaneously in our conversations.

Vinny continued to focus on injustice to the dwarfs; his empathy for the hobbit's "team" fostered his ability to notice gaps quickly: "The dwarfs go through all that stuff just to get to that mountain, and here comes all the rest of them just as easy. Why doesn't Beorn help them?" Later he wondered if Gollum were going to come and try to get something, too. And he predicted accurately that the goblins and wolves would soon arrive, causing more trouble. For his part, Mark soon noticed a better solution for the hobbit and dwarfs: "What they should have done is given the other people—Bard's people [of Lake town]—one part of twelve of the treasure and ask them to help them to fight the other ones now."

By the end of Chapter 15, "The Gathering of the Clouds," Tolkien's narrator was closing some gaps of text. We learned that Bard of the Lakemen was the heir of Girion of Dale, and Girion's wealth had also been stolen from Smaug and thus mingled with the dwarfs' wealth (thus Bard had a legitimate claim to the treasure and a reason for joining the impending battle). "Everyone's going to fight over the treasure," I said. "All of them want it—the elfin king, Bard, the Master, the goblins, the dwarfs." Vinny predicted that "the men will be there and also the goblins and the hobbits and dwarfs." Mark added, "Beorn will be there on their [the dwarfs'] team." Vinny also decided that Gandolf would return to save the day. And he remembered that Bilbo still had "that weird gem [the Arkenstone] in his pocket."

Suspense was building now; the actions code is particularly strong in Chapter 16, "A Thief in the Night." And both children began cheering when they heard that Dain and 500 dwarfs were "hurrying from the Iron Hills" (p. 253) and within two days would be in Dale. What would Bilbo do now? "Something with the gem," Vinny predicted. "I know," said Mark. "He's going to give the Arkenstone to the Bard." Why, I wondered. "For friendship," he decided.

As we finished the book, both children marched around the room cheering, after which Vinny announced, "I'm gonna write a story."

## CHILDREN AS RESEARCH PARTNERS

Vinny's story, told to us (and into the tape recorder) during the last weeks of our summer vacation, proceeded through four phases: invention, drawing, telling back stories of the main story, and telling the story itself. And his creative process was not all that dissimilar to that of Yep (1995) and other writers like Diana Wynne Jones (2004), who say they allow events and characters to influence the way the eventual story emerges and they revise original story plans when new ideas need to be incorporated.

His storymaking plans took root as he heard about Dain's armor in Chapter 17: "I was thinking of those dwarfs—Dain and his people—and how it described their armor. And then I was thinking I should make a Ninja that has a ring of invisibility and magic armor. And then I said maybe tonight I'll make my character." He was talking about one of his Dungeons and Dragons characters, but soon he was delving into his own story.

### Invention

As I listened to Vinny unfold his story plans, it was clear he was using his preferred way of story-creation: He would "borrow" aspects of a favorite story (just as Tolkien borrowed from Norse and Germanic sagas); change some details of plot, setting, or characters; and combine them with aspects of other sources—and inventions of his own—to produce an entirely different story. This particular kind of reshaping gave him more options for characters, a greater range of settings and plots, and allowed his imagination to roam freely around all the literature in his story "bank" (*intertextual* literacy). Here he was borrowing Tolkien's creation—hobbits—and adding to the mix legendary creatures like goblins and dragons and humans from Japanese history (ninjas and samurai) intriguing to him for their strength, mystery, and powerful weapons:

> *Vinny:* It's going to be Japanese hobbits and there's going to be ninjas and samurais in it. And there's going to be Japanese goblins and lots of dragons in it. And I was thinking I might make some other creatures.
>
> *Mark:* Japanese dwarfs or elves?
>
> *Vinny:* Yeah, maybe. And I'm gonna make some evil people that are like winged. They're not hobbits but they are like winged hobbits. These are evil. And they are not slaves but workers of an evil wizard who uses ancient magic, ancient powerful magic. And I'm also gonna make up another kind of creature, something really weird. I'm also gonna have the main foes of ninjas—this is in ancient Japan—what they're gonna be is winged, long-nosed goblins.
>
> *Mark:* By the way, they're in that book [he points to Tom McGowen's *Encyclopedia of Legendary Creatures* (1981), a children's information book that we had brought along on our vacation].
>
> *Vinny:* I'll show you a picture of a winged goblin [a griffin in McGowen's book illustrated by Victor Ambrus].

In the same way that small details of Tolkien's semic code had drawn Vinny into the book as reader, Vinny as storymaker began building his own secondary world (his own semic code) by focusing primarily on the appearance of his characters. (The winged goblins had long noses; the evil hobbitlike creatures would have wings.) There was little at this time about motivation for conflicts. The ninjas and winged goblins would be enemies of one another, but he had not said why. Thus his actions code (or some semblance of plot) was not yet visible.

He linked details of his semic code to both a cultural code (he was transplanting Tolkien's English hobbits to ancient Japan) and a symbolic code: winged goblins would be evil (they worked for an evil wizard who used powerful magic). And ninjas and Japanese hobbits (wingless—and therefore "good") would be combating the evil ones. From *The Hobbit* he was borrowing his character types (hobbits and goblins) and his theme of good versus evil, but he had added his own touches—an evil wizard and winged goblins.

When story time began the next day, Vinny's action coding was well under way: he had decided to borrow Tolkien's idea of folk creatures setting off on a quest, but they were trying to find a jewel they would use to defeat an evil opponent (rather than jewels stolen by a dragon). He was also beginning to fill gaps in his enigma code, although several things were still unclear to me. Were these hobbits retrieving stolen treasure, as in *The Hobbit*? How did they know about the jewel? How would the jewel be used to defeat the evil wizard? What were the magical powers of the jewel?

I asked him no questions at this time; I wanted simply to observe, not influence, his process. For the moment, his semic code remained a strong force for his thinking. He had created a magical gem (a ruby) as center-piece for his story plot, and the gem might have been at least partially inspired by Tolkien's Arkenstone.

As this session unfolded, it also seemed clear that Mark's interest was helping to generate ideas, even to influence the story. Mark needed to hear details about Vinny's characters to help situate himself in the story, and his questions and comments caused Vinny to pause in the planning of his actions code (events, scenes, causal links) in order to generate more details for the semic code. Clearly Mark's role as responsive listener was important: Vinny was taking great pleasure in unveiling his story-in-progress for an actual—and informed—child audience: Both children had shared knowledge of popular culture figures, a shared way of talking about them, and a shared history of appropriating these heroes and antiheroes for their play and storymaking. Therefore, in this invention stage, talking to learn was crucial:

*Vinny:* My story is gonna have—like *The Hobbit*—they are going on an adventure. They're going to find an important jewel to defeat an evil wizard and the evil wizard has the power to turn himself into a dragon. That's how powerful he is. And it [the gem] was split into two different parts like it used to be—one big ruby. It has two different parts and one part is in a deep volcano and that part is called a Lava Ruby. That's from one of my other stories. The other one is on the top of a very high mountain. This one is called the Sky Ruby. One part is red; the other is light blue. I'm connecting the bottom of the earth to the top of the earth—underground to almost in the heavens. And also these Japanese hobbits—

*Mark:* How tall are they?

*Vinny:* The same size as Bilbo and the dwarfs . . . And what they do is they go—first of all the people in it are four hobbit fighters and an elf that's undersized . . .

*Mark:* No dwarfs?

*Vinny:* Right.

*Mark:* Ohhhh! [clearly distressed]

*Vinny:* Ok, there will be a couple of dwarfs. I'll run them in some-how. They'll be called Dwarfs of Mushrooms. [We had begun reading Tolkien's *The Fellowship of the Ring* (1965a) after we finished *The Hobbit,* and Chapter 4, "A Short Cut to Mush-rooms," was becoming an influence for him at this point (Frodo loves mushrooms).]

*Mark:* [laughs]

*Vinny:* They'll be fat and chubby. There will be two of those. Ok, now this head hobbit is, he's a magician, and he's—

*Mark:* Like Gandolf.

*Vinny:* Yeah, and he's real good in magic . . .

*Mark:* Is he tall or real small?

*Vinny:* He's real, real old. He's small, 'cause he's old . . .

*Mark:* Are there any people you know like that, or did you make it up yourself?

*Vinny:* Yeah, but not good, just evil people. Ok, he goes to—yeah, there's one made up. He's a minidragon.

*Mark:* [laughs]

*Vinny:* He's a light blue mini-dragon. He sides with the hobbit. . . . Ok, this little guy, the head guy, the wizardlike hobbit, he goes to a temple and he meets Mr. Yamaguchi. Mr. Yamaguchi is a ninja; he's the head ninja, a Shidochi person, and he runs a school and they ask him for his help . . . and he brings three of the main people to the class . . . and what they do is, Mr. Yamaguchi has some people he knows too, and he's gonna get a Shogun Hobbit samurai . . . And there's one elf . . . And there's one more small dragon and they run into trolls that are called "trobs" and they're real big.

*Mark:* That's your story!

Vinny had his cast now and a sketch of his plot; the quest was faintly in place, too. What lay ahead was developing the adventure itself, actually dramatizing it with events and scenes (showing rather than merely telling), which he would soon do. Perhaps such scenes were beginning to run through his mind already, as when he said, "They run into trolls that are called 'trobs' and they're real big." And Mark was already visualizing the scene.

**Drawing as Storymaking**

"That's Night Hawk," Vinny told me one day when he was drawing. "He's part of your story?" I asked, wondering if this comic book superhero had entered his story about the magical gem. "Yeah," he replied. "He's a ninja. What they did, they captured one of the evil wizard's people."

"Who are 'they'?" I asked. "Who did the capturing?"

"The Adventurers," he replied, indicating his four Japanese hobbits; Mio, the small Japanese elf; and Night Hawk, one of his hobbit ninja characters. Then, as he continued to draw, he unfolded more about his story, his words decoding a picture that was telling him more about both the actions and semic coding of his story:

> They chained them up and they gave them wrong information—
> lies. He [Night Hawk] said, "Tomorrow we shall attack the village."
> And then another one [of the Adventurers] said, "Shhh, have you
> forgotten we have a prisoner in the room?" The other one says,
> "Don't worry, he'll never get out to return this news to them . . .

Because the scene was so well developed in his mind, I asked what part of the story this was, and I was surprised to hear him say "toward the end." Either he had fast-forwarded to the part he found most exciting to draw and dramatize, or because he was reliving some of his favorite events from *The Hobbit*—borrowing them for his story, as he said—he found this part the most "fun" to live through alongside his characters. In either case, his storymaking was fostering both *narrative* and *aesthetic* literacies.

"Who is he?" I asked about a mysterious figure in his picture.

"Well, it's sort of hard to explain," he replied, settling in to divulge— or develop—more. The ending of his story—inspired by the climactic battle scene of *The Hobbit*—and his middle part (the Adventurers retrieving gems an evil wizard had stolen from them, also inspired by *The Hobbit*) were now in place. So he could take time to unfold details of how all these things came to be, and this backstory of the large plot functioned the same way his main story did: He began telling it through the semic code, with details about characters—names, appearance, physical traits, clothing—at the foreground of his narrative meaning-making. (He needed to "see" the story he was creating, just as he needed to see any author's story, to walk around inside it or shape it, in terms of his own child's world, before he could read or tell it.)

"It started after they went through all this stuff," Vinny explained. "The Adventurers had two gems and the wizard had two gems, but the wizard gave one to a Goliath to hold, and the Goliath put it in his little leather sack. And Night Creature—these are little creatures; they sort of look like woodchucks, but they wear leather clothes and they can fight with weapons and stuff and also they're sort of like a platypus cause they can swim real well."

Then he showed me that the tiny Night Creatures climb up the Goliath's leg (the Goliath mistakes the creature for a cobweb) and gnaw on the Goliath's leather pouch, thinking it is food, before out drops a gem, which the Night Creatures take back to their own army. The evil wizard thinks the Adventurers have a gem, Vinny explained, so he steals a gem from them, leaving the Adventurers with one gem, the evil wizard with two, and the Night Creatures with one.

With his motivation for the story conflict in hand, Vinny was ready to tell more about his ending. I asked if he had thought all this up right then, as he was drawing and talking, or if he imagined it at some earlier time. "Uptown at the museum today," he replied, "when we were looking at the mammals and stuff." Then he continued explaining, in terms of the actions code, that the creatures will begin fighting when they learn what the gem can do when all four parts are put together.

Noticing a puzzle of his enigma code (What could the gem do when all four parts were put together?), I asked if he knew how the story ended yet. "Yeah," he replied. "I figured it out a pretty long time ago, when I started thinking about it." He also knew why the Night Creatures were stealing from the Goliaths: "So how it ends is they are fighting—the Adventurers have two [jewels of the gem], the [evil] wizard has one, and the Night Creatures have one." In other words, no "team" has any way to complete the fitting of the gem together; no group has all the power or the way to dominate other completely, but the Adventurers have at least two of the four gem parts now, as the story ends, and their allies, the Night Creatures, have another part—an uneasy balance of power, tipping toward the good guys.

## Telling Backstories

In several sessions after this, with no further conferencing with me, Vinny began telling his story. His initial words had a formal storytelling tone; he had a title, and it seemed clear he had thought about an appropriate or traditional opening. And once again, Mark served as active listener, asking questions for clarification. It was also becoming clear that talking was helping Vinny see when he needed to fill gaps. Then, as he backed up to engage in more story planning—and more backstories—the semic code became strongly visible to both him and his audience.

Because he was creating a quest fantasy, Vinny needed to create a secondary world that readers would accept as true. In other words, the semic code would need to propel the actions code; it stimulated the image-making that readers needed to become engaged in a new world. But in this case, because Mark needed to know how this secondary world came to be, Vinny had to produce a little more actions coding, a feat he accomplished by backing up in time, in his story opening, to tell how his magical gem came to be and about a character he described as a "fantastical lord" who originally owned the ring. And his inclination to blend details and ideas from other stories played a large part in this backstory.

The word "lord" and the character itself were not borrowed entirely from *The Hobbit* (a story in which Vinny had encountered a "Lord" of the Eagles) or even from Tolkien's *The Lord of the Rings*. Another book we had read that summer was Laurence Yep's *Dragonwings* (1975), a realistic story (historical fiction) having, as an inner backstory, a dream fantasy involving a lord who is a dragon king and whose throne is "encrusted with all kinds of gems, each as big as my fist" (p. 45). In Vinny's story, a gigantic lord similarly wears a large gem as a ring. Vinny might also have borrowed, for his own creatures, the idea of wings, richly described in Yep's work (and pictured in the griffin of McGowen's and Ambrus's book).

Thus *intertextual* literacy—the ability to see connections among several different texts—was playing an important role in Vinny's semic coding. Before he could tell what happened to the gem, he had to know—and let others know—what it looked like. So he pulled several semic details from his own child's world. To describe the size of his gigantic, magical gem, he drew, from his own *sociocultural* experiences, a basketball and one of his own favorite animals, the prairie dog. But knowing what the gem looked like was only the beginning. His description of a gigantic gem meant creating a larger-than-life lord who wore the gem "on his pinkie."

Because the lord loomed larger now, too large to live on the earth, Vinny placed him in the heavens, where his death sets the conflict in motion: when the ring falls off his hand, down to earth, it splinters into four separate parts, or jewels, thus fracturing its power. When Vinny saw this event posing another problem (how would anyone in the heavens die?), he created a world in which 20,000 feet below the gods [there] lived a "lord," a creature less powerful than the gods, and therefore mortal. And when he dies and his ring falls, it lands in four different places on the earth; thus it is discovered by four different creatures on the earth, who race to find the missing parts in order to unify its magical power.

All of these ideas were speeding through Vinny's thoughts as he set his story in motion, telling and then stopping to plan and fill in gaps, then resuming his telling of backstories in order to set his story opening in motion:

> The name of my story is "Journey to the Magical Gem." It's about a fantastical lord. This is how it starts. A fantastical lord once had a huge gem. This gem was not only beautiful but it had the power of magic—ancient magic—because this happened a million years ago.

And this fantastical lord ruled with his magical gem. He wore it on his finger . . . [He paused to describe the size of the gem as a basketball, then an animal (a wolverine? Mark asks), no, a "full-grown prairie dog" or "full-grown mole" or prairie dog "in width but it's very fat," Vinny replied.] The lord wears it on his finger. This lord is gigantic . . . and one day after he died—'cause lords do die—but gods don't . . . So then this beautiful gem went flying to earth from the heavens. When it hit the atmosphere, it just broke open in four different places—a volcano, an ocean, a mountain, and somehow it went through a rabbit's hole which is pretty far down, I'll say about five feet. Then it kept on going down, about five or ten more feet, about fifteen feet, 'cause it was going so fast.

At this point Vinny sensed a gap in his story and moved to fill it. He needed to interject a backstory telling about how these creatures found the gem parts and what they did then. And once again, he used the semic code to propel his actions and enigma coding. Borrowing from his Dungeons and Dragons game-playing and his reading of *The Hobbit*, he began unveiling more details of his secondary world—his Goliath characters, his six "races" of creatures, his poisonous mushrooms "for the tips of swords and stuff," his Dragon Fighters used by a tribe of monsters called Dragon Riders, and the five magical rings that his Goliaths wore—for power, telekinesis, walking on water, teleportation, and making three wishes.

"Ok, so that's how it is," Vinny said, bringing this phase of his planning session to a close. "And so my story is how to get it [the Great Gem]. And I'm about to start telling you the story of 'The Journey to the Magical Gem.'" Mark applauded: "He has a big audience here tonight!" (the Summer Olympics was playing in the background). "At least five hundred people!" Vinny added.

## Telling the Story

The same recursive pattern of Vinny's creative process continued as his story began. He told a part of it; then if he saw gaps, or if Mark's questions and comments caused him to see gaps, he backtracked to fill them with brief narrative comments or backstories. The story gradually emerged through this process of talking and telling. Creating his secondary world enabled him to give his small creatures—hobbits, Mio the elf, a small light-blue dragon, and his Mushroom Dwarfs—their own share of power. If a children's book is often about children struggling for power when adults are absent, Vinny's story was about child-sized adult characters, like Tolkien's Bilbo, struggling in a world where adultlike reason is absent.

And here the hobbits are clearly the heroes: They are slaying the "dragons" themselves—and winning:

> Once upon a time there was a god, I mean a lord, and this lord had a gorgeous gem. He lived in the heavens, and he had hold of this gem because it was magical and he was a very important lord; he was very powerful. So one day he died. His last request was that he would be pushed toward a new planet. That way none of his enemies could get their hands on it and rule unjustly. So it went flying . . . One part of the gem went fifteen feet underneath the ground; another part went on top of a snowy mountain. Another went in a volcano, and another one went into the Pacific Ocean, as we know it now. And there were rulers in these certain places that found the parts of the gem and these rulers were called Goliaths. Goliaths were giant half-orcs and elfish things . . . Goliaths were evil, so after their rulers died, all of them died. This is 1300 A.D. now, and word has gotten around that they died. Some people had actually thought they would go on a hunt and pick up the gem parts, and that's where I leave you off—at a small hobbit hole in Edo, Japan.

Telling a story about Japanese hobbits gave Vinny a way to weave together two of his favorite subjects—hobbits and Asian culture (he and Mark and their friends liked playing ninja and samurai warriors and reading about them in comic books and nonfiction information books). And just as Tolkien and Yep had shown him many ways of creating inner stories or backstories, Tolkien had taught him to begin a story about hobbits with many semic details about what they looked like and where they lived.

> And in this hobbit hole lived a little old man named Akasa Kashugi. And Akasa was known for his wizard powers. And he was named after his birthplace on the island of Akasa in Japan. So he was very wise and he knew about the jewels. So he pinned a note onto a small bird, a sparrow, and flew it—he tied it and sent it to three friends to tell them about the gem. And he invited them to some tea that day—green tea—and they were going to talk it over.

From *The Hobbit*, Vinny had borrowed such details and events as the bird-as-message-carrier and an invitation to tea, during which a wizard character tells a story about a quest for treasure. From a story, "Mr. Yama-guchi and the Troll," he had created earlier in the Gnome Workshop, in response to a collection of folktales from South China (Hume, 1962), he borrowed or transplanted a wise little old man, or ninja-hobbit, who values helpfulness and companionship as the foundation for friendship, survival, and prosperity. In addition, Vinny had fused two Tolkien characters, the small, childlike hobbit Bilbo (small, vulnerable, powerless, yet intrinsically powerful) and the elderly wizard Gandolf, as one character, Akasa.

> So the bird went off. And this is how Akasa looked like: Akasa was a chubby man, about two feet, not two feet, but one and a half feet, and he was sort of wrinkled. He had no beard or mustache, and he wore a silky, a black silk, a black cotton topcoat. He wore a velvet— a black velvet pajamas, really used as a jumpsuit, but it was covered by a black satin robe. And he wore straw sandals and under these straw sandals, he had a cotton lining, so he walked silently.

Vinny went on to describe Akasa's hobbit hole—his "castle," his "home" (with a round door, borrowed from Tolkien) that was "halfway in a tree and the other half was underground," his foyer ("a little room" where he kept a "little line of small velvet shoes [and] that way, what people would do was slip their feet into those shoes to keep his rugs clean"), his bedroom, with "a bookcase full of mysterious books" that "looked like a witch's cavern," behind which was a "secret little room "where he prayed, worked out and also casted some spells," his kitchen, with a "big pot hanging down from the ceiling, underneath a small fireplace," and his dining room, filled with "china plates and crystal goblets, cups and glasses. And of course he always kept a chilled wine bottle."

At the next session, he told about three brothers, hobbit friends of Akasa, arriving at the door, and he drew heavily on the semic code to differentiate their personalities, interests, and abilities. One thing he didn't like about *The Fellowship of the Ring* was that Tolkien had not described his characters as much as before. Reading *The Hobbit*, Vinny had reveled in Tolkien's passages about hobbits having "natural leathery soles and thick warm brown hair like the stuff on their heads (which is curly)" (p. 16). In *The Fellowship of the Ring*, Vinny was left with only Sam's "curly head" (p. 72) to visualize. Here, in his own story, he would correct all that.

Akasa tells his friends a story about the gem, a story that Vinny did not retell; he had told it already, he said. (He had noticed Tolkien using this same narrative strategy in Chapter 8 of *The Hobbit*, when Bilbo tells the dwarfs about his experience in Gollum's cave—but readers do not hear Bilbo's story, because they have already witnessed it.) In place of the story, Vinny has Akasa simply say, "And now that the four possessors of the gem have died, we must get it so evil will not reign in this forest of the land," signaling the major thread of his symbolic code, the clash of good and evil forces for control of the world.

Then Akasa shows his friends a map showing where the four gem parts are; they discuss an enemy (Yakamultia, an evil wizard) who might find the gem first, and they set off in different directions to find helpers for their mission. But before Akasa sets out, a fierce Dragon Rider appears on the doorstep he is sweeping, and Akasa's response is important for showing what he values—his home, nature, beauty, the creation and nurturing of things (Vinny's symbolic code again coming into play). Before telling what Akasa does, Vinny returns once more to the semic code, pausing to tell what his Dragon Riders looked like (three feet tall, ugly, with "large, papery ears"), where they lived ("high in the trees"; thus they have "huge wings" with batlike gray fur on their hands, feet, and their "short little beards"), what they wore ("green, silk, camouflage suits," "golden bracelets and lots of wings"), and what they were—"extremely mean." This Dragon Rider went right into Akasa's garden, "full of flowers and other plants and started hacking it up with his sword."

> Now that made Akasa furious. So then the Dragon Rider threw a large stone through one of his windows. So then Akasa pulled the top part of his broom off, and out came a large chain and then Akasa swung the chair around, and it wrapped around the Dragon Rider's feet. Then Akasa pulled him in, took out a few small pins out of the broom part where the bristles were kept, and jabbed away at the Dragon Rider. So the Dragon Rider then fell dead. So Akasa mended his window before he left on the little journey, and he planted some more seeds and watered them.

At this point, Vinny produced a series of five scenes in which Akasa and his brothers assembled their coalition and met enemy resistance to it. The scenes reveal the meaning of the story for him, or why he was telling it. Just as creating the scenes gave him a chance to bring together the semic and actions codes, or to place his characters "onstage" and let them do their work—to enlighten and entertain, as story characters must do, with their words, actions, and scheming—it gave him a chance to shape his story in terms of his own child's world. Not only could he, as any narrator, tell about his characters as he set them in motion, adopting the all-seeing perspective that Tolkien uses; but he could also as a "player" on his own stage step into their shoes and try out each role. In addition, he could create small—childlike—creatures that "can do stuff we can't do; they can spy easier; they have magical powers and weapons."

Each of the scenes is rich in the semic and actions codes, especially in conversational dialogue. And it is clear that he was enjoying the creation of his scenes; humor was an important part of the semic coding. He laughed as he produced words and actions of characters with broad comic touches, evoked vivid personal "pictures" of his many different characters, created sound effects for their humorous behavior, invented humorous words, and built scenes with humorous details, such as when he "paints" the picture of an Asian scroll showing a "cat swiping a bird."

The first scene revealed Yakamoto making contact with Mio the Elf. The second involved the Dragon Riders, one of whom was last seen lying dead on Akasa' s doorstep. The third told about Akasa setting off on his journey to Mr. Yamaguchi, his ninja friend. The fourth, Vinny's longest and most highly developed in terms of the semic code, took place at the ninja temple, and here, as he explained when Mark asked, he used the "God-type" point of view ("I go from Akasa to the little demon rider; then I go to Mio and Hakamoto; then I go to the Dragon Riders, the King") because "It's funner this way" (to go into many minds):

> It was a long time before Akasa got past the security of Mr. Yamaguchi's temple. But he finally did get there. And this is how it happened. He went in there and the room was full of scrolls on the walls. I'm not sure if they were magical or not. But I do know they were very large and beautiful.

The fifth scene focused on the Mushroom Dwarfs, and here he introduced a dwarf character, "King Mushroom of the East, also named Chubs," who became a favorite in stories he created when summer ended and he continued to make stories with his friends during the school year:

> They went to the garden and into the palace, where the room had silk curtains and gold thrones and a large ivory table. There was no one in this room. So the guard took them outside to the courtyard where Chubs was harvesting some mushrooms. So Chubs then waved to his old friends and said, "Hmmm, come on inside." Chubs then took a handkerchief and wiped off his hands and his face. Then he went into a different room and slipped on a fat robe with white fur made of a polar bear 'cause once in a while the ships will come in from the North . . .

## CHILDREN AND FANTASY CREATION

When children tell stories for pleasure, as Vinny was doing, they are engaging in a kind of vicarious "play" that can lead us to see more about what "matters" in their lives (*narrative*, *sociocultural*, and *personal/empathetic* literacies intersecting). From listening to Vinny's storymaking in all its phases, I learned what personal, social, and cultural issues were at stake for him. I also saw that the more literary experiences children have as they venture into storymaking—or the stronger their *intertextual* literacy—the richer the stories are in terms of authorial coding and *narrative* literacy, and the stronger their confidence for engaging in authorial plans.

We often identify children's books as those filled with action, or with descriptive passages kept to a minimum. But Vinny's storymaking reveals that he valued details of the semic code as much as, if not more than, other codes. He wanted to hear—and tell about—what characters looked like and what their clothing, houses, and weapons looked like. He couldn't really situate himself in stories until he saw these things, and he wanted to situate his listeners in the same way.

With such an extensive storytelling venture, he was balancing many things, not the least of which was the way events of the past were feeding into his main story. Inner stories are part of any actions coding, and both Tolkien and Yep, whose books Vinny had heard just before he began telling this story, had threaded their main stories with embedded inner stories. Yep's characters often tell stories to one another to illuminate ideas of the symbolic and cultural codes; Tolkien's characters and his narrators tell stories—and backstories—as part of the actions and enigmatic codes. Hearing these stories showed Vinny how to layer his actions code with inner stories. Telling backstories was one way he used to fill gaps of his enigma code.

Listening to Tolkien's narrator telling the main story also enabled Vinny to adopt the same strong all-knowing narrator's voice, one that often interrupted the action to provide opinions, explain, interrupt, and comment on the action. Vinny's chosen narrative perspective, the godlike one, as he called it, was "funner"; it allowed him to tell what he saw and heard and knew about, to let his listeners know they were seeing through *his* eyes and that they had the best possible guide. It gave him total control, and such power was "fun."

For his cultural coding, Vinny drew on Japanese ninja traditions discussed in several nonfiction information books, Tolkien's hobbit world, Asian folk myths about dragons as he had seen in *Dragonwings*, and life and literary experiences of his own child world. His blending of fiction and nonfiction sources, in fact, resonates strongly with the way Yep (1995) says he creates fantasy from many sources—Chinese folklore, historical accounts, and particular experiences (life and literary) he is having at the time of creation.

For his symbolic coding, Vinny relied, perhaps unconsciously, on quest fantasy traditions, which meant sending a hero on an adventure in search of something—in this case a valued treasure—and confronting this hero with evil forces. But he was also creating a story in response to *The Hobbit*, or inspired by it, and in some ways to Yep's *Dragonwings;* therefore he would borrow what he saw as thematically important from *The Hobbit* and early chapters of *The Fellowship of the Ring*.

Akasa's statements lead us to see Vinny's thematic focus or his symbolic coding: "We must go to those places [waves, mountain, volcano, burrow] and collect the different gems before other evil races get there first"; "We're on a search for a large gem to rule the world"; "We must get [the gem] so evil will not reign in the forest of the land." What Vinny took from Tolkien's work was the use of power for good. And what was "good" from a child's perspective? If we examine the scene in which Vinny introduced Akasa, we discover a great deal about how he was reshaping Tolkien's and Yep's stories in terms of his own personal way—his own child's way—of seeing the world.

"In this hobbit hole lived a little old man named Akasa Kashugi," Vinny said. And who was Akasa? A very wise man who knows about the fragmented gems and who invites his three friends to tea—green tea—so that they could talk about his concerns. In other words, Vinny began his story with a scene of peace and harmony, an idea that he developed further in his description of Akasa's home, which brings us back once again to his rich semic coding and the way that his semic and symbolic codes were strongly intertwined or mutually supportive.

Akasa's house has a round door, a circle like the gem ring that the lord once wore, suggesting the reconciliation of opposites, and a round window cut into four sections, similar to the magical gem that falls to the earth, breaking into four jewels. And it is a stained-glass window, like he had heard described in Yep's book, engraved with the picture of a dragon (culture and nature, art and life, human and superhuman in balance). There is also the balance of body and spirit (in Akasa's secret room is a wall, where on one side he prays and on the other he exercises), and of life and death. (Akasa's hobbit hole is built half in a tree and half underground; the tree is dead but he covers it with leaves "to keep it looking nice." The little wise man who values home, friends, and green tea also values beauty.)

Akasa's house has a garden, and here we find him confronted by a Dragon Rider, whom he ignores until the creature begins hacking at his flowers, which makes him furious. Then, when the creature throws a stone through his window, he has no choice but to fight back, to protect what he values most—his garden and his home. As Uncle in *Dragonwings* tells the boy Moon Shadow, "The superior man tends his own garden" (p. 179). Like Bilbo, who must go off on a fearful adventure to save his peaceful life, Akasa has the courage to do what he needs to do to preserve what he regards as good. Before he leaves, he plants more seeds and waters them. "A superior man can only do what he's meant to do," Moon Shadow later tells Uncle (p. 200).

Vinny found a space in his storymaking for scenes rich in semic details, and they tell us what was important to him. What Akasa valued, what he saw as good, were friends, green tea, small velvet shoes—and especially his garden and his home with a stained-glass window, a bed full of sheets and blankets, a bookcase full of mysterious books, a secret room, crystal goblets, and chilled wine. This is Akasa's castle, Vinny tells us, the place he must leave in order to save it and the place where, similar to Bilbo Baggins, he will return once the journey ends. And the question arises, did Vinny enjoy *The Hobbit* because it mirrored ideas that already matched well with his interior landscape, or did this book give him new ideas and images to think with, as *Dragonwings* was doing?

A few months later I asked him what he had thought of *The Hobbit*. "An adventure," he told me, is "not so much war as time—a place of mind." And certainly, Tolkien's book had taken him to a "place of mind" where he could live through the story with Bilbo, with all the attending excitements, over and over again, each time he picked up the book. Fitting him so well at this moment when he was leaving childhood and entering his teen years, the book inspired his own stories; it found its way into his extraliterary activities and conversations. He read and reread it; he played it; he remembered it long after his first encounter with it. Finally, he used it to make new worlds for himself—and his audience.

In doing so—after long-term immersion in words and word-pictures of the book—he adopted many of Tolkien's narrative strategies: intrusive, omniscient narrator; verbal and physical jokes; and child-sized hero, playful and impetuous, yet sensible and mature. At the same time, he revised or resisted another of Tolkien's narrative choices (*critical* literacy): His Akasa, unlike Bilbo, takes his place upon the adult stage, fighting the Dragon Rider even if it means being wounded—or possibly dying. *And Akasa wins.*

## FANTASY AND CHILD WORLDS

By their attention, by what they notice, question, comment upon, and story about, children show us which characters, scenes, events, actions, and ideas are the important ones for them, and understanding these interests, preoccupations, and personal meanings helps us to see better their worlds.

Vinny's pleasure in *The Hobbit* was undercut when the character for whom he had the greatest empathy was treated like a child, not allowed to fulfill his role as hero: Bard, not Bilbo, slays the dragon. Because Vinny was so closely aligned with Bilbo, and because he wanted to fight the dragon himself, he wanted Bilbo to do the actual fighting. To fulfill the quest, in his view, Bilbo needed to perform in all ways as the hero. And when Vinny told his own story in response to this book, he found a way to solve this problem by weaving a scene of a hobbit fighting a Dragon Rider into his own actions code. This was his reasoning, and once we unravel it, we see better how children's life and literary worlds meet.

Listening to children's responses, we learn which narrative codes are the important ones at particular moments in the story *for them* and at what point one code feeds into another to deliver insight or to stimulate new meaning-making, empathetic role-play, storymaking, or cultural connections. Of great importance also, their responses tell us where the story gaps are for them. Because gaps feed the enigmatic code, they foster children's *generative, personal/empathetic, sociocultural, literary*, and *narrative* literacies when children move forward to fill them.

The "best" books for adults are richly interpretive, meaning they are "writerly" or riddled with gaps and blank spaces. Most children's books have few if any gaps; instead they often insult children's intelligence and curiosity with overexplicitness. That Tolkien left so many gaps for readers may explain why so many older readers have enjoyed or appropriated the book. That so many children through the years have enjoyed the book shows us that they can navigate writerly books. Children's responses to *The Hobbit* also reveal that fantasy—particularly quest fantasy—is a special and important one for them.

Quest fantasy has first of all a plot pattern of adventure that brings with it mystery, life-and-death excitement, and the thrill of an unexpected outcome. Adding to the mix are a hero's quest to find some prize or attain some worthy goal; an intriguing collection of legendary, folk, and invented characters; and a mythic kingdom in a newly minted world, all of which make the genre particularly inviting for child readers. And judging by these children's responses, Tolkien's way of coding Bilbo's quest adventure—and the child's way of encoding it—makes quest fantasy especially important.

Details of the semic code drew these children into the book and kept them riveted. They found strong empathetic links to themselves in Bilbo's behavior and appearance and in Gollum's plight. These *personal/empathetic* feelings fostered *sociocultural* literacy when details of setting stirred their imaginations and allowed them to see gaps and to fill them through connections they made, based on prior life and literary experiences.

Events of the actions code—motivations and conflicts of characters—led to thoughts about personal/ethical choices (what they would do; what Bilbo should do). Thus *personal/empathetic* feelings led to *critical* literacy. Questions about the cultural code (whether hobbits were real) fed into the pleasure these children took in making up their own creatures. (Tolkien was doing what they liked to do.) Thus the author–reader relationship was strong.

Gaps feeding the enigmatic code produced a question-posing stance important for *critical* and *sociocultural* literacies. But *personal/empathetic* literacy carried the day; that the children saw Bilbo as a person in many ways like themselves served as a path into *literary* and *critical* literacies. Because these children were following Bilbo's fortunes so closely and responding to his quest, they noticed important narrative patterns and constructed ways of building narrative structure. Thus key scenes arose for them based on these perceptions, and the scenes, in turn, enabled them to make *intertextual* references, follow the actions code in all its semic intricacy, and remain invested emotionally in the story.

Ultimately, in exploratory conversations, ideas raying out of the symbolic code, such as Bilbo's ongoing conflict of whether to engage in adventure or to retreat from it, led to the children's even stronger empathy for the character. *Personal/empathetic* and *aesthetic* reading strengthened their desire to engage with the various strands of the authorial coding, finally to think like authors themselves, considering narrative perspective (who is telling the story, who is seeing the story) and narrative strategies like backstories, motivation, and plotting. *Narrative* and *literary* literacies interweave more easily for children if they are writing or creating literature at the same time they are reading it. And if they are composing in the same genres they are reading, so much the better.

It seems reasonable to conclude that these children liked reading fantasy for the same reason they liked creating it. "You can do anything you want," said Vinny when I asked why they liked making fantasy stories (as opposed to realistic fiction or nonfiction). "You can make up things, draw special things, let your mind wander anywhere as far as you can, and put it on paper. You can invent the people, the adventures. You can put anything in it; you can make anything you want for the plot. It's your story. You are being free. You can make up different kinds of characters, wars, weapons, treasures, and creatures like hags and werewolves." In a similar vein, Mark said, "With fantasy, you can do anything you want 'cause it's *your* story. You know you didn't do those things, but it's *your* story. I like to invent things no one ever thought of."

Fantasy enabled these children to go anywhere, as far as they could go, taking pleasure in the author's inventions, playing new roles, becoming many different otherworldly kinds of characters—or being, as Vinny said, "free." The objective for them was not a story product; it was the experience of entering more deeply into characters' lives to play the becoming game. Thus fantasy took them more deeply into *personal/empathetic* literacy, and it made them more responsive and more deeply engaged readers (*aesthetic* literacy).

## REFLECTIONS

If children find fantasy important, then they need to participate in this form in the role of author reading, writing, or telling it as often as they wish, to explore fully and deeply the conventions and narrative strategies of fantasy. Then, as they take even greater pleasure in this genre, they become more competent users of it. When they are exposed to rich literary coding or as they move from simpler to more complex coding, they internalize new ideas for stories of their own. And we should also value children as researchers. Vinny embarked on his project of reading, listening, and responding to *The Hobbit* at age 12, when many children might not be hearing stories read aloud (often adults stop reading to children as soon as children can decode print) and might not even be allowed to tell rather than write stories. And a great deal of creative energy is lost in the process. Some children write fluently and read unreluctantly very early on, and they should be encouraged to do so. Many other children need to tell or record their stories so that they see themselves performing as authors at the same time that writing fluency is building and catching up with ambitious storytelling ventures.

Had writing been the sole requirement for Vinny's literary output, he would never have seen himself as an author, a storymaker, and a creative person, with much to share about literature and child worlds. Had Vinny been creating this story in the Gnome Workshop school setting, he would have presented his taped story or some part of it and then decided for himself what he would do next: take a favorite part of his story and turn it into a piece for the classroom story collection (written or taped) or create new stories like his adventures of Chubs, from this one.

In other words, on the way to perfecting children's *print* literacy skills, we must not risk losing their growing strength in *literary* and *narrative* literacies. We need to open up spaces to talk—and tell—about what they find puzzling, incongruent, and important in stories, those of the author's and of one another. Children need to see things in terms of their own sociocultural worlds, even as their vision is being stretched beyond it; therefore they need opportunities in social contexts for sorting out story enigmas, testing unexamined assumptions about story worlds and real worlds, noticing details and patterns in stories, and then reshaping them in terms of their own child values and ideologies. They especially need to encounter and create fantasies.

Some educators are not fans of fantasy; even the most famous fantasy classics may not be well known to them. Some adults experience a strong fear of fantasy for various reasons (Mikkelsen, 1999), which often leads to acts of censorship. Even more adults, with good reason, may find children's fantasy writing difficult to understand and deal with—time-consuming at best, tedious and confusing at the worst. But beyond the simple fact that certain fantasy texts such as the Harry Potter books, although they might not be great literature, at least draw children into reading, the fantasy genre has exceptional value for children trying to make sense of the real world.

Inviting fantasy writing into the classroom does not mean trying to help children become better at writing or creating fantasy; it means helping children to become better learners generally. Children creating fantasy, as we have seen here, become better synthesizers, weaving life and literary experiences with feelings and ideas related to their own child worlds. In creating fantasy, children have opportunities to explore what they are learning through literature as it connects to their view of their world and their own personal/ethical choices. In the process, we learn more about children and their many worlds.

Drawing from Dyson's research (1989) involving the intersection of multiple worlds that children negotiate when they take on writing processes—real and imagined, artistic and intellectual, social and symbolic—Tom Newkirk (2000) identifies six worlds or "cultures" that he discovered in one student's stories: "outside expertise," "visual representation," a "toy or video culture," a "friendship culture or social world," a "curriculum culture," and a "culture of established literature" (p. 297).

I saw similar worlds intersecting in Vinny's reading of *The Hobbit*. He drew on "outside expertise" about the German *blitzkrieg* of World War II and of Russian-American antipathies during the Cold War in order to sort out aspects of Tolkien's story and to conjecture about authorial choices, and his historical interests had ties to school or the history "curriculum culture" without ever crossing the line into efferent goals (*using* literature to teach history).

He translated his reading to a "visual representation" of his own symbolic world when he painted a Dungeons and Dragons figure as Bilbo, fashioned his own ring of invisibility from a paper clip, and drew scenes for his own story. Knowledge of a "popular [toy/video/film] culture," including a cartoon picture book and film of Tolkien's work, enabled him to sort out puzzling aspects of the book.

Talking about the book, role-playing scenes of it, and singing the dwarf songs with Mark produced a peer social world or "friendship culture" that brought the two children closer together and closer to the book. Vinny's decision to produce a story as we finished the book revealed ties to the kind of storymaking he had previously done in extracurricular literacy activities like the Gnome Workshop. Books like Yep's *Dragonwings* entered his story and contributed to a "culture of established literature." And he could step back, thinking about other books and stories he had read, and decide that everything was a fantasy; everything was an adventure.

I saw other worlds too. One was a *world of play* that bubbled up from Vinny's personal/empathetic feelings, when he "became" Bilbo or stepped into the scene of Fili and Kili playing the harp. Closely related to this imaginary world was a *dream world*, where goblins from Tolkien's secondary world entered his unconscious "thinking" and one of his dreams involved finding an invisible ring of his own (life and literature interweaving). Interfacing with these worlds was the *fantasy world* of the book, filled with dragons that needed to be tracked down for connections to the *real world* of dinosaurs and lizards. (Were dragons, dwarfs, and hobbits real? How tall was a hobbit?)

There was also the *world of the author's cultural coding*, filled with puzzles about tea cakes, intriguing activities like making smoke rings, and drinking wine or beer, that intersected with the interests and preoccupations of his own real or experienced sociocultural world and the personal/ethical choices he faced. Tolkien's ability to engage him through the actions and enigmatic codes served an important function: Vinny paid close attention to the semic code, details of which fitted easily with his personality construct, developmental stage, reading style, and narrative meaning-making at this time and freed him to become a member of this new fantasy world quickly and easily.

There was, in addition, what Vinny saw as a *world of adventures*—psychic and real (looking for a bird, fighting a dragon, sailing the sea)—that intersected with the *world of the book* and with questions that arose for him as he entered more deeply into it. (What is a hero? Who should fight the dragon, Bilbo or Bard?)

All of these worlds led to meanings and understandings about a *world of authoring* (his own and that of others) where there were differences between adventures for characters and for readers, where inner conflicts could become adventures, and where an all-knowing narrator had fascinating power. In this world, a place where you joined others engaged in the literature and literacies process, you could question an author's narrative choices and speculate about alternative authorial visions (Who should kill the dragon—a man or a hobbit?). And if you didn't like the author's answer, you could re-"write" the story *your way*—putting something into the world that wasn't there before.

So it was not just that these children entered more readily into *literary* or *narrative* literacy because so many of their own child worlds were intersecting as they responded to *The Hobbit*. It was that the intersection of all these worlds deepened their *aesthetic* literacy. And this condition strengthened the effectiveness of all the narrative codes to work together for the children's meaning-making abilities, causing them not only to read a richly coded story but to reshape it in terms of their own child worlds. If fantasy lies at the heart of children's literature as its most inventive and exuberant genre, quest fantasy surely lies somewhere close to the heart of fantasy as its most enriching and important form, as we also see in the next chapter, when we examine children's responses to a work that blends history, folklore, fantasy, and multicultural aspects with a female quest figure—something *The Hobbit* certainly lacks and that might very well affect female responses.

*Chapter Seven*

# Into the Woods:
## *The Magical Adventures of Pretty Pearl*

THE SUMMER AFTER I read *The Hobbit* with Vinny and Mark, I found myself in a dilemma. Several months earlier, I had submitted an article focusing on Virginia Hamilton's *The Magical Adventures of Pretty Pearl* to a journal in the field of children's literature. To my surprise, the editor wrote to say that I would first need to establish that the book was a *children's* book, as there was some debate among the staff about its status. It seemed a simple enough task; the jacket said, "Ages 11 up." But how authentic were publishers' recommendations? What makes a book a *children's* book? Who decides these things—and how?

I wrote to the publisher and received no answer. Then I encountered Virginia Hamilton at a conference and told her my story. "The best children's books are for everyone," she told me, meaning that the best children's books had an adult audience too. But I still needed to know if this book would appeal to children.

To find answers, I could turn to those who had defined the term "children's book," based on theories and speculations about child readers. My own favorite theory of this subject was that of Myles McDowell (1976): "[A] good children's book makes complex experience available to its readers; a good adult book draws attention to the inescapable complexity of experience" (p. 143). Or I could turn to actual children to test McDowell's theory. As Margaret Meek (1987b) asserts: "We need particular examples of children reading, in order to test these [adult] guesses," and more comparisons of the "readings and rereadings done by both children and adults" (p. 111).

My own two children, ages 11 and 13 at this time, seemed to be at the most likely ages for the book, and one night at the dinner table I appealed to them. How could I know if this book was truly a *children's* book without their help? They readily agreed. Like all the children I worked with, they liked being invited to become researchers in response ventures; it meant their ideas were valued. Vinny read the first 50 pages, but summer was

well under way, with sports events and activities with friends taking up
his time.

Soon after the school year began, I found myself reading the book aloud
to both children, and they had enlightening responses from the beginning.
Mark, however, had an all-consuming fascination with Lloyd Alexander's
Prydain Chronicles at this time; whenever he had a spare moment, he
wanted to return to *The Black Cauldron* (1965). These books were funny and
adventuresome, he told me. "They have 'zing' to them."

When Vinny came down with a cold one week that fall, I seized the
moment, reading Hamilton's book aloud as he sat weaving an Indian belt
for a crafts project. He didn't mind listening to long books like this one, he
told me; he could do other things as he listened. And as Hamilton would
later tell me, "A lot of times my books have a degree of difficulty and they
have to be introduced and parts of them have to be read aloud before kids
feel very comfortable with them" (Mikkelsen, 1994a, p. 404).

## *THE MAGICAL ADVENTURES OF PRETTY PEARL*: ADULT RESPONSES

*The Magical Adventures of Pretty Pearl* is the story of a young goddess, Pearl,
who travels from Africa to America in the 18th century to help the Africans captured as slaves. Two centuries pass as she waits to see what she
can do. Once immersed in human culture, however, she succumbs to
human ways, forgetting the rules laid down for her by High John de Conquer, her older brother (and "best god") and losing her magical god power
to become human and dependent on human luck. The novel is essentially
the story of Pearl's growth (physical, emotional, moral, and mental), or
her passage from childhood innocence to young adult experience. And
what makes it exceptional is the way Hamilton blends nearly every kind
of fantasy—transformation, time, quest, folk, and historical—as she in-
scribes her readers into authentic and amazing African-American cultural
experience.

Her major characters are three mythic African gods who, in their
various magical transformations and special abilities, could mingle with
African-American humans to help them in one of the most turbulent
periods of American history, the post–Civil War Reconstruction era. But
two of those gods—John de Conquer and John Henry, linked here as god-
brothers—were also African American folk heroes. John Henry is the post-
war industrial hero confronting his adversaries, men or machines, with
physical power. John de Conquer is the legendary slave trickster, operating and surviving through secrecy, cunning, or mental power.

The third god is Pretty Pearl, god-sister of both heroes, created especially by Hamilton for this story. Thus the book is also a modern creation novel, for Pearl is prototypical, creating herself as she moves through time and allowing Hamilton great latitude for exploring many possibilities for child growth and exploration. In the beginning what moves Pearl and her quest into action is that she yearns to "come down from on high" (p. 5), as the novel states at the beginning. She is bored living on Mount Kenya, and in her growing god-power, she sees the African humans captured by other humans, and Pearl becomes curious and concerned. Creating folk gods as her characters thus enables Hamilton to show, in subtle ways, some not-so-pretty-parts of American and African history and to help readers see African-American heroes victorious in battles against injustice.

In Pretty Pearl's strong pride, competitive spirit, and childlike impatience lie the seeds of both potential weakness and strength, mixed as they are with her deep, caring spirit. All she can do is watch; she has no power to do anything else, until High John (John de Conquer) decides she is ready to move on to the next god-plane, that of god-woman in America. Deeply buried inside Pearl is a future self, an adult character and parent figure who materializes in Pretty's place when she needs to become the adult, yet is conceptually not ready to do so. (Unlike human children, as High John explains, god-children have different "parts" they must fit at different times, rather than parents to guide them, and they can call on these different parts when they need them.)

Pearl's having a powerful parent figure within (rather than over) her broadens her power: By exercising power she will be better able to conceptualize her growing power and make better personal/ethical choices. Her power is extended further when John allows her to choose four of his ancient, invisible African spirits to take with her on their journey to America: a tall, powerful woodpecker; a dog with a sharp tail for cutting trees; an ugly, two-headed monster to scare others; and a young, sensitive man-spirit, Dwahro, for brotherly protection. She can bring the spirits to life whenever she chooses, as long as she controls them. He makes Pearl a conjurer, one who uses magical power to summon spirits, just as he is an enchanter who turns them both into albatrosses (birds no superstitious white slaver would ever shoot) perched atop a slave ship that carries them to America; thus John and Pearl have a safe passage.

What makes *Magical Adventures* unique is not only the way Hamilton blends many kinds of fantasy with a multicultural subject, but the way she uses fantasy to show children and adults grappling with so many complexities of human experience. Pearl's moral growth depends on whether she will see that the wise use of magical power is determined by responsible and unselfish actions and choices. Creating a harmonious social order depends on following rules based on social principles that exist for the good of all, not just anyone who feels a need for power (communal versus individual needs). The question is, can children deal with these complexities? And if so, how?

### THE MAGICAL ADVENTURES OF PRETTY PEARL: CHILDREN'S RESPONSES

Vinny journeyed through the book in four stages, related to four different "chunks" of the book. In stage one (Chapters 1 through 3), both he and Mark had questions about the cultural and semic codes. Vinny began building a meaning base for the story with initial questions about Pearl (Who is she? What is she?) and comparisons to comic book characters he used as intertextual reference points.

In stage two (Chapters 4 through 8), he responded to the symbolic, cultural and semic codes by theorizing and speculating. *Sociocultural* and *personal/empathetic* literacies fed into *generative* literacy, as magical aspects that continued to emerge in the semic code led to deeper engagement with the text—or the emergence of *aesthetic* literacy.

In stage three (Chapters 9 through 15), the cultural and enigma codes, as they intersected with the symbolic code, were especially important for him, so he stepped into a period of deep wondering or questioning of pondering solutions. Again, magical aspects of the story, and other stories he knew—plus a strong *personal/empathetic* relationship with the child character, Pearl—helped him sort out the narrative coding. In stage four (Chapters 16 through 18), he was resolving the actions code in terms of the symbolic, cultural, and enigmatic coding, so he began drawing conclusions and bringing closure to his reading process through his strong alignment, his empathy, with the child character.

And a much later fifth stage emerged as a post-story exploration in which he began shaping the book to his life or drawing sustenance from it. *Sociocultural* and *narrative* literacies were strongly in play at this time, the result of his strong bonding with the John de Conquer character and his *aesthetic* engagement with the book as a whole.

### STAGE ONE: INITIAL QUESTIONS

**Chapter One**

As he hears the first lines of the novel, Vinny is filled with questions about Pretty Pearl: "Who is she? What is she?" he asks. Hearing the first page, that Pearl is a god-child living on Mount Kenya, he answers himself: "Pretty Pearl's a god," he says. "She's a goddess." Then he continues by comparing her with a cartoon character: "Reminds me of Storm. She's a lady in the X-Men. She comes from African Kenya; she's known as a goddess." Then he remembers a difference: "But she isn't really. She's a mutant. She had power over the land. She acted like a goddess, made everyone think she was. People would bring her chickens, sacrifice chickens and pigs to her and then she'd bring rain to the barest trees."

"How did she come to be?" I ask. "She's a mutant," he repeats. "She was born with certain powers that set her off from humans. She can change the elements. She can make rain suddenly appear, lightning, and snow. She can control the weather." As a mutant, Storm is a valuable character that Vinny can draw upon in his repertoire of intertexts: She helps him to know more about a goddess (Storm has power over natural elements, powers that set her off from humans, and she can change things). But Vinny knows that Storm is not a real goddess, so he wonders if Hamilton's characters are also mutants: "Are they really gods or what, or are they just saying they are gods?" A few pages later, he seems to have decided. When Mark enters the room asking what the book is about, Vinny answers with certainty, "Gods, different gods."

Moving into a book with so many new ideas embedded in the cultural code is not easy for these child readers. There is first of all the initial setting, long-ago Africa, where humans (white or black or perhaps both) are capturing other humans and sending them off to America, all the while that gods stare down at the horror. Mark is puzzled, as Vinny had been, about gods living on a mountain: "I thought gods stayed in the clouds." Vinny wonders if Africans are capturing other Africans.

Later in the book, the setting shifts to a forest in Georgia, where Pearl will find the hidden ex-slave community, during a time when lawlessness and racism resulted in white brutality against African Americans, and nothing in the children's repertoire of texts prepares them for this place or the inhumane events such as lynchings.

The language structures are not what they expect; Mark says he gets "all the words confused in my head"; Vinny thinks the characters should speak British English, as he has heard Africans speaking in movies.

Finally there are the characters, gods who are born complete and have parts they must fit and tests they must pass in order to take on these parts. That Pearl, a god-child, has two parts, rather than two "times" (childhood and adulthood), is certainly a challenging concept for these child readers. But talking together helps all of us to see more:

> *Mark:* The person when they grow up they're gonna have this part. But right now they don't have it and, like, when they go down

to earth, she's not going to need it because—I don't know why she's not going to need it. I know where the other part of the body comes from but I don't know why she wouldn't need it, the grown-up part. It may be because this is like, if you were an adult, it'd be so easy. But if you're a kid, you have to do something hard to get more power. Like they have to prove themselves good when they're young, so when they grow up they'll be good rulers.

*Vinny:* That's sort of like Indians. They had to take a test to become a man.

*NM:* He says he's going to leave the grown woman part to watch over the mountain. And he could do that because he was the [high] god and had the power. He could leave the woman part or call her [the woman part] later because he said the god-children need a mother to watch over them.

*Vinny:* Like he would sort of use half of her—like her soul.

I ask about "tests" in other books, to see if *intertextual* literacy can foster *generative* literacy, and they talk about samurai knights jumping into spikes. "Sharpened bamboo," Mark says, "and if you survive it, you become a warrior. If you don't, you die." Vinny says Indians had to climb 50-foot trees. They talk about Taran's tests in the Prydain Chronicles, and Bilbo passing the test of bravery, becoming "a good adventurer," as Vinny remembers.

## Chapter Two

When Mark returns to his Lloyd Alexander books, Vinny and I read on. He wonders what Pearl sees as she enters the forest and finds a charred shape hanging from a poplar tree. (Pearl, with her great empathy, says, "'Be my poor heart hangin' there—yes, it is!'" [p. 27].) I decide not to interrupt the flow of story to give answers at this point, reasoning that if this is really a children's book, the text itself will either unfold the answer as we proceed, or leave the image as a mystery the author intends—a blank space of text—that child readers like Vinny will continue to ponder. And ultimately the image (or the lack of explanation for it) does thread its way strongly into the enigmatic coding for him.

I read about John giving Pearl two shifts or dresses before she leaves (one is short, for the child part; the other is long, with an apron, for the adult part) and Vinny begins talking to sort out this new concept: "She's got two parts," he says, "the woman part and the girl part and the woman part stays behind while the girl part goes on the adventure. Like the woman part has to stay behind to look after the babies, while the girl part goes on the adventure." This two-part configuration will continue to resurface in his thinking as we move through the book. It is a dominant metaphor of the story for him, and he continues to revisit it, studying it from different perspectives, as he revisits other images that puzzle and disturb him, like the charred "shape" and Hunger, the personified shape that Pearl tries to beat to death.

## Chapter Three

"Remember when Hunger picked up that girl?" he asks as we begin Chapter 3. That John in his dreams rises up to help others and make their "spirits grow" (p. 43) is another complex metaphor that causes Vinny to double back to the event involving Hunger, a scene that is still puzzling and intriguing him. Through the actions and semic codes, Hamilton has made concrete an idea of the symbolic code (how invisible gods respond to human needs): John de Conquer has turned himself into a real person, battling hunger/Hunger by tossing a hungry child through the air to a caring person who will feed her. And suddenly the semic code is causing Vinny to see things from four perspectives—human, god, adult, and child:

> *Vinny:* I wondered if it was really like a person picking her up or was it like she stopped and the wind blew in her face? Like to the gods it would be him picking her up [helping her escape Hunger] but to the humans it would be her being stopped and the wind blowing. Could she see him? I know she could hear him.
>
> *NM:* The little girl would see it as—
>
> *Vinny:* Him picking her up.
>
> *NM:* Yes, as a real picture.

## STAGE TWO: THEORIES AND SPECULATIONS

## Chapter Four

As we begin reading Chapter 4, Vinny continues to sort out aspects of the cultural code, such as whether there is such a thing as a coachwhip snake. But when Pearl suddenly turns into Mother Pearl (the child needing her adult part now), after a wrenching inner struggle, he must also pay more attention to the symbolic code, or what things mean and why. And the way he does so, based on his own experiences (*sociocultural* literacy), gives him a chance to explore the personal ethical choices that confront him in his own child's world:

> *Vinny:* It's almost like her conscience, like if you're gonna do something and in a way you don't want to do it. And like you have something like a fight with yourself inside. Let's say I want to jump off the house, I'd say yes but another part would say, no, you might get hurt. Her conscience.
> *NM:* Would the part that told you not to jump win over the part that told you to do it?
> *Vinny:* For some people it's difficult. Some would say, "Smoke! Have a puff; have a smoke." Inside says, "Yeah, go ahead."
> *NM:* So you think there are parts of her and one part tells her not to do things and one part—
> *Vinny:* Conscience, good and bad conscience.

Mother Pearl tells Dwahro, Pearl's spirit-brother, about the work they will be doing when they reach the forest place where the Inside People are hiding; then she reminds him that he will be working for both her and Pretty Pearl, meaning that he must respect Pearl's power, even though she is a child. As the chapter unfolds, Vinny extends the discussion by thinking further about how Pearl's two-part construction works and using *sociocultural* references to his own life (his own two-part construction or his child-to-adult continuum) to navigate textual complexities.

> *Vinny:* In between one and two, you're both one *and* two; like she's halfway between adulthood and childhood. It's like one and one half; if you're rounding, it would be two, but more or less, it's two *and* one.
> *NM:* So she's something like an adult and something like a child—
> *Vinny:* If you had two books and could refer to either one of them, instead of just one, ok, if you were halfway reading both of them—like you're a kid and you only have one book and you've finished with that one book. You can only refer to one book. When you're an adult, you've read the other book, a higher-level book, and you can refer to that book. But when you're in between, you can refer to either one of them. Or you could use, like if you're doing a project, you could use information from this book or this book, instead of just being an adult with this one or a kid with this one.
> *NM:* You have choices.
> *Vinny:* Let's say your birthday comes around and you want to get a

new bike, but you've already got one bike. Ok? Your old bike,
ok, so your birthday comes and you've got two bikes. Now see,
the whole thing is, you just don't, well you could just throw
away the old bike, but you don't want to. It's sort of like one
day you could ride the new bike and one day you could ride
the old bike. You'd have two bikes. You just wouldn't ride one
of them if you had two. Like let's say you want to go to a
friend's house. You want to show off your new bike.

*NM:* Yes.

*Vinny:* Or let's say one of them is a ten-speed that's your new bike
and your old bike is a three-speed. Ok? You've got this hill.
And you can change bikes at will.

*NM:* Yes.

*Vinny:* You get halfway up the hill and you're getting tired with
your three-speed. It's not doing you that much good, so you
just change to your ten-speed. And you go all the way up it. So
it was getting too confused for her and tiring and her young
self. She had to go to her older self.

Using details of the semic code to explain Pearl's two-part construction, Hamilton again takes complexities of the symbolic code—growth,
change, ability, power, and wise use of power—and makes them visual and
accessible for child readers. Similarly, Vinny, in order to sort out the continuum of child and adult, innocence and experience, powerlessness and
empowerment, creates "pictures" of bikes and books, things from his own
life experiences, to explain Pearl's puzzling experience in the forest. He
adopts Hamilton's narrative strategy for his own reading strategy (he reads
the world in order to read the text).

**Chapter Five**

When in Chapter 5, Mother Pearl asks Dwahro to paint her picture on
the apron, picture within apron picture, Vinny helps himself to understand the "infinity" picture, which will later enchant or mesmerize the
murderous white bandits so that they can do no harm to Mother and
Dwahro, by producing a concrete picture of his own. "It's like me standing in front of the TV," he says, "and inside the TV picture, there's
another me standing inside the TV. And inside that TV is another me
standing inside that TV. And in that TV there's another me in the TV. It
goes on forever; I'll draw you a picture." And he does. (Again he adopts
Hamilton's narrative strategy for his own reading strategy: it opens up
the pictures of complexity.)

I read the passage in which the bandits march Mother Pearl and Dwahro to the poplar tree at gunpoint and Dwahro agonizes about his predicament, and I wonder what Vinny will make of it. He tells me, but then veers back to his major interest, the two-part construction of child-gods, and this time he is thinking about why, not how: "I've got something to say about one and two and why she can be a woman and a child." He has been studying the jacket painting for the book (Romare Bearden's "Under Morning Skies"), with its vibrant colors of blue sky and a tall woman in red, and it causes him to construct more pictures for the continuum of both child and adult and human and spirit worlds, pictures that show people not as compartmentalized but as fluid states, just as colors bleed together—or mix—to make new colors:

> *Vinny:* 'Cause if you're the color purple, you're just not purple, you're red and blue.
> *NM:* Oh, uh-hum, yes, wait a minute. Who's the purple?
> *Vinny:* She is.
> *NM:* Pretty Pearl. And who is red then?
> *Vinny:* She [Pearl] is blue and the lady [Mother Pearl] is red, and I guess the [god] spirit is purple.
> *NM:* Which spirit?
> *Vinny:* The spirit when she's not in any form at all.
> *NM:* When do we have that in the book?
> *Vinny:* In the beginning [on Mount Kenya].

Once the apron picture muddles the bandits' minds, Mother Pearl and Dwahro prepare to tie the humans up in the poplar tree. I ask Vinny how he feels about this event (this ironic reversal of the lynching we had earlier seen in the charred shape hanging in a poplar tree), and he replies: "They probably won't [kill the bandits] 'cause they're gods; [they're] supposed to be good."

The paradigm of fairytale morality—clear-cut good and evil—shifts here to a different way of seeing, an adult way: gods (and humans made in their image) are mixtures of good and bad. But Hamilton keeps the child's perspective in mind: Mother Pearl and Dwahro pull the ropes under the bandits' arms, not around their necks, leaving a possibility for someone to cut them down. "Do you think they'll die?" I ask. "No, well, I guess they do," Vinny replies. "I don't think they would, but they probably would." I ask how he would feel about them dying. Would it bother him? And he says, "No, they're evil."

## Chapter Six

As we continue, having left the bandits (never to see them again, as it turns out), he continues to ponder their fate, saying later, "I wonder if those people are still hanging on the tree." Still later, he returns also to the charred figure hanging on the tree, saying, "I'm still wondering what was that thing hanging on the tree." The two hangings, the two horrific images of violence, may be one of the things that causes adults to wonder if this is a children's book. I decide to respond to Vinny's question about the bandits with another question: "Do you think they're still alive?"

"I think animals probably ate them," he replies. "Snakes crawled on them."

Mark, who has dropped by to listen, adds, "Vultures got them." Does that make them sad, I ask. "No," Vinny says. "They were evil; they [the bandits] were going to kill them [Mother Pearl and Dwahro—and possibly the Inside People], if they had stumbled into their hiding place in the forest."

Vinny has questions about the cultural code: Are the Inside People black or white, is this happening *after* the Civil War, and if so, why would white people make black people work for no pay, and we talk a little about residual feelings of anger and racism after the war.

> *NM:* Do black people today enjoy the same rights as white people?
> *Vinny:* They don't make them work [without pay].
> *NM:* But do they get paid as well?
> *Vinny:* Yes.
> *NM:* Do they get the best breaks?
> *Vinny:* No.
> *NM:* So back then, right after the war, how can we suppose they
> were being treated?
> *Vinny:* They weren't getting any pay.
> *NM:* They had been slaves and the white people were going to try
> to get what they could out of them, weren't they?

He asks how the Inside People remain safe in the forest, and we talk about the strategies they use to stay hidden. He wonders if High John will come back into the story, and says he wants to see the "little Hide-Behind thing" (the spirit in Pearl's necklace that can frighten people if it escapes). He is also intrigued by the questions Dwahro continues to ask about the two-part configuration of Pretty Pearl: "But how'd they *do* that?" Dwahro asks. "How'd they *divide* in two like that?" (p. 110), and Vinny draws once again from his intertextual repertoire, thinking this time about another one of his comic book characters, Kitty Pryde of the X-Men, who also appeared in two ways:

> *NM:* You said yesterday when you were watching cartoons, you thought of Pretty Pearl being in two parts.
> *Vinny:* It was something to do with the future and present and Kitty Pryde, who was young in the present, like a teenager, went into the future. The "future" Kitty Pryde, who was older, went into the present, and the older Kitty Pryde helped them out during battle because she was experienced—from the future. From fighting, she knew all this stuff . . .
> *NM:* What was she like in the present [her teenage self]?
> *Vinny:* She was young, un[in]experienced. She didn't know how to do stuff . . . The way she walked and stood was more like a woman than a girl . . .
> *NM:* And that's like Pretty Pearl?
> *Vinny:* Yes, 'cause there's almost like two of them, the older one and the younger one.

**Chapter Seven**

In Chapter 7, after Pearl has entered Promise and met other children, she begins asking herself the same questions Vinny asked about her when the story began: "What am I, Pearl Perry, first from Mount Highness, now from de forest? One moment she would feel the feelings of the Mount; the next she would know her heart as a runaway heart finding safety inside a great, continuing darkness of trees. Pearl sighed. Who want to be of a lonely Mount Highness?" (p. 123).

Pearl's fractured sense of self (divided as she is between two locations—Africa and America) places another lens on her two-part configuration of child and adult, one that Vinny notices:

> *Vinny:* She could be talking to herself, saying "I like this place." Another part of her said, "It's not as good as Mount Kenya." And then she said, "Who needs that place." The child inside of her says, "Who needs that place, 'cause she wants to go—all that stuff on the ground" [the brambles in the woods that hide them].
> *NM:* And the grown-up [part of her]—?
> *Vinny:* She needs to go back and see it.

And this is just what Mother Pearl does as the book ends, although Vinny has no knowledge of this scene yet. What he notices in Pearl's sighing is a child growing up and away from certain times and places. The growth metaphor—leaving childhood behind to take up adult life—is what he focuses on—and what Dwahro also continues to revisit.

## Chapter Eight

At the end of Chapter 8, Dwahro finally has his moment alone with Mother Pearl; she has promised to tell him how she and Pearl were able to split in two when they arrived in Promise. And Vinny continues to sort out how Pearl and Mother Pearl can coexist in two separate forms now, perhaps because he, like Pearl, is a child involved in the same child-to-adult continuum of growth, a child who, in terms of his own *personal/empathetic* literacy, can use aspects of his own reading of the world to sort out aspects of the actions and symbolic code as they are intertwined:

NM: She was divided in two now—

*Vinny:* Maybe she wasn't sure which one she was going to be so she turned into both like which one she needed the most, like she decided she needed both of them. If she'd brought the other one there, maybe the mother part is the spirit too, just the spirit of her own self. Like they said, she was in the root, and they rustled her out, brought her out. Maybe she's just another spirit—a spirit of her own self.

NM: Yes.

*Vinny:* She wasn't real sure which one she needed.

NM: Have you ever felt that yourself? Some kind of struggle inside yourself over things that you wanted and knew you needed to do?

*Vinny:* Yeah, to make up a test or go home and watch TV.

NM: And what did you do?

*Vinny:* Went home and watched TV.

NM: It didn't split you in two? One Vinny stayed and took the test and one Vinny came home?

*Vinny:* The smart one would have stayed and made up the test.

NM: She was struggling with both too, wasn't she?

*Vinny:* Last year I had two favorite shows I used to watch, *The Master* on Friday and *Matthew Star* on Saturday. He was an alien. But he looked just like humans, and he could, when he was in big trouble, or had to get through something, he'd just

lie down and concentrate and he'd stay there and another him
would go to that place. One would be like a dead trance, and
the other one would be walking around.

*NM:* How did he do this?

*Vinny:* He had magic powers. Alien ability, because one part he
was in a car accident, about two seconds before the car crashed,
he did it [transport himself], and everybody thought he was
dead, and he went back and found himself in a coffin and he
got out.

Once more, Vinny draws on references from popular culture to sort
out the story. And it is magical power, he reasons, that enables both Pearl
and Matthew Star to exist in two different places at the same time, a fascinating ability he would also like to have. At this time, when he is growing
and wishing for more power, magical power is his vital interest and preoccupation, and it is also the centerpiece of the story. Almost immediately,
as the book began, he noticed the narrative perspective ("You get to see
everything that's going on," he had said, "it's got the god-type point of
view"), which is closely linked to the magical powers of the gods: "John
de Conquer," he observed, "could turn them into birds. He could make
spirits and keep part of her [Pearl] home."

Power to cast spells, make transformations, transport oneself into two
separate parts at once: All of these fascinate him and keep him not only
moving through the book alongside the characters but delving behind the
characters' words and explanations to see more (the intersection of *personal/
empathetic*, *literary*, and *aesthetic* literacies).

### STAGE THREE: DEEPER QUESTIONS

Vinny is following many different characters as we travel through the book:
He is moving through the story *with* Pearl, feeling what she is feeling because he, too, is a growing child. Yes, this is a children's book; but it is also
something "else," a rich, multicultural fantasy for all ages. Vinny is listening to and trying to answer Dwahro's questions, because like the spirit god
who wants to become human, he is moving—or growing—between two
different states or spirit worlds, childhood and adulthood; and he is wondering when High John will reenter the story, because, as "best" god, John
de Conquer is the one with the greatest magical powers. He is also continuously concerned about the charred shape hanging in the poplar tree
and he is still thinking about the bandits hanging from a poplar branch;
both present lingering questions for the enigma code. And he may be

making a connection between the shape and the bandits when he continues to wonder about each.

He continues to be intrigued by the personified, magical shapes that Hamilton brings to life: the spirits of the root necklace, especially the Hide-behind, "the little thing that can run around and scares people," as he calls it, and Dwahro. He is balancing all of these characters, keeping all of them in mind as the story unfolds. He needs to do so to "read" the actions and symbolic codes, and he can do so easily because the story moves in a recursive pattern, circling around to pick up the threads of characters and events as things move forward (Mikkelsen, 1994b).

### Chapter Nine

At the end of Chapter 8, Mother Pearl mentions the Hodag and the woodpecker (the Fool-la-fafa), to remind Dwahro that he is not alone in his own fractured state: He is neither god nor human, he constantly complains. And Vinny is reminded of the root spirit she does not mention, the Hide-behind: "Does that Hideaway thing really do something in the book?" he asks. "Does he actually appear?" The Hide-behind will appear later, in Chapter 11, when Pearl sets it free to scare the children and show her magical importance, an act that breaks High John's rule and causes her to fail the test for god-womanhood; but for now it lies dormant in Pearl's root necklace.

At this time, Vinny is also wondering about new characters he is encountering from among the Inside people—Black Salt, father of Pearl's new friend Josias, and Salt's friend Old Canoe. Thus he is forming new empathies and interests with both adult and child characters, just as Pearl is doing.

Wondering is what Vinny does most often now, in this third stage of his journey through the book, now that suspense is building and magical power will be important for the actions code. "I wonder if Black Salt will come back," he says as we are reading Chapter 9. A few pages later, he hears the phrase "Josias, son of Black Salt" (p. 156), and he makes a new intertextual connection, between the way they describe relationships of elves in one of his comic books (reading it aloud to me to demonstrate his point) and people in this book. In both, he says, "they give you background, so you know who the characters are related to. They also did it in *Beowulf* [children's versions of this ancient legend that we read in the Gnome Workshop]—a whole bunch there."

### Chapter Ten

"I wonder what's happening to Black Salt and Old Canoe," he says as we begin reading again. "They've got Dwahro behind them, and he's invisible." The word "invisible" reminds him of magical aspects of *The Hobbit*. And when he hears about Maw Julanna, disguised with leaves in the underbrush so that she can warn them about intruders, he is similarly intrigued. "I'm going to think of this the next time I go to the woods and it's real quiet," he says. The pigeons that carry messages from the Inside People to the Cherokees outside Promise also remind him of *The Hobbit*: "It's like that bird in *The Hobbit* that could talk, the raven that brought the news back to the hunter so that he could kill Smaug the dragon." Again, drawing parallels from his prior fantasy reading helps him sort out details of the narrative coding.

**Chapter Eleven**

When we reach the chapter in which Pearl lets out the Hide-behind, Vinny learns from the semic coding that this spirit is ugly and he doesn't like it. Still, the creature is important to him for its magical properties, and he asks if the Hide-behind will reenter the story. In his transitional state from child to adult, Vinny can see—from an adult perspective—that what Pearl did was wrong: "I know what the older Pearl would say—that it was foolish to waste it, the Hide-behind, to use it [her full power] when she didn't really have it yet." But, like Pearl, he cannot see why the Hide-behind has escaped—that in letting it out, she has not only wasted her god-power, she has lost it. "Do you think she'll be able to get the Hide-behind back?" I ask. "Yes," Vinny replies as Pearl is also thinking at this point: "All she has to do is touch the necklace."

   Although he sees Pearl hunting for the Hide-behind in vain, Vinny, like Pearl, doesn't see Pearl's fallen state in the withered root necklace, so he ponders a solution: "I wonder if she scraped some off the root and made a [John de Conquer] bush, could she make another one to keep it in?" And when nothing seems to work for Pearl (to make matters worse, the Hodag has now escaped the necklace on its own, further proof that Pearl has lost her god-child powers), Vinny says, "It's weird. Somehow it got out without her letting it out." (He shares her child's perspective, that she had done nothing "wrong"; thus, as she begins to see more about her situation, so will he.)

**Chapter Twelve**

When Pearl finds herself stirring the cook pot (Mother Pearl has gone to the woods to bring back the escaped spirits), she watches the human children: "Wish I was you! she thought. Thought I was, but I ain't!" (Pearl has godly responsibilities, not total freedom, and she is beginning to see this.)

"They had different morals," Vinny decides. "One released the Hide-behind. The other wouldn't have. The mother wouldn't have lost her temper; she would have been patient." Like Pearl, he is beginning to see that Pearl, in violating one of High John's rules, has made a mistake. (One part of her thought only of herself; the other part thought of the consequences.)

But like Pearl, he still doesn't see that she has lost her god power. "How do you suppose the mother [Mother Pearl] could bring back the Hide-behind and she [Pearl] couldn't?" I ask. "She knew how to do it; she was more experienced, like Kitty Pryde was," he says. (As Pearl will later see, however, the Hide-behind knows that Mother [Pearl] still has power and authority, and it shows respect for that power by obeying her.) Like Pearl, Vinny doesn't understand why her foot aches at times (she doesn't see that High John has sent this painful warning the day she let out the Hide-behind), and Vinny's reasoning remains closely intertwined with hers. "When she's in danger it aches," he says. (High John is now angry that she has let the Hodag escape.) "It was a warning of what might happen," Vinny says.

**Chapter Thirteen**

At this point, when Pretty Pearl wilts in appearance and won't touch her food or talk or sing (her "fallen" state, concretely "pictured"), things slow down; and Vinny becomes bored, or similarly disengaged, alongside her. "Do they ever move on [leave Promise for the outside world]?" he wonders. "I want them to be safe, but it gets boring." He confesses that he could read the book to himself, "'cause the words aren't that hard but it's just too long. I can't stand long books." He doesn't mind hearing it read aloud, he says.

*Magical Adventures*, like all of Hamilton's books, is not plot-driven; it is a story of unfolding character and drama, humorous wordplay, intriguing moral dilemmas, hard facts of history subtly introduced, and a carefully constructed enigma code that is becoming stronger all the time now and keeping Vinny strongly engaged. "Maybe the reason they're having trouble keeping the Hodag in and controlling it, maybe the reason the root is crumbling is [that] there's two roots at one time now," he says. An interesting point: Pearl's power was weakened when the two parts of herself split—and because her sense of direction is lost, her quest of helping the Inside People is faltering, too. This we see when the Hodag destroys the forest trees.

John Henry has entered the story now, and Vinny needs further explanation of the cultural code, so I tell about him blasting mountains to make tunnels, the Big Bend in West Virginia, the railroad coming through. "You know all the tunnels we go through going to Grandma's house?" I remind him. He has heard folk tales about John Henry, but he listens with interest as I recall details of the story, like John Henry dying with his hammer in his hand. And when John Henry tells the Inside people about the "Ku Kluck" riding every night in Kentucky, Vinny wants to know more about the KKK: "I don't understand how the KKK can still live [today]," he says, "'cause they said most of them were Civil War people." And we talk about inherited and acquired factors of racism:

> Vinny: Are they relatives [of the original members] or new members or what?
>
> NM: No, it's just like a club that's always been around, like the DAR [Daughters of the American Revolution]. Well, that is inherited. But the KKK is probably inherited, too. If your father was a member and you grew up around that, you could get in, if you had the same attitude.
>
> Vinny: What was Black Salt supposed to do? [in terms of the risks that the KKK presented at that time]
>
> NM: What effect do you think John Henry had on him? [Black Salt, who didn't want to leave the forest place where they lived in hiding]
>
> Vinny: Probably changed his ideas about hiding.
>
> NM: Made him feel like if he did leave, that—
>
> Vinny: That he might be able to find some way.
>
> NM: To survive, yes, maybe, although it wasn't going to be easy, because he said one half million of the black people were in the North; the rest—four and a half million—were in the South. And between Georgia where they were and the North, you've got to go through Kentucky where the KKK were riding every night, and they killed people, and slaughtered people. If you can get to the North, he's saying, it's going to be a little bit better for you.

## Chapter Fourteen

"Somebody reminds me of John Henry," he says suddenly, returning to his intertextual collection of popular culture figures: "Power Man, a black superhero, has a headband; he's real strong, muscular. Also, Colossus is an X-Man. He's strong. The Hulk." He is finding a way to visualize John Henry, to place a folk hero into the story, alongside the gods, John de Conquer and Pearl, and spirits like Dwahro.

## Chapter Fifteen

The Indians have their own appeal, too. Thomas Groundhog, who guides
the Inside People to the outside world, gains Vinny's notice when he hears
that "With his bow and arrow he [Thomas] would bring them prizes of wild
game, turkey and rabbit . . . He never once had to shoot his gun" (247).

"They don't have guns," Vinny says about the Indians, with approval.
"I might make up an Indian mutant named Thomas Groundhog."

High John is on his way to the Inside place of the forest, too; his drum-
beat sounds, but Pearl doesn't hear it. "I don't know why she can't hear,"
Vinny says, further evidence that, like Pearl, he still does not see her god
power waning. But he senses it. "Funny how gods can dream and sleep
but spirits don't," he notices. "Dwahro is always *practicing* sleep." I mention that Mother Pearl doesn't sleep either, but Pearl does. "She's not a full
spirit yet," he decides. "She hasn't fully taken responsibility yet."

Then he begins thinking again about how Pearl became divided into
two beings, and suddenly he reverses the visualizing process Hamilton has
set in motion with her images of two shifts and two Pearls to represent the
two-part child-to-adult continuum. He can see magical power as *psychic*
power now, revealing that he is starting to conceptualize the complexities
for himself, without benefit of concrete images (complex fantasy books enable children to grow in *literary* literacy as they navigate the complexities):

> *Vinny:* At the beginning of the story, they said usually people can't
> separate themselves, that normal gods couldn't make people
> split in two, but since he was John Con-care he could. Since he
> was John de Conquer, the big master, he could do it; he could
> make them able to split. I wonder if he wouldn't have put the
> spell, if there probably wouldn't be two Pearls. Instead of
> becoming two of them, she'd just *think* to herself. They'd [the
> two Pearls] would be inside her head instead of outside her
> head, when he gave them the power to split in two.
>
> *NM:* He said they had parts they fit into—
>
> *Vinny:* But only he could actually make them appear, 'cause he was
> John Con-care.
>
> *NM:* He said he was going to leave one part on the mountain; is
> that what you mean?
>
> *Vinny:* Yes, I wonder what would happen if he wouldn't have
> given them that power. They would just have changed places
> inside her head [as adult and child feelings often change places
> in human heads]. And they [the gods] would have the same

form but two different spirits [inside their heads], instead of two different forms, but one spirit [one individual person]. It wouldn't be two different people, not a mama and a girl. It would need a new character. One person.

*NM:* Would she have been a child or an adult?

*Vinny:* Both—a child, confused a lot, going with her mama intuition and her girl intuition. She'd get mixed up a lot, deciding what she ought to do. [She'd be a child with both childlike and adultlike feelings.]

Vinny's ability to turn the concrete into the abstract reveals his strong empathy for Pearl's imminent realization of her fallen state, his recognition of High John's authority—what she will also soon see—and his strong belief in High John's magical abilities. The suspense has been building up to the scene of High John's visit to the forest, where he confronts Pearl about her lapse into human behavior. "What' s going to happen to Pretty Pearl for letting the Hodag out?" Vinny asks.

I read the next passage, about John de Conquer weighing their actions on a scale of Mount Highness godlike behavior: "He put each one of them on one side of the scale and their deeds on the other. The one who did not balance the scale with the proper deeds would have to answer for it" (p. 255). I ask him if he thinks Pearl's deeds would balance on the scale. "It probably would," Vinny decides, taking the same forgiving stance as Mother Pearl. "She was young and not experienced."

But John is not so lenient. Pearl was never supposed to hurt any human children out of spite or anger, High John reminds her. "She didn't hurt them," Vinny protests. "She just scared them." I ask if scaring the children could have hurt them, and he remembers that some of the children tripped and fell in the brook. High John clarifies this idea of hurting children as one of feelings or intentions, rather than consequences: "You felt like hurtin' and scarin' child'ren on de long path . . . You was bein' mean, and so you did it" (p. 258). And John's comment enables Vinny to connect Pearl's feelings with her appearance after letting out the Hide-behind and to understand better the complexities of the symbolic code that Hamilton has been unveiling through the semic code: "She got ugly 'cause she was mean," Vinny decides. "Sometimes people get ugly when they get mean. Maybe it was a punishment from the gods, John de Concare. Maybe a sign." (He sees multiple possibilities.)

At this point, as Pearl sobs: " 'I forgot . . . I was just . . . livin' like a free chile, and I forgets all about de god child. I just forgot everythin'!" (p. 259), I ask, "Wasn't Pearl free, as a god-child?" And Vinny makes the connection that a "free" child is a "regular child, a regular human child." When I ask again, "Isn't a god child free?" he says no, a god-child has "more rules." He is beginning to see more clearly the difference between a human child who has freedom of choice and a god-child whose freedom, like that of human adults, is limited by responsibilities, and the gravity of Pearl's mischief-making with the root spirits, just when he needs to see this: High John is ready to make his decision about Pearl—that her bad deeds outweigh her good ones.

When John places his hand on Pearl's head, producing a sharp pain that causes her to become suddenly pretty again, Vinny says, "I guess she became ugly when she disobeyed him, and when she learned and was punished for it, she became pretty again." But Pearl still doesn't see that she has fallen into humanness at this point (that High John cannot or will not restore her to her original god state). *And neither does Vinny.* What he notices and emphasizes instead is that she has learned from her lapse. Hearing the words, "No longer was she Pretty Pearl of the Mountain. But this she had not come to realize" (p. 260), Vinny, his perspective still closely entwined with Pearl's, says in surprise, "She's not a god-child anymore?"

## STAGE FOUR: DRAWING CONCLUSIONS; BRINGING CLOSURE

### Chapter Sixteen

Near the end of Chapter 16, John Henry helps Pearl see his fate—that he will trade immortality for life. The god trick, he tells Pearl, is that High John knows what he will choose—to beat the steam drill—and that is his punishment for "bein *bad*" (p. 277). Thus John Henry prepares her for her own punishment, telling her that " 'To be human is about worth de whole world, to my mind'" (p. 277).

Vinny understands why "John Henry's face was resigned and sad" (p. 277). "They'll become human," he says, seeing what Pearl herself will see in the next moment, when I read: "Pretty Pearl was rigid, holding herself in. She started trembling. She couldn't form the question she had to ask" (p. 278). "What is the question?" I wonder. And Vinny knows: "Are you human?" he replies. But for him at this time, being human does not mean that Pearl loses her power entirely. Neither he nor Pearl notices at this point that she no longer has her magical god power. Both believe—or want to believe—that the new John de Conquer root that Mother Pearl tied to Pearl's necklace for good luck is not a "sad" thing.

"She could still turn them invisible," Vinny decides. "You think she still has her power?" I ask. "Yeah," he replies, "but we won't know till she uses the new root." No sooner does he say this than he hears that when "Pretty touched the de Conquer root Mother Pearl had given her . . . Nothing at all happened" (p. 278).

"It doesn't work," Vinny says sadly, foreshadowing Pearl's next words: "It don't have de power" (p. 278). And as both Pearl and Vinny are beginning to see now, she doesn't have her power, either. (The root has lost its magical power because she has lost her power over it; now—like all humans—she must simply depend on it for good luck.) "Is she turning human, too?" Vinny finally asks. And when John Henry tells Pearl, "It never did have as much [power] as you" (p. 278), he says in surprise, "Was it really her doing all the power things that time and not the root? The root was just—probably before—she thought it was the root doing all the power. Was it *her*?"

## Chapter Seventeen

He is, like Pearl, adjusting to Pearl's new human state. When Mother Pearl fills Pearl with stories, just before she and High John fly back to Africa once again as albatrosses, and Pearl, who is not sure if she is awake or asleep, tries to remember something she has forgotten (her life as a god-child), Vinny understands her feelings, and he says: "She isn't sure if she is human or not." Finally, when the birds fly away, he adds: "The god part went up, the human part stayed down. Her god adult part went back to the mountain, Mother Pearl."

"Will she grow up to be an adult here in America?" I ask him. "Yeah, as a human," he replies. "Her soul is now going back to the mountain." I wonder if what happened to Pearl (that she lost something so important, her god state) was fortunate or unfortunate. And his answer echoes a theme running through so many time fantasies: that children can see parallel worlds of the past or future, but once they become adults, the ability to see those worlds is gone.

> *Vinny:* Only one part of her became human, the part that had already passed, like your childhood is now a spirit, like a god, cause you're not that anymore. You grow up.
> *NM:* Is there still a part of her that's a god?
> *Vinny:* Yeah, Mother Pearl. It's like there's a part of you that's human, that's with you right now.
> *NM:* Is human?
> *Vinny:* Uh-huh.
> *NM:* You don't think that she and Mother Pearl were separated at the end.

*Vinny:* I did, but it's just like maybe your child part of you is now somewhere else in a different time zone. It's the past.

## NARRATIVE CODING, MULTIPLE LITERACIES, AND CHILD WORLDS

Older children who are traveling between the worlds of childhood and adulthood have a great deal to tell us about books like *Magical Adventures* that emphasize the continuum of child to adult growth and the past as a place in the mind. And I counted myself fortunate that I was present to hear Vinny's responses at this time. Reading the book alone, I could never have seen or expressed things in the book just this way. Guessing or even theorizing about a child's responses, I would never have foreseen these responses; they stand alone as those of a child journeying toward adulthood, and listening to them, we learn more about both the book and the child and about both a child's world and a *child's* way of reading.

Vinny's way for this book, and this reading of it, began with his puzzlement about the actions code of the book, although the cultural code, as it played out in the actions and semic codes, was producing his questions at this stage. (The enigmatic code was just beginning to surface for him.) He drew upon life and literary experiences to make initial meanings of the story (*generative*, *sociocultural*, and *intertextual* literacies weaving together).

He continued with more questions and long, extended comments about the symbolic code as it played out for him in the semic code (the cultural code was still causing puzzlement, too). Empathy with the characters, particularly the god-child Pearl, deepened his ability to tell his own story of the story alongside the author's (*personal/empathetic, sociocultural, intertextual,* and *literary* literacies intersecting).

As the story continued to unfold, he moved into a speculative, wondering phase. At this point, the cultural and enigmatic codes were playing into the symbolic and actions codes, but he was able to build his own scaffolding for meaning-making because he had a firmer grip on the story now. His storying about the story took him deeper into the story; he even wondered what might have happened had John de Conquer not given Pearl her two-part configuration. He stepped into the authorial role, considering alternative narrative strategies (*narrative, aesthetic,* and *literary* increasingly strong *personal/empathetic* literacies).

Finally, he began drawing satisfying conclusions about the story. The actions code was resolving itself for him in terms of the symbolic and cultural—even the enigmatic—coding, although he was still puzzled about the charred figure on the poplar tree. Near the end of the book, when he wondered aloud once more what this figure was, I asked what *he* thought it was. "A heart," he said, referring to Pearl's saying when she saw the charred figure, "Be my poor heart hangin there."

"Her heart?" I asked.

"Her soul," he replied.

And in many ways Pearl's caring heart, her spirit, her strong empathy and deep involvement with the Inside People, was her most distinguishable part from beginning to end. Vinny's *personal/empathetic* literacy was at its strongest now, and for a child who did not know that those who were lynched in this era were also set on fire (and nothing in the scene of Mother Pearl and the bandits supplies this knowledge), his interpretation was a sound one. The all-knowing god-child Pearl would have had this cultural knowledge, but neither Vinny nor the fallen god-child Pearl—in her innocence now—had this knowledge. So both he, the reader, and Pearl, the character—the children-turning-into-adults—had to make meaning of things through the way they read the world at this point in time.

And this wasn't the end of his reading.

## STAGE FIVE: POST-STORY EXPLORATIONS

All the time Vinny was hearing the story, he was shaping the book in terms of his own child worlds. But as the last pieces of the puzzle fell into place, he was free to begin reshaping his own child worlds in terms of the book, a process—or fifth phase—that took place over the next 10 months, at least the part that was visible to me. (The deep structure of children's responses go on to affect their friendships, social values, moral development, ethical perspectives, life work, and lifelong reading.)

As the book ended, Vinny told me that Dwahro was his favorite character and that the Hide-behind was his favorite creature, although it turned out uglier than he liked. If he could have had a creature of his own, like Pearl had, he would have liked a dragon that flew and breathed fire, he said. And soon after hearing the book, he began making a book of his own, one he called *Gods, Volume I.* He began with a God of Falcons, with large eyes that "can see a rabbit from two miles up and spot an ant at night and could mentally change from arms to wings." Then he added a God of Polar Bears, with magical spear, "small ears, thick fur for heat under water, and thick pads to allow silence for stealth." Both of these creatures, because of their magical power, had more affinity with John de Conquer than Dwahro or the Hide-behind. It was clear, even some 10 months later, that High John had left a powerful impression on Vinny.

The next summer, after a day at the beach, we were heading home, driving down a four-lane highway in North Carolina, when his father—with nearly magical eyesight, or foresight—heard a kitten's cry and stopped abruptly, double-parking on a four-lane road that runs through Morehead City. "Steer the car," he told me as he ran back, scooped up the kitten where it had wandered into the busy street, and ran back to the nearest house, dropping it at the door, then rushing back to the car. "How did you even hear the cat crying?" we all kept asking, but my husband seemed to have no explanation. He simply heard the sound and knew the cat would be killed at any moment.

"Dad is like John de Conquer," Vinny mused that night, clearly in awe of what he interpreted as a magical act:

*NM:* Really?

*Vinny:* Dad said he knew when the cat's time had come, and John de Conquer had something to do with life too. He knew when and when not to save it. He knew when the time had come, the right moment.

*NM:* For intervening in the slaves' lives?

*Vinny:* Yeah, John knew when the time hadn't come for death and birth and everything else.

*NM:* In Georgia, you mean.

*Vinny:* Yes, he waited two centuries. He could have come down and killed all the white people and saved all the slaves, but he knew the time had not come yet to save them, so he sent down two spirits to help them—Riley and Johnson. He saw that all things were in the right order—orderly for Mount Kenya—and the whole world.

Two weeks later, Vinny was still thinking of John de Conquer, even though it was nearly a year since he first heard the story. Once again we had made a day trip to Emerald Isle, where he had spotted a shark. He told his father about it; then he and Mark accompanied their father as he walked up and down warning swimmers of the danger. And just as Pearl assumed her place in the world as a cultural storyteller of her family history, Vinny and his brother found their own place in the larger social community that day, helping to save lives. Afterward, Vinny could only marvel again: "First Dad saved the cat; now he's even got more magical powers, 'cause he saved four humans.

"And I'm somebody, too," he added. "'Cause I saw the shark."

By this time, John de Conquer had become Vinny's favorite character: "'Cause he is real powerful," he told me, "he can do a lot of stuff—turn into an albatross, make people turn into two different people, and make a root to help the spirits." Magical power was what fascinated Vinny about the fantasy genre, and this fantasy was no exception. If he could be anyone in the book, he said, it would be John de Conquer, and he'd want to have the same powers. Pearl was important to him because at the beginning she had magical power, too, and it was through her eyes that he took in and absorbed all these magical experiences. Dwahro was nearly as important because his questions kept Vinny sorting out Pearl's actions and feelings (and Dwahro is a particularly appealing character). But for Vinny, John de Conquer had ultimate and *lasting* magical power.

## REFLECTIONS

John Henry, the character that I, an adult reader, had found so moving in his struggle to test his god strength, never surfaced in Vinny's repertoire of favorite memories of the story, perhaps because John Henry had chosen to turn his magical god power into human willpower. And it was *magical power* that drew Vinny into the book and kept him there throughout. As Dorothy Strickland, reviewing the book for *Language Arts*, said, "Children who are lovers of fantasy are most likely to gravitate toward this book and stick with it" (1984, p. 298).

Geraldine Wilson, writing for *Interracial Books for Children Bulletin*, also commented on the magic: "Don't miss *Pretty Pearl!* The book will provide you with magical spiritual moments, some belly laughs" (1984, p. 18). She was concerned, though, about ambiguities that deserved greater authorial explicitness: the role of white slavers that Hamilton never identified as white and the charred figure in the poplar tree that remains unexplained.

Most children's books are written explicitly to fill all gaps; most are also written to connect with and safeguard children's sensibilities. In Hamilton's book, many sensitive passages, such as the bandits' harassment of Mother Pearl and Dwahro, are also compelling for their explicitness; others have deliberate ambiguities. And the question arises, should children's books—as a rule—have to be explicit? Might they at times leave gaps and blank spaces for children—the ultimate *writerly* text? Might they accept and trust child readers to construct satisfying and logical meanings on their own terms? Says Jane Yolen (2000): "Some critics would have us believe that opacities have no place in children's books; that a story must be transparent or apparent, that a child must not be frustrated in his or her understanding of a tale. But to filter out the opacities for the child reader is to rob the tale of its magic" (pp. 32–33).

For Hamilton to produce an authentic multicultural experience, she needed to propel her child readers into this traumatic time quickly and without explanation, in order to convey this jarring moment of the past with all its horror—and all its sublime spirit. What Vinny talked about most easily was what engaged him in terms of his own child's world—the magical powers of Pearl and High John. And what makes this particular fantasy exceptional is that Hamilton was able to sculpt a story so strongly in tune with children's sensibilities and yet, at the same time so important for them, in multicultural terms.

Multicultural fantasy is one of the richest untapped veins of children's literature. Its ability to break away from, play with, and expand conventions promises to become one of the best ways for helping children become more perceptive about ethnic literature. Insiders of various parallel cultures can not only share their histories, tell their stories, and enlighten children about the American scene in all its color and diversity, but they can do so in magical, mind-bending ways.

Yet two decades after Hamilton published this book, there are still few examples of this particular—and important—genre. And when children have few models for a genre, they must use all their resources as they go along, including popular culture. Thus they need a wide array of intertextual sources—both fiction and nonfiction—from which to draw, and they need adults as co-partners to help bring their ideas to conscious awareness, through talk and creative ventures.

Adults need to bring alive books like Hamilton's, with all their complexities, either by introducing them with an opening chapter or by reading them aloud in their entirety. It is not usual for 11-, 12-, and 13-year-olds to be read to by adults, but these two children did have teachers who read aloud up through their sixth-grade years, just as I read aloud in the Gnome Workshop, and they always welcomed this story time with great pleasure.

With books such as Hamilton's, adults might also want to have on hand works related to lynching and other racist acts of the Reconstruction era, outlying communities of freed slaves, the Middle Passage, legendary figures like John Henry, and folk characters like John de Conquer. Joyce Hansen's *"Bury Me Not in a Land of Slaves": African-Americans in the Time of Reconstruction* (2000) is a particularly good reference book for children in this respect. And Hansen's fictional portrait of Gustavus Vassa (Olaudah Equiano), *The Captive* (1994), the African kidnapped and sold into slavery in 1788, explores the complicated interweaving of African and white American and European complicity in the slavery trade. Then, if questions arise about the historical background of the book, adult and children can investigate sources together.

Exploratory conversations about all these books are particularly important for helping children grapple with images of violence, whether subtly revealed in fiction or explicitly narrated in reference books. Children whose lives are very insecure, children whose families do not read fantasies—or who do not read together at all—and children touched by real-life violence might read fantasies such as Hamilton's very differently from children who have experienced violence only through the prism of literature and popular culture. Talking together in social contexts, they could help one another to see more.

Adults also need to make spaces in the day for writing about and dramatizing scenes that focus on puzzling events of the past and mythic and legendary characters and for creating art and stories to extend children's literary experiences—including stories that resist the text. (Hamilton's fantasy world is certainly a patriarchal one; High John is a male god who must "rule" on Pearl's lapse of judgment. What might female readers produce as stories in response to this book?) Given the rarity of multicultural fantasies, children's contributions to the genre would be especially welcome and would tell us more about how children, given their particular genders, ethnicities, cultures, and nationalities, view themselves as self-actualizing persons.

What makes this book so important is that it enables readers of all ages to conceptualize their own potential power in the world, based on—or inspired by—the power that multicultural children and adult characters possess. Just as I was inspired by John Henry's courage, Vinny was deeply engaged by Pearl's and High John's magical power. Vinny not only grew as a reader as the book unfolded, but he began exploring the idea of power as it played out in the folk legends and multiethnic history of the book. He was dealing with issues that mattered to him (humanistic concerns) or exploring personal ethical choices, therefore revealing growth in what we might call *ethical* literacy, as when children see the vulnerability of mice, grieve for a melting snowman, recognize injustice in the lives of fish and meat, defend the right of "little people" to slay a dragon, and learn about the use of power for good or evil.

Vinny took the journey *with* Pearl: What she saw he saw, just as she saw it. What she learned, he learned, just as she learned it. He was never one step behind or ahead of her; he time-traveled with her into the Georgia forest to relish her power, and when she lost it, he relished the power that High John, her god-brother, still had. Magical power was what engaged him deeply in fantasy stories—the transformations, the casting of spells, the risk-taking, the adventures, the all seeing eye that can outsmart Hunger— all of which he found in abundance here. And because Pretty Pearl made the journey from childhood to adulthood, and Vinny was skating between these two times, the emotional content of the book tapped into his personal, social, cultural, and narrative worlds, and he was able to make greater sense of the larger world, in terms of the way he read the book. He used the book to make sense of the world, and the world made better sense because of the book.

We can scarcely ask more of any book, and that is why, if the best children's books are those for everyone, it is important that we consult with children when trying to determine whether a book is really *for* children. Children are a significant—if not crucial—part of the "everyone"—very likely the most important part. The best books might, in fact, be those that adult and child read together. It is not simply that some books are complex and need at times to be explained. It is that children's books are better understood by adults if children are our partners in learning. Children have a great deal to teach us about their worlds, and children's books can be magical gateways to what children know and see and *are* in those worlds. *Children will listen*, as the Stephen Sondheim song title says; the question is, will we?

# Conclusion:
# Embracing Fantasy, Inviting Response

THROUGHOUT THIS BOOK, my thesis has been that children have a great deal to teach us. As collectors—"word-catchers"—of children's responses, we learn more about children, books, children's ways of reading, and their ways of viewing the world. If we are reading children's books alone or with other adults, we produce only partial "works": We need children's words and ideas to complete our own readings. By eliciting many responses—from one child or any number or children—we discover there are countless, constantly changing worlds within any one child and multiple worlds within the body of people we designate as "children." Thus we need to value difference and variety above convergent thinking about what children—as a monolithic body—should be saying, doing, or feeling.

We also need to value sustained time with children to develop full and rich pictures of response. Because of the current emphasis on literature-based teaching, there has been a great deal of discussion about ways of using children's books in school settings. But if we are going to talk about classroom use of literature, we first need to conduct in-depth studies with children or to produce portraits, rather than mere snapshots, of response. Such studies must take place in both personal and social contexts, and often they must occur outside the classroom where adults have time to evoke and extend children's responses to literature.

With greater knowledge of child worlds, we will be supporting children's natural learning during a reading event, rather than influencing or predetermining that learning. If we are reading to children or entering into their meaning-making with natural and spontaneous responses of our own, we will be extending their—and our own—meaning-making by the questions we ask, the modes of response we invite, and the conversations we encourage. As partners in thought, we will see not only what meanings children make of texts but how they are doing so. And we need to know how in order to make our practices better. Children show us the various

literacies in which they are likely to engage as they respond to literature—
and the more literacies that emerge, the better.

## LITERATURE, LITERACIES, AND RESPONSE

As we listen to children responding to texts, in a rich reading, strands of
literacies can rarely be separated; interweaving is everything. But we need
to separate—or unbraid—these literacies in order to talk about them, or to
see how they interweave—and do so easily—when readers make meaning of complicated texts.

We see children producing texts in different ways, depending on their
strategies and intents at a particular moment or reading. If they are building some satisfying meaning for themselves, through the choices they make
to shape and reshape their ideas in preliminary readings, they are involved
in what I have called *generative* literacy. From the start, they will be bringing to bear their *sociocultural* knowledge, experiences, and associations
about the world upon the text, and the text will be, in turn, reshaping their
knowledge about the world.

*Sociocultural* reading allows *generative* reading to happen. The more
children understand about the world, the more easily they will generate
meaning. Then, as they read and reread, they will weave strands of story—
or stories—into more meaningful and more satisfying textual patterns; they
gradually will move into *literary* and *intertextual* literacies, depending on
their interest in the story or the characters from this and other stories they
have encountered.

From the beginning, however, children are drawn into generating texts
by their immediate or gradual building interest in the characters and their
ability or desire to engage with characters in *personal/empathetic* ways. Then,
if they have a particular book or story that invites "walking" around inside the text, inventing a text with the author, as they puzzle out what they
make of the world and of themselves, as well as of the story, they will be
engaging in what we might call *narrative* literacy. And the more writerly
the text they are reading (the more gaps, the more blank spaces), the more
engaged they are likely to become in this particular kind of literacy.

The more absorbed they become, living through the story as one of
the characters, the more actively and deeply involved they become in the
reading event, the deeper the pleasure they take in the story, the more
strongly they will be engaged in *aesthetic* literacy or what we might describe
as being lost in the book—what we hope will happen in any reading event.

Children might accept everything about a text just as it is—and they
will be more accepting when they are concentrating merely on decoding

words. Or they might question or resist an author's evaluation of the world, especially if the author's ideas deviate widely from the realities of their own lives or values. Thus they will be engaging in *critical* and at times *ethical* literacies.

What causes any one of these literacies to emerge or become noticeable during a particular reading is very likely the intersection of several factors:

- the reader or readers (age, gender, reading interests, reading experiences, personality construct, sibling position, sociocultural background, ethnicity, nationality all play a part) and the interaction of the reader with other readers in social contexts;
- the text (with its unique characters, plot, setting, and genre) and the intersection of that text with other texts the child has encountered;
- the reading event (time, place, duration, kinds of questions or ways of questioning or conversing that occur, peer involvement, additional activities or modes of response);
- the mediation process that the child or adult chooses for the event;
- the narrative strategies or coding that the author and/or illustrator use.

Although there is no predictable sequence in which literacies emerge, the general sorting out of texts often gives rise to *generative* literacy early in the reading event. A reader's interest in a story, the result of *personal/ empathetic* bonding with characters or *sociocultural* meaning-making, arises early to strengthen *generative* literacy. Increased interest also leads to the emergence of *aesthetic, narrative, literary* or *critical* and *ethical* literacies, in a recursive pattern of readers circling around to pick up different literacies as the event moves forward. A tapestry of interwoven literacies is thus the result. And it is just this interweaving that we will want to see as often as possible if *aesthetic* literacy is to develop and deepen. When many literacies are operating simultaneously, the response is richer, and the insights readers gain are more plentiful, striking, and memorable.

## LIVE CIRCUITS OF RESPONSE

What causes this burst of literacies is often some special moment of insight arising in a reader, or among readers responding to a work together as they help one another to see or to see more—a very visceral relationship between child and book. As Rosenblatt (1990) has asserted, the reading event is "dynamic," not static, a "transaction" producing "the active role of both reader and text in interpretation" (p. 106), rather than an "interaction." Instead of a fixed merging of author and readers' ideas, it is an ever-changing, "to-and-fro relationship" (p. 104) between reader and text during any particular reading, which gives rise to the work itself. In other words, a book is not a "work" until the reader's personal interpretation brings it into existence.

When children produce full and rich responses to literature (spontaneous, sustained, enthusiastic, meaningful), we can look at particular books to see how they read the textual coding and how they deal with complexities of innovative texts and illustrations. Exploring the narrative coding leads to questions like: Is the book especially rich in any one code or codes, or is there a strong interplay among them all? Is there a pattern of expectation and surprise as the events, scenes, and conversations unfold (the actions coding)? Is there a pattern of growth and change in details of character and setting (the semic coding)? Is the book rich in a child's world of cultural coding (what children know and accept about the world)? Does the emotional content of the story tap into child worlds? What scenes, events, details, mysteries, and puzzles are stimulating children's meaning-making in terms of the symbolic code (the overarching ideas and themes of the story)? What codes are most important in terms of *child* readers, or is there strong interplay among all the codes?

Did the semic code evoke the child's imagining (often a sign that the book is engaging the children or—for children—the book is really a *children's* book)? Did the enigma code (what is left implied or unsaid) elicit children's interests and keep them moving through the story, filling gaps and blank spaces, telling stories of their own alongside—or within—the author's story? Did aspects of all these codes gradually help to generate ideas for a symbolic code (overarching ideas for the story)? Did the child reader move alongside the child character, discovering more about both real and fictional child worlds, as the story unfolded?

Richly coded books elicit many different literacies in children's responses when children are involved in naturally emerging reading conversations and storymaking ventures. But unless we elicit and study children's responses, we can only assume a book is richly coded based on our own responses. A good book, from a child's perspective, means that children are extending literature to fit their own meaning-making strategies and their own child worlds—and that the book is extending their field of literacies.

Children shape literature in terms of their own worlds and reshape their worlds in new and different ways after reading books that evoke their deep engagement with the book, or their *aesthetic* literacy, which emerges when many other literacies are arising and interweaving with one another.

*Personal/empathetic* literacy is often the strongest instigator of all the other literacies, particularly of *narrative* and *aesthetic* literacies. The emotional content of a book is its primary value for child readers.

*Sociocultural* literacy (how children bring their worlds to bear on the text and the text to bear on their worlds) is, on the other hand, important for affecting *generative* and *literary* literacies. (Children shape the story to their own worlds to make sense of both literature and life.) And *narrative* literacy, in turn, leads back to all of these literacies. How much richer children's *aesthetic*, *literary*, and *sociocultural* learning is when children are invited to perform as authors, making their own creative choices, which in turn show adults which books are the "best" ones. Children are capable of discovering the best books for themselves in terms of their own *personal/ empathetic* and *sociocultural* needs.

## LIVE CIRCUITS AND CLASSROOM PRACTICE

When teachers invite children to respond naturally and spontaneously in many ways to literature, and when children negotiate complexities of stories and explore personal and ethical choices as they talk, draw, create stories, and engage in role-play and exploratory conversations, they produce rich responses, and teacher and children both learn more because they are working together as response partners in an ongoing cycle of response events. If teachers invite children to become partners in response, if they allow children to become researchers of their own literature and literacy processes and make space in their curriculum for the children's research choices, everyone grows through response.

Eliciting and observing children's responses, teachers see that stories change from child to child and from reading event to reading event; they also see that children's responses can differ significantly from their own, and that children can articulate their own meanings and values, bring unconscious ideas and feelings to conscious awareness, and produce a more complete knowledge base for the entire group. Children's resistant reading and storymaking opens up even more doors to child worlds for all to see and learn about.

The simple question, What would you like to do (draw, write, role-play, talk about, sing, dance, investigate, think about, learn about, read more about, make, tell as your own story) after hearing or reading this story, is often all we need to ask to keep the response cycle going. The simplest prompt is the best; children immersed in literature do not flourish from our agendas. We simply need to provide many opportunities for reading and conversing about many books (children make greater strides in navigating complexities of literature when they draw from a rich bank of *intertextual* sources).

Talk is the crucial link between children and their books and their storymaking. Children as co-researchers reveal which books they like. What they notice, see, remember, and story about show us what is important to them. *Aesthetic* literacy evokes *narrative* literacy because child readers often want to extend the pleasure of the reading transaction with storymaking, if invited or allowed to do so. What children notice and remember in a book and how they fill gaps and blank spaces to make sense of puzzles, tell us how children are reshaping the book in terms of their own child worlds. Their ideas tumble out easily when they decide to respond with stories; then we see what they find interesting. If we do not know what sustains children's interest in books, we are at a loss for ensuring children's passage into *narrative* literacy.

The desire and ability to make stories of their own—to alter the world and produce social action—is very important for child readers. Of the many literacies in this field, the *narrative* one is so important that oracy becomes a literacy of its own. Children learn new and different ways of storytelling and expand their own literary talents when they are invited to engage in storymaking responses. Those who are encouraged to read in terms of their own preoccupations and to tell their own stories alongside the author's develop a kind of agency that frees them to change the world (creation as social action). Children hearing stories tell stories that shape literature to their experiences of the world, just as their experiences shape their stories. And fantasy is a particularly meaningful genre in this regard.

## THE IMPORTANCE OF FANTASY

Fantasy helps children explore new worlds far from home through adventures that involve risk-taking and danger, and it allows them to explore disturbing questions from a safe distance, such as, What is important—safety or freedom, what is a hero—or heroine—, What does it mean to have an adventure, What does it mean to be brave or to be really free, and What does it mean to have power, especially magical power? Rescuing something of great importance—a special friend in *Alexander and the Wind-Up Mouse* or a magical object or treasure in *The Hobbit*—adventuring with a friend in *The Snowman* or *The Hobbit*, or wrestling with important personal choices with characters like Louis or Pearl, children can examine the world in deep but exciting ways.

Transformations in fantasy stories appear to have a special attraction for children, perhaps because they are undergoing so many transformations in their own growth processes and they are witnessing so many changes in themselves and their worlds that have no logical explanation. Magical power gives children strength at shaky points in their lives when they need it most. Adventuring with a fantasy hero or heroine and composing fantasy adventures of their own are important ways for children to come to grips with overpowering emotions. The sense of imagined magical power helps them and their characters through frightening, puzzling, and oppressive conditions they often face. It is a talisman to guard against the dark moments. "I am fighting the dragon, and I am winning," Mark, age five, wrote on his drawing of a tiny knight and a large green dragon. And the same spirit reemerged for both children as they read *The Hobbit* together five years later.

Reading fantasy is both a way to make meaning about life and literature and a way of altering the world, and children exposed to rich narrative coding in fantasy works internalize many new ways of seeing for stories of their own. The more shapes of fantasy children encounter, the more they understand about life and literary worlds. But they need time to talk about what they find puzzling in the enigmatic code or disturbing in the actions and semic coding. And they need many ways to deal with texts that do not match their conceptions of the world.

Mark created a new ending for *The Snowman*, a happier ending that he needed to see, and in doing so he dealt with emotional complexities on his own terms, just as Keith resisted this book entirely, choosing another more in tune with his own child's world. Brooke talked back to Louis's mother as she read *Louis the Fish*. Rhoda and Amy reshaped *Alexander and the Wind-Up Mouse* for a different gender emphasis. Vinny rewrote the ending of *The Hobbit* so that his hobbit character was fully in charge, and he drew on a rich bank of intertexts for generative meaning for *The Magical Adventures of Pretty Pearl*.

In terms of narrative complexities, children need time to notice details and patterns of the semic code that support the actions and symbolic codes and produce key scenes for them. And because key scenes contain deeply engaging mysteries of the enigmatic and cultural codes, they show us where the emotional content of the story is for children. Children who become deeply engaged with the semic code build a sense of place, in terms of the author's created secondary world, and stronger feelings for the characters, thus fostering *generative* and *narrative* literacies that will ultimately help them sort out the actions, enigma, and symbolic coding.

Children puzzle out the narrative coding, especially the actions code, by drawing on life and literature experiences (*sociocultural* and *literacy* literacies); at the same time, they reshape their own child worlds in terms of their chosen books. They use literature to make sense of the world, and the world makes better sense to them because of their encounters with literature and their talk, drawing, role-play, and stories in response to it. When that literature is fantasy, as I have observed, their responses are often full and rich, thus revealing more about them, their books, and their ways of reading and seeing the world.

## THE IMPORTANCE OF CHILDREN'S RESPONSES

Children's words about literature show us what they notice: what events, scenes, and conversations are important to them, what small details about characters and setting evoke their imaginings. Children's words show us how they step into the book world and test the facts of it against their own life experiences; how they fill gaps in words and pictures to make broader meanings; and how they decide what the story is about to them. Children's words show us the narrative codes that are evoking particular literacies and the intersection of many literacies.

In these interwoven symmetries are the secrets of child worlds—children's interests, preoccupations, understandings, and ideas. When we call these children's ways of seeing and knowing out of silence, we see that collecting and preserving children's words and ideas is well worth our time and energy. As word-catchers, we see that children sometimes read as we do, but more often they read differently. We also see that children sometimes read similarly to one another, but quite often they read differently. Children's responses teach us more about children, collectively and individually—their books, their stories, their reading transactions, and their attraction to particular genres like fantasy.

To the question, which children's responses will we study, so many different children will have so many different responses, the answer is simple: any child has a great deal to tell us—not about *the* child's world (there is no such thing, nor is there one monolithic adult world), but about child worlds. And we sacrifice authentic reading if we do not avail ourselves of every opportunity to learn from even one child.

To the question, which book will we choose for studying children's responses (there are so many choices, which ones will be the "right" ones, the "best" ones), the answer is equally simple: The books that children choose (or that they find special once they encounter them), and the stories they themselves tell, are the best for their—and our—purposes. The important thing is that we open up exploratory conversations—rich, full responses—in both personal and social contexts, so that children teach us more about the books, themselves, their worlds, and their reading and storymaking transactions.

And to the question, which adults will write and talk about children's books (if we must ask, "Which child?" why aren't we asking, "Which adults?"), the answer, while not so simple, is still possible. In an ideal world, we might hope that any adult who has some decision-making role in children's reading would take time and interest in eliciting some child's response to a book before passing judgment on it during the writing, editing, marketing, reviewing, prizing, teaching, or learning process. But this is not an ideal world, and expediency, self-interest, practicality, and cultural traditions often set the terms for our priorities. What if it were otherwise?

What if all adults with connections to the world of children and children's books began by sharing just one children's book with one child and noticing what the child said or did or drew as she or he read, or afterward? What if they jotted down these children's words and thought about them in terms of how they themselves read the book? What if they engaged these children in more talk and storymaking about the books and what the books called up in the children's minds? What if they learned just a little more about child worlds in the process? Might it encourage them to want to know more, to invite more children into the conversation—and more books? Would it cause them to collect more words, to generate more ideas?

What if they stopped making guesses about children, their feelings about stories, and their transactions about them, and opened up a portal right into children's worlds, through children's own words and pictures, their "becoming" games, and their gestures and expressions? What might they see? Pioneer researchers like Hugh and Maureen Crago, Don Fry, and Carol Fox assumed the role of preserving children's words and ideas so that those who valued children's responses learned more about literature and child worlds. And researchers like Anne Haas Dyson, Shirley Brice Heath, and Vivian Paley, focusing on children from parallel American cultures in urban and rural settings, have continued in this role. Their ideas taught me, and I hope that ideas here help others see more about how they, too, can become word-catchers of children's responses.

I set out on this journey to see more about the colors that fade so quickly in that rainbow span of time when children are stepping into the world of literature, getting their first glimpses of what it means to sort out the world with stories that they hear and stories they themselves tell. I kept traveling this road for the same reason. Even after children were well on their way to becoming readers and storymakers, what they said told me so much more about children's books than I saw reading them alone or with other adults.

Far too often we value only the end result of children's engagement with literature—the "gold"—the adultlike behavior children exhibit when

they are taking on our literary competencies, interpreting stories as experienced readers, producing the most eloquent, the most "finished," the most
accomplished responses. So often what we don't seem to value is childhood itself, just as it is, before it fades. We don't seem to value children for
their own integrity, what they stand for as important persons with value
apart from anything they grow into later. We become so busy training
children to be like us as quickly as possible that we miss what children—
and only children—can produce. Their insights will be different later, but
not necessarily better—not more insightful, just insightful in different ways.
And for those who care about children and *their* worlds—for seeing literature through *their* eyes—difference is what matters.

   Difference produces the prisms of response we need to learn more
about literature and child worlds. Difference produces the rainbow, its
colors amazing—no comparison with the gold.

# Children's Books Cited

Alexander, L. (1965). *The black cauldron*. New York: Holt.

Arnold, K. (1998). Pictures by V. Suteev. *The adventures of snowwoman*. New York: Holiday House.

Babbitt, N. (1977). *The eyes of the amaryllis*. New York: Farrar.

Briggs, R. (1978). *The snowman*. London: Hamish Hamilton.

Cleary, B. (1965). *The mouse and the motorcycle*. New York: Morrow.

Cleary, B. (1982). *Ralph S. Mouse*. New York: Morrow.

Cleary, B. (1970). *Runaway Ralph*. New York: Morrow.

Dahl, R. (1964). *Charlie and the chocolate factory*. New York: Knopf.

Dahl, R. (1961). *James and the giant peach*. New York: Knopf.

Hamilton, V. (1983). *The magical adventures of Pretty Pearl*. New York: Harper.

Hansen, J. (2000). *"Bury me not in a land of slaves": African-Americans in the time of reconstruction*. New York: Franklin Watts.

Hansen, J. (1994). *The captive*. New York: Scholastic.

Hume, L. (1962). *Favorite children's stories from China and Tibet*. Rutland, VT: Charles Tuttle.

Hunter, M. (1964). *The kelpie's pearls*. London: Blackie.

Hunter, M. (1975). *A stranger came ashore*. New York: Harper.

Lewis, C. S. (1950). *The lion, the witch, and the wardrobe*. New York: Macmillan.

Lewis, C. S. (1951). *Prince Caspian*. New York: Macmillan.

Lewis, C. S. (1952). *The voyage of the "Dawn Treader."* New York: Macmillan.

Lindgren, A. (1950). *Pippi Longstocking*. New York: Viking.

Lionni, L. (1969). *Alexander and the wind-up mouse*. New York: Pantheon.

McGowen, T. (1981). Pictures by Victor Ambrus. *Encyclopedia of legendary creatures*. Chicago: Rand McNally.

Miller, A. (1963). Pictures by Emily McCully. *Jane's blanket*. New York: Viking.

Mosel, A. (1972). Pictures by Blair Lent. *The funny little woman*. New York: E. P. Dutton.

Potter, B. (1904). *The tale of Benjamin Bunny*. New York: F. Warne.

Sendak, M. (1981). *Outside over there*. New York: Harper & Row.

Tolkien, J. R. R. (1965a). *The fellowship of the ring*. Boston: Houghton Mifflin.

Tolkien, J. R. R. (1965b). *The hobbit*. New York: Ballantine Books. (Originally published in 1937)

Tolkien, J. R. R. (1984). Pictures by Michael Hague. *The hobbit: Or, there and back again*. Boston: Houghton Mifflin. (Originally published in 1937)

White, E. B. (1952). *Charlotte's web*. New York: Harper.
White, E. B. (1945). *Stuart Little*. New York: Harper.
Yep, Laurence. (1975). *Dragonwings*. New York: Harper.
Yorinks, A. (1986). Pictures by Richard Egielski. *Hey, Al*. New York: Farrar.
Yorinks, A. (1980). Pictures by Richard Egielski. *Louis the fish*. New York: Farrar.
    (Originally published in 1980)

# References

Barthes, R. (1985). On S/Z and the empire of signs. In L. Coverdale (Translator), *The grain of the voice: Interviews 1962–1980* (pp. 74–75). Berkeley: University of California Press.

Barthes, R. (1974). *S/Z*. R. Miller (Translator). New York: Farrar, Straus and Giroux.

Bartlett, F. (1932). *Remembering*. London: Cambridge University Press.

Belinky, M. (1986). *Women's ways of knowing*. New York: Basic Books.

Booth, W. (1988). *The company we keep; An ethics of fiction*. Berkeley: University of California Press.

Bruner, J. (1986). *Actual minds, possible worlds*. Cambridge, MA: Harvard.

Cambourne, B. (1992). *Whole language strategies that build student literacy*. Torrence, CA: The Education Center.

Chambers, A. (1993). *Tell me*. Exeter, England: Thimble Press.

Chukovsky, K. (1971). *From two to five*. Berkeley: University of California Press.

Clay, M. (1989). *Position statement for IRA nominations and elections procedures*. Newark, DE: International Reading Association [unpaged].

Crago, H. (1995–96). Serious reconsiderations. *Children's Literature Association Quarterly* 20 (Winter), 186–191.

Crago, M., & Crago, H. (1983). *Prelude to literacy*. Carbondale: Southern Illinois Press.

Dillon, D. (1985). Quoted by G. Boomer in S. Tchudi (Ed.), *Language, schooling and society*. Montclair, NJ: Boynton/Cook.

Dombey, H. (1982). Learning the Language of Books. In M. Meek (Ed.), *Opening moves* (pp. 26–43). London: Institute of Education, University of London.

Dyson, A. (1989). *The multiple worlds of child writers: Friends learning to write*. New York: Teachers College Press.

Dyson, A. (1993). *Social worlds of children learning to write in an urban primary school*. New York: Teachers College Press.

Dyson, A. (1995). The courage to write: Child meaning making in a contested world. *Language Arts* 72 (September), 324–333.

Dyson, A. (1997). *Writing superheroes*. New York: Teachers College Press.

Egoff, S. (1981). *Thursday's child: Trends and patterns in contemporary children's literature*. Chicago: American Library Association.

Fox, C. (1993). *At the very edge of the forest*. London: Cassell.

Fox, C. (1988). Poppies will make them grant. In M. Meek & C. Mills (Eds.), *Language and literacy in the primary school* (pp. 53–68). London: The Falmer Press.

Freire, P. (1973). *Education for critical consciousness*. New York: Continuum.

Fry, D. (1985). *Children talk about books: Seeing themselves as readers*. Philadelphia: Open University Press.

Frye, N. (1984). Literary and linguistic scholarship in a postliterature world. *PMLA* 99, 990–995.

Gardner, H. (1983). *Frames of mind: The theory of multiple intelligences*. New York: Basic Books.

Genette, G. (1972). *Narrative discourse*. Oxford: Basil Blackwell.

Graham, J. (1990). *Pictures on the page*. Sheffield, England: National Association of Teachers of English.

Harding, D. H. (1977). Response to literature: Dartmouth seminar report. In M. Meek et al. (Eds.), *The cool web: The pattern of children's reading*. London: The Bodley Head. (Essay originally published 1968)

Hardy, B. (1977). Narrative as a primary act of mind. In M. Meek et al. (Eds.) *The cool web: The pattern of children's reading*. New York: Atheneum. (Essay originally published 1968)

Heath, S. (1983). *Ways with words*. Cambridge: Cambridge University Press.

Iser, W. (1978). *The act of reading*. Baltimore, MD: Johns Hopkins University Press.

Jones, D. W. (2004). Birthing a book. *Horn Book* (July/August), 379–394.

Kafka, F. (1972). *The metamorphosis*. New York: Bantam. (Original work published 1915)

Lehr, S. (1991). *The child's developing sense of theme*. New York: Teachers College Press.

Lionni, L. (1989). Alexander and the wind-up mouse. In V. Arnold & C. Smith (Eds.), *Friends aloft* (Unit I; Caring; 2-2; Reader Level 7). New York: Macmillan. (Original Lionni work published 1969)

McDowell, M. (1976). Fiction for children and adults: Some essential differences. In G. Fox (Ed.), *Writers, critics, and children*. London: Heinemann. (Originally published 1973)

Meek, M. (1982a). *Learning to read*. London: The Bodley Head.

Meek, M. (1982b). What counts as evidence in theories of children's literature? *Theory into Practice* 21 (Autumn), 284–292.

Meek, M. (1987a). Playing the texts. *Language Matters*, 1–5.

Meek, M. (1987b). Symbolic outlining: The academic study of children's literature. *Signal* (May), 97–115.

Meek, M. (1988). *How texts teach what readers learn*. Exeter, England: Thimble Press.

Mikkelsen, N. (1994a). A conversation with Virginia Hamilton. *Youth Services in Libraries* 7 (Summer), 392–405.

Mikkelsen, N. (1994b). *Virginia Hamilton*. New York: Twayne.

Mikkelsen, N. (1999). *Words and pictures; Lessons in children's literature and literacies*. New York: McGraw-Hill.

Newkirk, T. (2000). Misreading masculinity: Speculations on the great gender gap in writing. *Language Arts* 77 (March), 294–300.

Paley, V. (1997). *The girl with the brown crayon*. Cambridge, MA: Harvard University Press.

Rosen, H. (1984). *Stories and meanings*. Sheffield, England: National Association of the Teaching of English.

Rosen, H. (1988). The irrepressible genre. In M. MacLure, T. Phillips, & A. Wilkinson (Eds.), *Oracy matters* (pp. 13–23). Philadelphia: Open University Press.

Rosenblatt, L. (1976). *Literature and exploration*. New York: Noble and Noble. (Originally published 1938)

Rosenblatt, L. (1990). Retrospect. In E. Farrell & J. Squire (Eds.), *Transactions with literature: A fifty-year perspective* (pp. 97–107). Urbana: National Council of Teachers of English.

Rosenblatt, L. (1994). *The reader, the text, the poem: The transactional theory of the literary work*. Carbondale: Southern Illinois University Press. (Originally published 1978)

Stibbs, A. (1993). Teacherly practice of literary theory. *English in Education* 27, 50–59.

Strickland, D. (1984). Critic's choice: Virginia Hamilton's *The magical adventures of Pretty Pearl*. *Language Arts* (March), 298.

Tolkien, J. R. R. (1965). *Tree and leaf*. Boston: Houghton Mifflin.

Wells, G. (1986). *The meaning makers*. Portsmouth, NH: Heinemann.

Wilson, G. (1984). *The magical adventures of Pretty Pearl*. *Interracial Books for Children Bulletin* 15, 17–18.

Yep, L. (1995). A garden of dragons. In Dianne Johnson-Feelings (Ed.), *Presenting Laurence Yep* (pp. 108–113). New York: Twayne. (Essay originally published 1992)

Yolen, J. (2000). *Touch magic: Fantasy, faerie & folklore in the literature of childhood*. Little Rock, AR: August House.

# Index

# About the Author

NINA MIKKELSEN received a Ph.D. in English from Florida State University, after which she completed studies in children's literature and literacy at Ohio State University, Columbia University Teachers College, and Columbia University School of Library Science. She has taught children in the elementary and middle grades in the areas of literature, writing, and storymaking as well as college students in the areas of children's literature, literacy methods, writing, and literature. As an independent researcher, she has published about children's responses to literature, children's writing and storymaking processes, literacy through literature as a classroom teaching approach, cultural contexts of children's literature, and multiethnic American literature. She is the author of three books—two literary biographies, *Virginia Hamilton* and *Susan Cooper*, and a children's literature textbook, *Words and Pictures: Lessons in Children's Literature and Literacies*—and many articles. She lives in Emerald Isle, North Carolina.